D1503239

You Better Watch Out

You Better

GREG MALONE

Watch Out

a memoir

Alfred A. Knopf Canada

PUBLISHED BY ALFRED A. KNOPF CANADA

Copyright © 2009 Greg Malone

www.randomhouse.ca

Every effort has been made to contact the copyright holders of material
reprinted here. Grateful acknowledgment is made to Alfred Publishing Co., Inc.,
for permission to reprint portions of the lyrics to "The Happy Wanderer" by
Friedrich W. Moller and Antonia Ridge and "Santa Claus Is Coming to
Town" by J. Fred Coots and Haven Gillespie.

Library and Archives Canada Cataloguing in Publication

Malone, Greg
You better watch out / Greg Malone.

ISBN 978-0-307-39674-7

1. Malone, Greg. 2. Actors—Newfoundland and Labrador—Biography.
3. Comedians—Newfoundland and Labrador—Biography. 4. St. John's
(N.L.)—Biography. I. Title.

PN2308.M34A3   2009 792.02'8092   C2008-905079-7

Text design: Terri Nimmo
Maps: Beate Schwirtlich

First Edition

Printed and bound in the United States of America

2 4 6 8 9 7 5 3 1

I dedicate this book to Whitey. It is safe to say that
without her unwavering support and dedication,
this book would not have appeared in its present form,
and perhaps not at all. I have relied heavily on her kind
wisdom, her unerring judgment and her love.

And to Dad and Mom and their grandchildren—
Anahareo, Django, Dashiell, Luke, Christopher Scully,
Keelin, Declan and Finn.

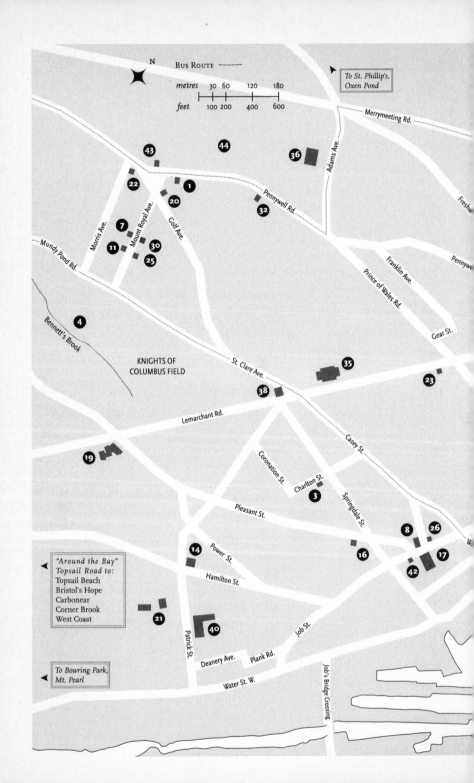

N

BUS ROUTE ·············

To St. Phillip's,
Oxen Pond

metres   30 60   120   180

feet   100 200   400   600

Merrymeeting Rd.

43

44

36

Adams Ave.

Freshw

22

1

Pennywell Rd.

20

32

Morris Ave.

7

Mount Royal Ave.

Golf Ave.

Franklin Ave.

Pennyw

11

30

Prince of Wales Rd.

25

Mundy Pond Rd.

Gear St.

4

Bennett's Brook

KNIGHTS OF
COLUMBUS FIELD

St. Clare Ave.

35

23

38

Lemarchant Rd.

Casey St.

19

Coronation St.

Charlton St.

3

Springdale St.

8

26

Pleasant St.

16

17

14

Power St.

42

"Around the Bay"
Topsail Road to:
Topsail Beach
Bristol's Hope
Carbonear
Corner Brook
West Coast

Hamilton St.

21

40

Patrick St.

Job St.

To Bowring Park,
Mt. Pearl

Deanery Ave.   Plank Rd.

Water St. W.

Job's Bridge Crossing

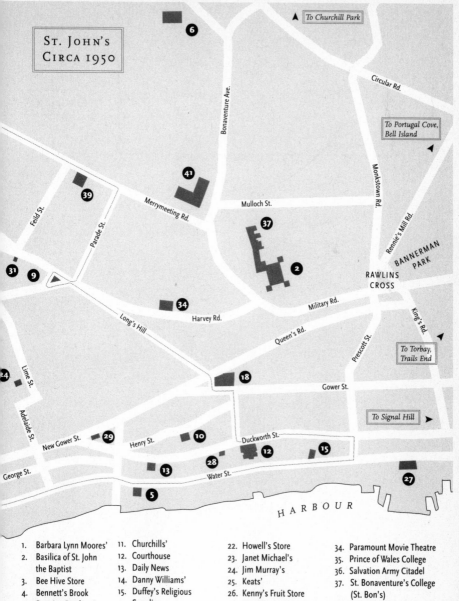

St. John's
Circa 1950

To Churchill Park

Circular Rd.

To Portugal Cove,
Bell Island

Bonaventure Ave.

Monkstown Rd.

Rennie's Mill Rd.

BANNERMAN
PARK

Merrymeeting Rd.

Mulloch St.

Feild St.

Parade St.

Harvey Rd.

Military Rd.

RAWLINS
CROSS

Long's Hill

Queen's Rd.

King's Rd.

Lime St.

Prescott St.

To Torbay,
Trails End

Gower St.

To Signal Hill

Adelaide St.

New Gower St.

Henry St.

Duckworth St.

George St.

Water St.

HARBOUR

1. Barbara Lynn Moores'
2. Basilica of St. John
   the Baptist
3. Bee Hive Store
4. Bennett's Brook
5. Bowring Brothers'
   Department Store
6. Br. Rice High School
7. Braces'
8. Brownsdale Hotel
9. Bus Terminal
10. Capitol Movie Theatre

11. Churchills'
12. Courthouse
13. Daily News
14. Danny Williams'
15. Duffey's Religious
    Supplies
16. Ewing Fur Factory
17. George St. United Church
18. Gower St. United Church
19. Grace Hospital
20. Hodder's Store
21. Holy Cross Monastery
    School

22. Howell's Store
23. Janet Michael's
24. Jim Murray's
25. Keats'
26. Kenny's Fruit Store
27. King George V Institute
    and Swimming Pool
28. Lawyers' Row
29. Majestic Theatre
30. Malones'
31. Marty's Restaurant
32. Miss Snow's
33. Murphy's Barber Shop

34. Paramount Movie Theatre
35. Prince of Wales College
36. Salvation Army Citadel
37. St. Bonaventure's College
    (St. Bon's)
38. St. Clare's Hospital
39. St. George's
40. St. Patrick's Church
41. St. Patrick's Hall
42. T. J. Malone's Grocery
43. Walshes'
44. Walsh's Field

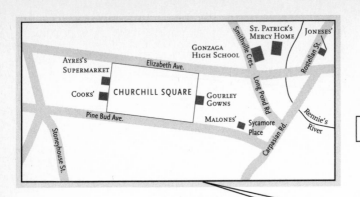

AYRES'S SUPERMARKET

COOKS'

CHURCHILL SQUARE

Elizabeth Ave.

GONZAGA HIGH SCHOOL

Smithville Cres.

ST. PATRICK'S MERCY HOME

JONESES'

Rostellan St.

GOURLEY GOWNS

Long Pond Rd.

MALONES'

Sycamore Place

Carpasian Rd.

Rennie's River

Pine Bud Ave.

Stoneyhouse St.

CHURCHILL PAR

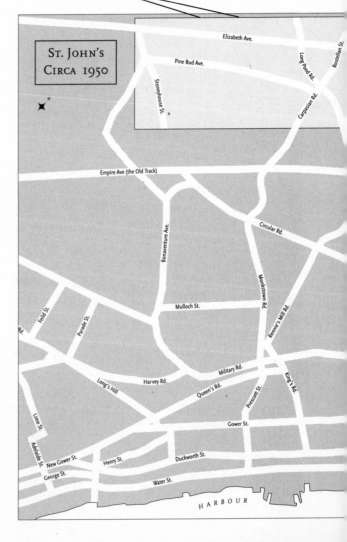

ST. JOHN'S CIRCA 1950

N

Elizabeth Ave.

Pine Bud Ave.

Long Pond Rd.

Rostellan St.

Stoneyhouse St.

Carpasian Rd.

Empire Ave (the Old Track)

Circular Rd.

Bonaventure Ave.

Monkstown Rd.

Rennie's Mill Rd.

Mulloch St.

Feild St.

Parade St.

Rd.

Military Rd.

King's Rd.

Harvey Rd.

Queen's Rd.

Prescott St.

Long's Hill

Lime St.

Gower St.

Adelaide St.

New Gower St.

Henry St.

Duckworth St.

George St.

Water St.

HARBOUR

Contents

Author's Note

THAT THE MALONES were the perfect family was a fact universally accepted by friends and relations alike. Bill Malone was handsome, energetic and dedicated, and his wife, Ada, was glamorous, smart and passionate. In the family albums, with their four handsome boys, each exactly three years apart, arranged next to them like steps, they were the very picture of 1950s optimism.

However, it is, I contend, no small achievement to survive the perfect family. It is certainly a wonderful thing to survive a great shipwreck, unless, like my unfortunate great-uncle Will, you afterwards died of your injuries, or my equally tragic great-grandmother Margaret Kennedy, who lived two fretful years after her abandonment on the windswept coast of Labrador before succumbing to the stress of that ordeal. But those great seafaring epics are not the focus of this volume.

These are stories of little disasters, small betrayals, secret dramas and the fierce storms that rage in the undefended heart of the young. None of this would matter except for the great love, my great love, for the old Town of St. John's, and all my beautiful friends and tormentors within it.

I have been amusing family and friends with many of these tales of school and Scouts and home life for years. Others I have not told before now. The stories of "The Dentist," "The Truck" and "Marilyn and the Monster" were written some time ago and still stand like stepping stones in the roiling river of my reality. The rest of the book is my attempt to put them into context, to understand what really happened and what it meant, to create an emotional history in chronological order, or as close as I can come to it. There were times I believed I might drown in that past, but this book would seem evidence to the contrary.

Greg Malone
Cow Head
May 2008

The Sunset at the Beginning

.

I didn't want to be tied to a bush, an easy prey for bugs and mosquitoes with only a pair of underpants on my head to protect me. It was hot, the leather straps of the harness were twisted, my tears were wet, my cries unheeded. What torment was this?

It was the Imperial Oil summer picnic. I wanted to go and play with Wayne. But Wayne wanted a break. He had been minding me, holding my harness, making sure I didn't wander off, since we had arrived. Now he wanted to go with Gary Mooney around the picnic site and have fun. Mom let him go. I understood all this but I cried after him all the same and tried to follow.

The Imperial Oil picnic was a grand affair if only I could reach it. That summer they had booked a train to transport everyone, truck drivers, tank men, mechanics, dispatchers, secretaries, managers and families, along with tents, wooden cases of soda, insulated duffle bags full of hot dogs and ice cream, stoves, pots, kettles, dishes and flags, all to a rocky field on the Salmonier Line just past Holyrood.

In no time, poles were cut, tents pitched, refreshments prepared and games organized for prizes to be won. The field and tents were lined with red, white and blue triangular flags, which hung stupefied in the rare heat. From the centre of the field came the sound of metal clanging and a great cloud of dust rose up, followed by the roars and groans of the men playing horseshoes. Dad was in their midst, laughing, focused, pitching. Mom chatted with the other women and prepared our spot, then took me on a controlled tour of all the games and glories of the day.

That evening, as the little train, packed full again, crossed Holyrood Beach and turned northeast on its way back to Town, the swollen sun came to rest on the hills along Conception Bay. Suddenly everything, the Bay, the water, the hills, the train and everyone in it was drenched in a dazzling golden orange glow, and for a moment, the whole world and everything in it seemed to be made out of the same shining material.

The Bee Hive

Before we had our own television set, Mom would take Wayne and me down to Nanny and Pop's house on Charlton Street to watch *Disneyland* on Saturday evenings. The shop on the ground floor was rented now to someone else. In the upstairs hall, under the archway leading into their sitting room, Nanny set up a card table and served us triangular sandwiches with the crusts cut off, cake, cookies and tea. She made us gingerbread men so perfect they looked like a picture in a book. Too good to eat, we thought, but she laughed at us and said she made them for us to eat. She would rouse Pop with pretend impatience.

"Get up and play something for the boys. You're lying down too long. You won't be able to sleep tonight. He's deaf," Nanny explained to us with a sudden girlish smile, "so I got to talk loud to him. The boys are here now," she repeated in her clipped Bonavista Bay accent, dropping h's and almost adding a syllable so that "here" became 'ere, but was pronounced 'ayere.

Pop steadied himself and focused on his small visitors.

3

"How are my girls today?" he inquired in his polite English accent.

"Don't be so foolish, they're not girls," said Nanny with a frown. "Don't mind him. That's Ada's boys, you know that," her frown suddenly twisting again into a little smile.

"I know them," he said, settling in to the old upright piano in the corner.

He enjoyed performing and still played every day, and after warming up his old hands with a few scales, he launched into a non-stop medley of show tunes, songs from the war, or Chopin and Mozart, rocking back and forth until he was tired or *Disneyland* came on.

Nanny, in her early sixties and almost twenty years younger than Pop, now held the whip hand, although lightly. Pop still continued his daily walks. If the weather was fair, he would walk the three miles out to Bowring Park and back. Sometimes Wayne and I would see him on his walks around town, but we did not go up to him. If he did recognize us, he would only call us "the girls" and laugh. But his calling us "the girls" had little to do with us, we felt. It was just another eccentricity of our remote English grandfather.

"You can stop now," Nanny yelled over the music. "That's good, you can go on upstairs and I'll bring you up your tea. Their show is coming on."

She closed the venetian blinds for the main event.

Since we had no television of our own, to be able to watch our favourite show in undisturbed comfort every Saturday evening was a great luxury and the high point of our week. If the show on *Disneyland* that week came from Adventureland, it meant a Western like *Davy Crockett*, or even a dog story, which was good. And if it was from Tomorrowland, it meant science fiction, which was also good. But if it was from Fantasyland, it meant Mickey Mouse or Donald Duck or another magical cartoon, and that was the best of all.

Pop had bought a television set as soon as they came out for sale. He bought every new gadget for Nanny. They were among the first to have an electric kettle, a Mixmaster, an electric can opener and steam iron. While we watched our show, Pop went upstairs and sat in his easy chair on the next landing looking out over the felt roofscape of the hill below, past New Gower Street to the harbour. Nanny would bring him up his tea and he would read.

Mom returned for us later in the evening and sometimes stayed to watch *Cameo Theatre*. Dad did not usually come with us. He had been there many times before, of course, and was a great favourite with Nanny, although this had not always been the case. His visits were, at first, very definitely unwelcome even by his own account and he had required a focused plan to gain entry and more effort than he had imagined when he first stopped by to look at the candy.

Sometimes on warm summer evenings, Dad and his buddies would climb Springdale Street to Charlton Street and the Bee Hive Store, where the owner, an Englishman named Arthur B. Walker, made superb homemade ice cream and sold the best bonbons and Turkish delight. They were hungry for it all, but these sugar plums were not the visions that had brought them there. They had come for the unexpectedly perfect sight of Vera Walker, the owner's daughter, with her fine features, her thick, dark blonde hair clipped back and her exotic hazel eyes that seemed always ready to laugh. She was tall and moved with an easy, lively manner. They watched her scoop out vanilla, chocolate and strawberry ice cream as she danced around the little shop of confections and entertained them with anecdotes about her customers. Vera, the Goddess of Goodies, laughing at them and ladling out Turkish delights.

Of course, Vera was entirely aware of her beauty and charms. She dressed in the latest fashion, posed for pictures like a movie star and laughed at the results. They were bedazzled, smitten by this English witch. Oh, those cool Protestant girls from Prince of Wales College. They were exactly the forbidden fruit that a tortured Catholic boy from St. Bon's longed for.

Dad and the boys were secretly converted. The Bee Hive became their shrine. Observances were frequent and well attended, but not always successful. Vera was not in regular attendance on the main altar of the shrine. Usually there was just the girl minding the shop, hired help without any of the secret charms that had drawn them. So dazzling was the goddess Vera that it was many moons before these savages were even aware of the younger sister.

Ada was barely fifteen and her full head of rich, caramel-coloured curls fell on her shoulders framing a gentle, smooth face with full cheeks and classical features. Like her older sister, she too was quick to laugh, but her hazel eyes, though full of humour like Vera's, looked out on the world with more caution, and there was even a trace of sadness in the corners of those perfect, dreamy eyes. There was a vulnerability to her look that provoked in males between the ages of fifteen and fifty an overwhelming desire to protect and a passion to possess such mysterious and fragile treasures.

But this spell had not been cast at the Bee Hive, because Dad had not yet seen Ada there. In fact, the first time he saw her was on Bell Island in the middle of Conception Bay. It was only a short drive from Town and a crossing from Portugal Cove to Bell Island, where the Wabana Mines would soon be pressed to even greater production to meet the demands of World War II for iron ore. But even in 1937 they brought much-needed employment and prosperity to the Bay. It was also a popular destination for sailboats and picnics and other recreational events. Dad, a star athlete in track and field and on the basketball court, was there to compete in a track meet. It was a big event with games, races, prizes, food and drink concessions, and lots of people, both competitors and spectators.

Bell Island itself was like a fortress. It appeared in the middle of Conception Bay, a high plateau rising out of the sea, a rocky mesa in a liquid blue desert ringed with steep, red cliffs that plunged straight down onto a rocky shoreline. At only two places were there openings in the rock wall with a beach and coves, which allowed for a landing, and an incline gradual enough for a road, a steep and dangerous one, but a road nevertheless, to the plateau above. There the harsh rocks of the coast gave way to rolling, silky meadows, grassy roads, small woods, a deep, dark pond and small sheep farms.

The town of Wabana on Bell Island was booming with new shops on Main Street. It even boasted a large new drugstore with a soda fountain, comics and movie magazines. The broad boardwalk, which ran down both sides of the dirt road, gave the place a Western air and added character as well as convenience to the mining metropolis. It was on this stage that Bill first beheld Ada as he crossed the street with some friends.

"She was dressed up like a movie star when I saw her," said Dad, "in a fancy satin outfit with a jacket and bows and gloves and a fancy hat. And then she had the face and the figure to match it. You couldn't miss her. It was like she just appeared in front of me. I still can hardly describe it today."

Ada was five years younger than he was, but they spent the day together. Dad won all his events. He had to. He was not going to lose in front of this exotic creature that had suddenly appeared to him like a mermaid out of the middle of Conception Bay. Bill simply could not leave her. He would have accompanied her to hell, and certainly back to St. John's, but Ada was not returning to Town that day. She was staying over on Bell Island, there to sink back into the apricot ocean whence she had come, after he had sailed away on the little ferry. Her father,

Neptune, was there on business. They were very comfortably situated in a boarding house, where Mr. Walker always stayed when he came over to Wabana. The landlady, who had two small children of her own, was particularly attentive to Mr. Walker's pretty daughter. It would be some time before Bill saw her again.

While Bill floated back to Town, Ada returned to Mrs. Buckley's boarding house to have dinner with her father. At this point, the story is not complete and exactly what happened and what it meant is still surrounded by some mystery. The day was so long and sunny and Ada had been so engaged that it had been easy to forget the time, and when she got back the meal was over and the table had been cleared. Her own dinner was covered on the kitchen table.

There was no one in the dining room or the kitchen but there were voices in the pantry. She looked in through the partly opened door. Mrs. Buckley was facing away from her, working at the counter, and Ada's father was behind her with his arms around her waist.

"I can't put the jelly on it if you're going to keep on doing that, Arthur," she scolded.

Ada's father mumbled something into Mrs. Buckley's ear, which made Mrs. Buckley laugh and turn around into her father's arms. Ada pulled back from the door before Mrs. Buckley could see her. She knew they were kissing now, although she could not see them. She knew because they grew very quiet except for the rustling of their clothes and then the shocking sound of lips. She remained motionless until jolted by the mention of her own name.

"Come on now, Ada will be back soon," said Mrs. Buckley.

Ada carefully backed out into the hall without a sound and went out the door straight into the meadow where she lay in the tall grass and looked back at the deadly house. Did her mother know? Maybe that's why she was sometimes so unhappy and why she and Pop sometimes fought. But her mother could not know what Ada knew. But what did she know? Who was this Mrs. Buckley? She was very familiar with Ada's father and now Ada could see why. Pop had been coming to Bell Island for years now. And who were these little children of hers? Were these children Pop's? Her half-brother and half-sister? Would Pop come here to live one day, leave her mother and her and Vera and her brothers on Charlton Street? What would she do? What could she do?

She felt more danger to herself than to her father from revealing what she now knew. He might be irritated and just continue on with Mrs. Buckley. If she told her mother, it would certainly make her mother unhappy, perhaps even angry with her for knowing what her mother only guessed. And there would be fights, and, who knows, her father might really leave them, not for one of his many trips, but for good. Perhaps her mother would leave too. No, she could not confront him or tell her mother. She could tell no one about this threat they were all living under, which might any day destroy their own family.

Mrs. Buckley was kinder than ever and at a loss to understand the sudden shift in Ada's mood. She had certainly been in high enough spirits the day before. Perhaps she had overexerted herself. Did she feel well? No, not really. Nor did she have much of an appetite for food or going out. And her glamorous satin suit and hat with the shiny bows would not come out of the closet again this trip.

Ada's mood did not improve. She was sick after all and continued to deteriorate until she was hospitalized with a complete nervous and physical breakdown. What the cause of such extreme stress was could only be guessed at. Nanny had no clue, and if Pop did, he was not forthcoming. Ada herself did not enlighten them. The breakdown was attributed to an excess of physical activity. Too much bicycling was the final conclusion, with a prescription for complete rest, but there was no other reason for it ever found, according to Dad.

*

Dad's shock was complete when he discovered the address of his Mermaid was actually the Bee Hive Store, the Temple of All Earthly Pleasures. How could he not have noticed her on one of his many visitations? He no longer resented Ron McGrath, the brooding policeman from St. Mary's Bay who had become Vera's fiancé. Vera was smashing and dynamic and a lot of fun, but Vera could take care of Vera. She didn't need Dad, but Ada, he had felt from the very first, did need him. Hearing that she was up at St. Clare's Hospital only confirmed this instinct and occasioned the final transfer of all his feelings from the older sister to the younger. The Mermaid lay ill in a hospital bed, for God's sake, of course she needed him, and so, with every ounce of energy, passion and dedication that raging hormones and a hungry heart can generate, it was Dad to the rescue, then and ever after.

He threw himself into Mom's recovery as only a true-believing Boy Scout could, and her improvement was rapid under his continuous infusion of compliments, solicitations, gossip, jokes and outright ecstatic proclamations, and she was soon home again on Charlton Street. Deeper and deeper he fell into the seductions of the Bee Hive. Vera had been the honey. Now he had discovered the Queen. Getting into the shop was nothing, but access to the living quarters upstairs would not come so easily.

Sweet William

Bill Malone from New Gower Street was a Catholic and, as such, regarded as some form of gypsy by the Wesleyan mind of Mary Walker.

"You don't know what they're doing in there behind those curtains, bowing down to statues, burning candles and strange-smelling things, and chanting in foreign tongues."

It was as close to devil worship as you could come and still pass for Christian.

"And you know they're drinking. I suppose he must drink because the whole crowd down there drinks. And he's twenty years old! He's a man for heaven's sake and you're barely fifteen and not out of school. No, you're not going out with him. You're not going out with anyone yet."

This was the firm and decided opinion of Ada's mother, Mary Walker, née Winsor, from Wesleyville, which was as properly Protestant as its name declared, with all the accents and prejudices of seventeenth century England.

Every summer of their childhood, Ada and Vera boarded the

SS *Sagona,* or one of the other coastal boats, for their mother's childhood home in Wesleyville, a day's voyage from Town on the north side of Bonavista Bay. Nanny always sent a barrel of goods with them from the Bee Hive for Nana and Papa Winsor. There they slept on feather beds in their grandparents' house. Japhet Winsor had married Lydia Vincent from nearby Swain's Island, who was by now bedridden with rheumatoid arthritis, and so there was always a girl there to care for her needs, and for his, of course.

Young Ada thought the boys around the Bay were very forward.

"Well, what else was there to do, I suppose. The boys would come up to Vera and me and say, 'Hello maid, how's your broach?' and laugh, or 'Hello maid, how's your fish?' and laugh again. I didn't know what they were talking about and Vera wouldn't tell me, so I asked Nana Winsor . . . Well!"

She did not get a direct answer, but by their averted expressions and warnings, guessed quickly at the location of broach and fish, and that they referred to the same part of the female anatomy. She would avoid those boys and spent her time instead with Cluny Blackwood, the merchant's son, who was more refined and reserved. They liked each other immediately and were teased mercilessly for it by the other boys. "Ada and Cluny, Cluny and Ada. Ada loves Cluny. Cluny, Cluny, Cluny," until they finally stopped seeing each other altogether.

But she liked Wesleyville with its pretty white clapboard houses and white clapboard church, school and stores, its dusty dirt roads and summer winds, which ruffled the tops of the shiny black-blue waves as they pushed in across the long sandy beaches into the tall green and golden grasses, spotted with sapphire ponds. The rugged and delicate shore had been settled in the 1600s and 1700s by the English, who gave the name of their serious new faith to the community they founded. Wesleyville was the home of the Windsors and the Blackwoods and the

Hanns, God-fearing English fundamentalists. And indeed, with his thick white hair, his good black suit and starched shirt, Japhet Winsor looked the part of the patriarch, and this picture of him Ada would have accepted forever except for the comments she began to hear, and the allusions to him and young girls. Ada began to realize that, while Nana Winsor lay twisted in bed with rheumatoid arthritis coming to the end of her knitting, Papa Winsor was chasing young girls, and not at all the pillar of the community he presented.

"I don't know, perhaps he was the biggest whoremaster in Wesleyville," said Mom with a puzzled laugh, much later.

Years earlier, before Ada was born, when Nanny was just a girl of eighteen, her father, Japhet, had enjoyed the company of one Arthur B. Walker. The dapper, well-educated Englishman was travelling the Newfoundland coast, giving piano recitals. He also played the mandolin guitar, which he sold along with sheet music. He was a widower and had a small shop in Town, and a daughter almost my grandmother's age called Nellie, of whom he carried a picture showing an extremely pretty young girl of sixteen with thick curls and large, sensitive blue eyes.

Arthur and Japhet got on very well and Mr. Walker ended up staying with the Winsors whenever he came to the northeast coast. He even brought Nellie to visit. He grew fond of young Mary Winsor and thought she would make an excellent companion for his only daughter when he was away. She could also help run his little shop. And so it was that Mary Winsor came to live in Town with the Walkers. Mary was only two years older than Nellie, who found her to have a quiet dignity and a sisterly, even motherly concern that drew in her confidence, and when her father's attention to Mary increased, it was Nellie who encouraged them. She was the go-between and passed notes for them of proposals and intimacies too fragile to risk in open conversation, and before long Nellie's companion became her stepmother. At twenty, Mary was eighteen years Arthur's junior.

They went back to England for their honeymoon, where her reception at the Walkers' in Windsor was as warm, no doubt, as his first wife's had been years before.

The story of Pop's first family was a mystery to us. We knew there was another family, of course, because Mom and Auntie Vera had a stepsister somewhere who was almost as old as Nanny. But they were rarely spoken of, and even Auntie Vera, the source of all stories, gossip and knowledge, was silent on this subject, but only because she did not know it. She would make it her business to find out years later.

Pop's English family had come over with him to Canada, where he played concerts and recitals and sold his instruments around eastern Canada from Montreal to Halifax, and did very well, but his young son died suddenly, then his wife died shortly after. He returned briefly to England with his surviving daughter, Ellen, "Nellie", to what was generally understood to be the stifling formality of the Walker home in Windsor. After only a short stay, he returned to Canada with Nellie, where his travels eventually brought him to Newfoundland. It was a British Dominion like Canada, but they still drove on the left, and it reminded him of home with its West Country accents. The people were hugely friendly, the girls pretty, and he did well in the numerous outports that had to depend on the one general store for their needs, if there was even that. He liked St. John's with its old, colonial mid-Atlantic ways, and its connections with the United States and Britain and Canada, so he set himself up in the Newfoundland Hotel and sent for his little Nellie. Pop was very protective of Nellie. He doted on her and loved to dress her in expensive clothes, especially blue velvet and furs.

He opened his own store, the Bee Hive, at 27–29 Charlton Street, a shop with an apartment above. His first purchase was a piano. He imported all kinds of delicacies for the store: Scottish shortbreads, English tea in fancy tins, good china and hundreds of postcards, which he hired young boys and girls to sell for him, and, of course, confections. In the summer, Pop added his delicious homemade ice cream, a new flavour each day. But the burden of running the shop fell heavily on Nellie when Pop was travelling in the outports.

When Pop met and married Mary Winsor their little household settled down to a pleasant routine. But within a year of the marriage, though not because of it, there came a terrible and irrevocable break between Pop and his adored daughter. The only evidence of this rupture was an advertisement in *The Daily News* in which he, Arthur B. Walker, disclaimed all responsibility for the accounts and debts of Ellen V. Walker at Bowring's Department Store, Ayre & Sons and the Royal Stores.

Nellie, horrified and humiliated at this public spectacle, eloped with her new boyfriend, Baxter Hann, Mary's cousin from Wesleyville. They moved to the United States, and she and Pop did not see or speak to each other again. The story of Aunt Nellie was only known to us because of that notice in the newspaper, and we were shocked. How could Pop do such a thing and how was such an irrevocable breakup possible? Auntie Vera and Mom did not see their stepsister until many years later when Auntie Vera sought her out. She did come back, as an old woman, for a brief visit to our house in St. John's. She and Pop were polite, but not warm, and no longer close. The intimate feelings of those long-ago days would not be reclaimed.

After Aunt Nellie's dramatic and traumatic departure, Pop's attention was turned to the concerns of a new family. Mary presented him with a son, Raymond Vivian, who, despite all efforts, failed to thrive. He was small and shrivelled and Nanny had to put him in the oven as a makeshift incubator. Pop was always health conscious. A disciple of health guru Bernarr Macfadden, he ate carefully, never smoked, was a teetotaller and always preferred to walk rather than drive. He ordered the best tonics and formulas, but they were all tried in vain on baby Raymond.

Nanny was at her wit's end. Across the street Mrs. Whiteway had a house full of fat, rosy-cheeked children and they were poor. How did she manage it? So Nanny went over and asked her.

"I feeds them all pap," was Mrs. Whiteway's quick reply.

"Pap!" said Nanny.

"Yes," said Mrs. Whiteway. "I just break up some bread and soak it in warm milk with a bit of sugar and mix that up and they love that."

Pap, thought Nanny in utter astonishment, as she stumbled back across the street. Who would have thought it? It was Ray's next meal, and sure enough, he was soon as fat as the Whiteways, and remained hale and hearty all his life.

After Ray came Vera Madeline, and then another son, Hershel, who died in infancy. There was nothing pap, or Pop, could do. The day before Vera's fifth birthday, on April 15, 1922, Ada Constance was born, a birthday present for her, Vera said. Last came Leonard Bertram, of whom Vera and Ada were very fond. Leonard, the "peacemaker," was a ray of sunshine, his bright eyes always squinting in a smile. Once when he was barely yet able to talk and their parents were fighting, each sitting in separate rooms, little Leonard went to Pop, took him by the hand, and led him into the next room to Nanny. He put Pop's hand in hers and pushed them together.

"Daddy love Mommy." Then he took their heads and pushed their faces together.

"Daddy kiss Mommy."

He refused to leave until they made up.

"Well, what could we do?" said Nanny. "We were so overwhelmed that we had to make up for him."

This story, like most others, came to us from Auntie Vera, who was more forthcoming than Mom on the subject of their family.

"But what were they fighting about?"

"Oh, I don't remember that now."

"Did they fight often?"

"Oh no, we had a good life really. Mom was good to us, and we used to have a great Christmas. Mom would make fruitcakes and gingerbread men and a goose and a turkey and a pudding, and she'd fill your stocking with all kinds of stuff, and there'd be presents wrapped up beautifully. She really went all out. So we had a good time. We had our bad times too, of course. Sometimes, now, if things weren't going well, Mom might take a turn, you know. She'd put on her coat and hat and she'd say, 'That's it, I'm going up to Mundy Pond and jumping in and that's the last you'll see of me,' and then she'd go. And that was it, we wouldn't see her again all night, or maybe not till the next day even. I knew she'd be back, but Ada and Len would be worried, especially Len. He'd screech and cry. So we'd have to calm him down."

"Why did Nanny leave? What was wrong?"

"You know, Pop was away so much and she was left alone, a young woman. And Pop was so much older than Mom, I suppose. He didn't want to do a lot of the things a young woman wanted to do, and he was set in his ways. They were so different really. So they had their problems," was as much as Auntie Vera would offer on that subject.

Many years later a neighbour of ours offered a more pointed explanation.

"We knew the Walkers," said Mrs. Howell. "'Lock up your daughters if Arthur Walker comes around,' is what my mother and her friends said, so she must have suffered, Mrs. Walker. She didn't seem to go out much or to have many friends."

"Eventually Mom would come back home and everything would be fine," Auntie Vera continued. "We'd have Len asleep and she might make hot chocolate then. I'd have to tell Len a really good story to get him to sleep, probably 'The Ruby Ring.' That was their favourite."

"'The Ruby Ring'! Oh tell us about 'The Ruby Ring,'" we cried.

"Gosh, you boys sound just like Ada and Len. Tell us about the Wooby Wing, they'd say. So I'd start in, you know, I don't know where I got it, but I'd tell them some long, complicated story and it would always end up with, 'what do you think they found in the box, or in the cave, but . . . a wooby wing!' That was my best one. I'd keep that going, night after night for weeks. The Wooby Wing. But we loved Len. He was so cute and we'd dress him up. I used to knit everything, socks and mittens and hats and sweaters, so we'd have him bundled up," and she laughed.

I searched for the right key to unlock the next story.

"You made sweaters for him? I didn't even know you could knit."

"Yes, I made sweaters for everyone then, and one day Ray noticed this and he says to me, 'How come you made a sweater for Len and Ada and everyone else and you didn't make one for me?' Well, I didn't want to make a sweater for Ray, you know, we didn't get along. So I said, 'Okay, I'll make you a sweater, but you have to buy the wool, and do my chores, wash the dishes, clean the floors, while I'm knitting the sweater.' Well Ray agreed to all that and he got me this black wool, and I started knitting his sweater, and Ray did my chores.

"He washed the dishes and the floor, and he was good at it, so I thought, well, this is great, I should keep this going a bit longer. So he'd see me knitting the sweater in the day, and then at night I'd unravel it and take out some of what I'd done that day, you know, to keep Ray doing my chores a little longer, and I thought it was a good punishment for Ray anyway for all the mean things he'd done to me. So after a while Ray started to ask, 'Vera, when is that sweater gonna be ready?' so I'd say, 'Well, it's a big sweater, you know. You're a lot bigger than Len, so it's taking me longer and I need more wool.' I just added that to make it more convincing. I didn't need more wool, but he bought it and it worked for a while, but then, eventually, I had to finish it up. Ray got his sweater but he paid for it, and I had enough black wool left over to make a sweater for myself," said Auntie Vera, and she had a good laugh, pleased with herself all over again.

Ray had his father's musical talents and, as a teenager, helped Pop with his concerts and recitals in St. John's. Once, he told us, when Pop was playing a concert at Pitt's Memorial Hall, a man in the front row lit up a cigarette. Pop made a great display of taking out his handkerchief and tying it around his nose and mouth, and then continued to play until the man relented and put out the cigarette.

"Ray was a lot older than me but whenever he made money he always gave me a dollar, which was a lot of money then," said Mom. "He and Vera didn't get along, but he was good to me."

My family laughed a lot at Uncle Ray, who despite his early generosity to Mom developed a reputation for being cheap to a comic degree. He sent us a festive tin of hard candy for Christmas once, which Mom thought was pretty good for Ray. Another year he promised Wayne a cowboy suit, which had Wayne dancing in expectation until it arrived and turned out to be nothing but a string tie with cowboy boots for a clip. Wayne couldn't believe this was the promised cowboy suit, but on his next visit Uncle Ray asked about it.

"How did you like the cowboy suit I sent you, hey Wayne?"

Wayne looked like he'd just smelled a fart, but managed to answer.

"Oh it's great, Uncle Ray, thank you."

"That's good. Go put it on and let me see you in it."

Another fart, but he went off and put on the string tie and came smiling back to model it for Uncle Ray who was well pleased with the entire effect and kept calling it "the cowboy suit." We were speechless but laughed about it for years after.

The case of Ray was not as clear as it seemed. One winter night, just after Len was born, Raymond was sliding down the hill behind Prince of Wales College on Lemarchant Road. He slid under a fence at the bottom, which caught the top of his forehead and tore his scalp back. There was a lot of blood and some time recovering, and poor Raymond was never quite the same again. His grades at school fell and he became just a little odd. After this story emerged we curbed our judgments of Uncle Ray but not our laughter.

But it was Vera who was Mom's main support, her big sister and second mother. When Mom contracted diphtheria at the age of five it was Vera who carried her around, upstairs and down for days, because Nanny was afraid to touch her. She was taken off to the Fever Hospital, where Nanny, Vera and Len couldn't visit. They would stand outside below and she would wave to them from the window, the same window she would scrape her porridge out after the matron left.

Vera had taken care of Ada when she was little, but as she got older Vera developed her own busy social life. She was very popular and had lots of suitors, and now there was another protector, waiting on the doorstep ready to serve Ada.

The Majestic Theatre used to have live entertainment and the Fourth St. Edward's Scout Troop and the Fourth St. John's staged plays there regularly, evening performances and matinees.

"The girls would come to see the boys. We had good singers, the Andrews boys and the Michaels, most of whom I knew," said Dad. "I took Ada to a play and I gave her a kiss and she slapped me. She thought I was fresh. She was sixteen and I was twenty-one."

Nanny didn't want Ada dating at all. She saw them walking together once and gave Ada a bawling-out. But she finally agreed to let her see Bill occasionally, and one afternoon they were all scheduled to go to a garden party. Nanny was not impressed.

"What kind of job is that he got that he can just take time off in the middle of the day? He won't have it for long."

"But Bill wasn't stupid," said Mom. "He came up for me, but he didn't look at me. He had eyes only for Mom. 'What! This is Ada's mother? Really? Not her sister?,' like that. He brought her a big Jersey Milk chocolate bar, her favourite, and then confessed that, unfortunately, he would not be able to come to the garden party with us because he could not take the time off work! But he would make it up to her, and he left us all laughing."

Bill was a charmer who never came empty handed. He brought flowers to Nanny on her birthday and always chocolate bars, and even though Nanny had her own store, she liked the thought, and the bars, and before long she eagerly awaited his visits.

"You better hurry now, Ada. Bill will be here for you in a minute and you're not dressed. I'll give him his supper while you get ready.'

"The change was so gradual you didn't notice it," said Mom.

And in a few years Nanny would say, "I'd rather go out with Bill than any of you," meaning her own children! They became very close.

"Bill would help her out too," said Mom. "He had Nanny around his little finger. He could do no wrong, and before long, if something went wrong, it must be my fault, not Bill's, sweet William."

✦

Uncle Ray joined the Army and fought in Italy with the Newfoundland Field Regiment of the Royal Artillery. Uncle Len lied about his age and enlisted too. Dad tried enlisting with the Royal Newfoundland Regiment but was rejected because of his ears. You could never tell, but Dad had been kicked in the head by one of the horses when he was a delivery boy, and knocked out. He had to learn to crawl and then walk and talk again. Everything came back eventually except he didn't have complete hearing in one ear. And then he was knocked off the trestle by the train in Bowring Park, and he'd also had a sucker stick driven into his head, which he swore went in one side of his head and out the other. None of this improved his hearing and, all told, he was judged too big a risk for the Army.

Dad became a driver for the Canadian Army and took the brass careening in jeeps over the gravel hill into Portugal Cove to watch for German subs, which sometimes came into Conception Bay and attempted to disrupt iron ore shipments from the mines on Bell Island to munitions and armament factories in the US. He had other jobs too. His older brother Ken had a good position at Mammy's Bakery and got him a job as a baker, which he hated. But it was a better job with better money than he made driving for the Canadians and he was good at it, so Ken and Dad set up their own bakery. The lack of flour due to wartime rationing forced them to close, but not before the bleach and chemicals in the flour caused Dad to lose all his hair. His friends started calling him Scully, which was his middle name, after Dr. Scully who delivered him, and even though his thick black eyebrows and raven hair all grew back, it was Scully from then on to all his gang.

It'll Do

Their wartime courtship was a golden time for Dad and Mom, and her little scrapbook of "Snappy Snaps" was filled with sepia pictures of them and their burgeoning gang. The Fourth St. Edward's Scout Troop's main campgrounds were outside St. John's, in Mount Pearl. After camp was over, Dad and some of his Scout buddies collected what money they had, sold bottles and raised enough to rent one of the cabins for the rest of the year. It was simple affair with a wood stove and a verandah, standing in a clearing in the woods near the banks of the Waterford River. There was a waterfall nearby, which fell into a large pool where they would dive and swim. They had parties and picnics with scavenger hunts when the whole gang was out, and in the winter they went cross-country skiing. It was a paradise, and a perfect escape from the troubles of Town. They called the cabin It'll Do after answering every objection to the place with that phrase, until It'll Do became the place for them and their gang.

There was Bill, Gandhi Royal, Cam Eaton, Dad's brother Kit and Ladd Bursey. The girls were there as much as they could be,

Ada and Vera, Florence Mercer and sometimes Dad's sister
Sheila, who came out with her husband, Vic Wiley, and their
Newfoundland dog, who ate rubber balls. Ada and Vera posed
like their favourite movie stars on a gold satin eiderdown in the
field for Ladd Bursey, who captured it all with his camera. These
friends, with their strange, exotic names, were the chosen family. From the faded photos their eager faces still shine out, their
arms around each other, all tumbled together, laughing and
smiling. Whenever Dad could get a vehicle from his father's grocery store or from work they drove, but usually they bicycled or
walked the seven miles in to St. John's for work in the morning
and back to Mount Pearl again in the evening for a game of tennis and the night.

There was a club in Mount Pearl too, not officially exclusive,
but mostly the preserve of the well-off Protestant merchants and
bureaucrats, such as the head of the Church of England School
Board, who disapproved of a bunch of Catholic Scouts renting
cabins and living on their own. They were living fast, entertaining girls, having parties and they were Catholic. They'll destroy
the place and it won't be fit to come here, was the general gist of
Mr. King's view.

His wife's view was not so fixed. She would watch the boys
hiking off to Mass at Corpus Christi Church in Kilbride every
Sunday. Sometimes there were fifteen of them, singing songs as
they marched along. One Sunday it poured and Mr. King was-
n't going to Church. Mrs. King, looking out through the tor-
rents of rain, saw Dad and several of his buddies come trooping
along on their way to Mass, singing in the downpour.

"There, Mr. King," she said. "It's too wet for you to drive to
Sunday service, but look at those Catholic boys, walking miles
in the rain to church and singing. And they didn't destroy the
place, did they? They fixed up those cabins and they even made
a playing field, and are nothing but courteous. Go on out now
and give them a ride to Mass. It's the least you can do."

So out he came in his big black car and pulled up alongside the boys.

"Get in," he said, "and I'll give you a lift."

"Oh no, Mr. King," said Bill. "We don't want to get your seat wet."

"Damn it, get in," he said, "or my wife will never let me hear the end of it. Come on."

They piled aboard. Mr. King waited outside the church till Mass was over and drove them all back to the cabins.

"Well, you've got a holy show made of me. The wife won't let me alone. 'The boys are this, the boys are that.' I'll tell you the truth, I wasn't sure about you when you moved in, but she was right. Come on down to the club this week and we'll have a game of horseshoes or tennis if you like."

And so they did, and Dad was happy to report his gang beat them at their own games, and they all got along great after that.

Dad recounted all this with great delight. Perhaps because he was about to marry his own Protestant Princess, he was happy to report on all such ecumenical and humanistic epiphanies, where differences, especially religious ones, were overcome by camaraderie and common sense, and all came together as one. It was all in how you played the game, for Dad, but I don't know if we ever would have heard the story if Dad had not won both the game and the girl.

All golden ages must come to their end, and so after a respectable period of restraint, the inevitable was reported in *The Daily News* on September 2, 1944.

"A beautiful and impressive ceremony was performed at the Oratory of Our Lady of Mercy, Military Road, at eight o'clock Monday evening, August 28, when Reverend Fr. R. Murphy united in the holy bonds of matrimony Ada Constance Walker, daughter of Mr. and Mrs. Arthur B. Walker, Charlton Street, to William Scully Malone, son of Mr. and Mrs. Thomas Malone, New Gower Street."

It was a wartime wedding and material was in short supply. The fashion was for summer suits, in the bride's case "a costume of heavenly blue with white accessories and . . . a corsage of pink roses and maidenhair fern . . . The bride's mother looked very becoming in an afternoon dress of cocoa-cocoa tan with matching accessories and a silver fox. Her corsage consisted of carnations and sweet peas . . . After the ceremony, the wedding party motored to Smithville, where the reception was held." It was reported they had an "excellent supper." This would mark the first, and last, time that the Malone and Walker families sat down together, not that there was any animosity or sorrow attending the union, even though the groom's mother was "attractively gowned in black." It was simply that the Walkers were United Church and English, and the Malones were Catholic and Irish and older in their ways. When Dad first brought Ada home after a tennis game to meet his parents, his mother looked at her in her short shorts and sleeveless top and said to Dad, "Tell her to go home and put some clothes on."

But Dad liked her the way she was. Father Murphy had done his duty and applied all the appropriate pressure on Dad to renounce his Protestant preference, but he had come this far and would not lose his prize. The reception was all affability and warmth. Father Murphy, triumphant from the Catholic service, and with Mom's name not yet dry on the document containing her agreement to have all her children raised and educated in the Roman Catholic faith, "eloquently proposed a toast to the bride and groom." The fathers of the bride and groom both spoke to the assembled guests and found enough to say to each other afterwards, as did their wives. Both were shopkeepers and had grown children married and sons overseas, and all were optimistic that the war would soon be over.

Mom and Dad had a brief honeymoon in Holyrood, all recorded on Ladd Bursey's Brownie Hawkeye. It seemed very natural to them for Ladd to come along—after all, they were all bosom buddies, and Ladd was a laugh and made himself very useful. Indeed their little gang seemed to revolve around Bill and Ada's romance, and Ladd in particular was devoted to them. Nevertheless, after the honeymoon, Mom decided it was time to find Ladd his own girlfriend, which they did. After all these celebrations were over, Bill and Ada rented two very unsatisfactory apartments before they eventually moved in with Nanny and Pop and Uncle Len on Charlton Street with Baby Wayne. But with baby number two on the way, they would need a place of their own. The year was 1948, the war was well over and the City was filled with the expectations of all the opportunities offered by the new age.

Mom and Dad

Mom and Dad were thrilled to finally have their own house on Mount Royal Avenue, even though they had to rent the second floor out to tenants to make it work out.

"It was Nanny who gave us the money for the down payment. We paid her back, but she gave it to us without any conditions," said Mom.

Dad was a route man now for Imperial Esso, delivering stove and furnace oil in a big oil truck. He walked home in the dark, all the way from the wharf on the south side of the Harbour. He was big and strong, and so tired, smelling of furnace oil and the cold, in his blue delivery jacket and hat. Mom would rub Vaseline on his cold, chapped hands as he sat next to the oil stove.

In the long winter evenings, Mom read us *Lassie Come-Home* and *Black Beauty*. She sat in the big armchair in the living room, with me and Wayne sitting on either arm. As Beauty's perils and sufferings increased, I started to cry and slip down into the chair with Mom. Then Wayne would cry and then Mom would start to wipe tears away too.

"That's really sad."

"People can be very cruel. Okay, that's enough for tonight, I think."

"What happens to Black Beauty?"

"We'll find out tomorrow night."

"Aw!"

Mom and Dad slept on the big pullout sofa in the living room, and Wayne and I slept in the little back room. There was only a toilet under the stairs. The tenants had the large bathroom upstairs, and by arrangement, Mom and Dad had the use of it once a week for bathing. We children were bathed in a great production in the kitchen sink. There was no wall along the stairs, so the tenants came in and left through our hall. Even so, the apartment upstairs was large and clean, and it was not hard to find tenants from the American base at Fort Pepperrell, usually young couples, like Grace and Don.

They were a little younger than Mom and Dad, and Grace stayed home and visited with us sometimes, while Don worked on the base. One morning, Mom was very worried about something going on upstairs. It was very tense. Then Grace came down the stairs, dressed to go, crying quietly. Don followed her with suitcases, but he was not dressed to leave. Halfway down Grace broke down sobbing and turned back to Don.

"Don't make me go, Don," she begged. "Please let me stay."

She didn't care that we were standing there. She didn't seem to see anyone but Don. He took her hands from his chest and put his hand on her shoulder.

"We talked about this and we agreed," he said.

"I didn't," she sobbed. "I don't want to leave, Don. I'm afraid," cried Grace.

"It's only for a short time, come on now," said Don, and he picked up her suitcases again.

It was terrible. She was in such grief. She hugged Mom and cried, and begged Don again before she was finally persuaded to leave in the taxi alone. I was shocked at her suffering. What could hurt her so much? Was she sick? Had she done something to Don? Was there an accident? No. Don had decided he wanted to live on his own, here in Newfoundland. He and Grace hadn't been married long and Don wasn't sure about living with someone else. He found it hard to change his ways. So he decided to send Grace back to the States. Dad and Mom were very sorry for poor Grace and so was I.

After that, it was very quiet upstairs. At first, Grace wrote long letters, which Don enjoyed getting, and he started to write her back, and talked about her more and more. Finally he decided he missed her and wanted her to come back. But Grace was happy at home and wasn't sure about going back with Don. Don was desperate. He sat crying at our kitchen table.

"I've lost Grace," he choked out.

"No," soothed Mom. "She'll come back."

"I'm not sure I'd come back," said Dad, after Don had gone back upstairs.

But after a good while, Grace did come back, and she was so different. She had new clothes and was confident. I was amazed. We had all been so sad for her when Don had sent her away. She had been so broken, I thought she might even die, and now here she was laughing, with everything much better than before. Don would hardly leave her side.

★

Wayne was in school now. He was three years older than me, but Mom dressed us in matching outfits like twins, and took our picture on the front steps. Wayne didn't mind being dressed like me, even though I was younger. He put his arm around me and took care of me. Wayne was my protector. He was tall and handsome and even won the Beautiful Baby Contest in the *Daily News* one Christmas. Mom cut out the picture with the caption from the paper and put it in the album. "William Wayne Malone, 4 ¼, hangs an oversized stocking over the fireplace. The hammer was kindly donated for the occasion by his dad, W. S. Malone, a route salesman in St. John's."

They both went all out for Christmas, but when we hung up our stockings and went to bed on Christmas Eve, there was no sign of a tree. It appeared magically, full of mystery in the morning light, its boughs glinting with fat, blown-glass ornaments of red, green, turquoise and gold. Hundreds of strands of individually placed silver tinsel hung motionless, and strands of unlit Japanese series coloured lights, collared in their metal reflectors, poked through the boughs from the bottom to the top where a red and silver, five-pointed star stood. Under the tree lay all the presents, in their bright Christmas wrapping.

Mom and Dad were very particular about the tree, and if there was a bare spot, Dad would get his brace and bit from the basement, drill a hole in the tree trunk, whittle the end of an extra branch with a knife, fit it in the hole and tie it to its neighbours for support. All day long he laboured to keep the series lights lit, reaching in carefully around the delicate ornaments, unscrewing and testing light after light until he found the dead one. When he replaced it, the whole set would light up and we'd send up a cheer. But before the New Year he was grumbling more and more at it until the magic was worn out and put away for another year.

✦

Our new little brother was named Kerry. He was skinny and small and they were worried about him. I don't know if Mom gave him pap, but he managed to survive. He was very pretty and affectionate, and Wayne and I devoted ourselves to his protection and amusement. Kerry ushered in the new fashion of Irish names. His full name was Christopher Kerry, but we were all called by our second name for some reason. Wayne was William Wayne, after Dad and John Wayne. I was David Gregory, after some David on the Winsor side, and Gregory Peck, of course. Mom loved the movies, and would take us to the Paramount or down to the Capitol to be amazed by *Magnificent Obsession* or *Mildred Pierce*. She took Wayne to *Snow White*, but he panicked and cried at the Wicked Witch, and Mom had to take him out, but that was before I was allowed to go.

Sometime after Kerry was born, Mom stopped getting up in the mornings with us. But Dad was a good cook and produced a hearty breakfast of fried eggs and bacon, or bologna or sausages and toast, or even pancakes with molasses and tea. Sometimes he'd make just porridge with milk and brown sugar or molasses, and tea, or sometimes refried fish and brewis with bacon, which was better than fish and brewis, but not much. There was always fish and brewis on Fridays, the non-meat day of the Catholic week. Dad then took over Sunday dinner as well, and sometimes at Christmas, and on special occasions, he would even bake up a batch of his delicious homemade bread. He still had the baker's touch, and made small, golden loaves and dinner rolls, cinnamon rolls, and braided-rope breads with nuts and cherries and a white glaze down the middle. The whole table would be full of fresh-baked treats, and Dad took every delight in garnishing them with great aplomb to our ecstatic approval.

He put fresh milk and eggs in his bread so they were very rich, almost creamy. The fresh milk for these delicacies was delivered daily by Kelsey's Dairy, which took the empty bottle with the milk ticket pressed inside the neck, and put a fresh bottle of milk in its place, which we were quick to retrieve.

"Now don't just pour off the first glass and drink it," warned Mom. "That's all the cream there. You have to shake it up to mix it through."

"Just this once, Mom."

"No. Definitely not. Here, let me open that."

Mrs. Nash brought the eggs and fresh butter. Mrs. Nash from Nash's Farm in her big slope-back Nash car. Wayne and I struggled vainly to penetrate the hidden meaning of this cozy coincidence.

Barbara Lynn

Around the corner on Pennywell Road was the well-kept, pale yellow, clapboard duplex where the first love of my life lived. Barbara Lynn and I first met in our carriages. Mrs. Moores and Mom met on the street and admired each other's new babies. Barbara Lynn and I expressed an interest in each other, Mom said. Mrs. Moores and Mom had both gone to Prince of Wales College, the United Church High School on Lemarchant Road. The Mooreses were Protestants, of course. Their house was perfectly arranged, spotless, and was run like clockwork.

Every day I went down the driveway, past the pale grey doorway to their immaculate, painted basement, and up the long wooden steps to the back door to call for Barbara Lynn. Standing on the small gallery at the top, I peered into the tall, double-hung kitchen window to see Mrs. Moores in her neat apron, tending to her morning tasks. The good, dark, red and black battleship linoleum gleamed in the morning sunlight. To the left, off the kitchen, I could barely see into the pantry, filled with jars of preserves, crocks of flour and sugar, and carefully wrapped leftovers. There was always fresh homemade bread, toasted with butter and soaked in warm molasses, which I never tasted, and still crave.

"No, Barbara Lynn is in school today. She has school in the mornings now. So if you want to see her, you'll have to come back this afternoon."

And so I did.

On the first morning of her summer holidays, Barbara Lynn came to the door before I had finished my breakfast. I had eaten all the crust off my bread as usual and was ready for the un-encrusted joy of the soft, buttery centre. Mom and Wayne laughed at me for this but Mom said we had to eat all the crusts, so that was my solution. But that day I was so excited to go and play with Barbara Lynn that I totally forgot the soft centre I'd been preparing and ran out the door after eating just the crust. Mom and Wayne really laughed at me then and told everyone the story.

I loved Barbara Lynn. Her sunny, tanned face was slightly freckled. She had blue eyes and her straight, caramel-blonde hair was pulled back and tied with a ribbon, showing her high, smooth forehead. She had even, regular features and a smile that showed her perfect white teeth. I sought her out every day and, I have to say, she sought me. We explored the neighbourhood, down every laneway, trespassing every possible backyard, and made hideaways in the tall grasses and low bushes of the open fields between the backyards of Mount Royal Avenue and Golf Avenue. We minded Kerry together for Mom and ran messages for her. We bought Cracker Jacks for the prize, waited for pineapple popsicles to come out, skipped rope, went running and sliding, and played house every day for endless summers and into the long winter's night, when she took her big, big brother Basil's long, long toboggan without asking, so the two of us could go sliding together, down over the hill at the bottom of Mount Royal Avenue, across St. Clare Avenue under the pole light and down into the Knights of Columbus field where the full moon glittered on the mounds of glazed snow, and the toboggan flew along forever on the longest slide we'd ever had.

Barbara Lynn was almost a year older than me, but when we were found to be playing "doctor" behind Keats' Mattress Factory, it was me who was blamed.

One warm, idle, summer morning, after doing a forbidden pee among the discarded wrappers, broken glass and faded cardboard molded over the green rocks by many rainfalls in the shaded alley behind Keats' little factory, I said to Barbara Lynn, "Why do you have to coopy down to pee?"

"Girls are different than boys," she said.

"I know."

"Do you know what the difference is?"

"Yes."

"What is it?"

"Girls don't have a topper."

"What's that?"

"What you pee with."

"Yes, they do, but boys have it on the outside and girls have it on the inside."

"How can you have it on the inside?"

"Do you want to see?"

"Yes, show me."

"No, I won't."

"I'll show you mine if you show me yours."

"Okay, I'll show you mine if you show me yours first."

"No. Then you won't show me."

"Yes, I will."

"Let's do it together."

We slowly pulled down our short pants with their elastic waistbands.

"All the way," I said.

"I will."

Mine were down.

"There, see?"

"Oh."

Her eyes widened.

"You have to go all the way, Barbara Lynn."

I quickly pulled my pants back up.

"You didn't show me yours."

"Yes, I did," she said.

"I didn't see it."

"Well, I showed you."

"No, let's do it again."

"No."

"But I showed you mine."

"Okay."

We lowered our pants again, getting more used to the situation.

"See?" she said.

"Oh," I said, as I gazed in fascination at the two smooth, pale mounds with the cleft in between them.

"What's that?" she asked, pointing to my scrotum.

"There's little round things inside."

"Round things?"

"They're like eggs."

"I have eggs too."

"Where are they?"

"My eggs are on the inside."

"You mean we both have eggs?"

"Yes."

"You have to be careful of them," I said. "You can hurt them easy."

"We better be careful not to break our eggs then."

We laughed.

"Where does your pee come out?" I asked.

"From here."

"It's like a little bum."

"I like the way mine is. I wouldn't want it all on the outside."

"I don't mind it. Come on. Let's go down in the field and make a house."

"We should check on our eggs again," Barbara Lynn said, "to make sure they're okay."

"Okay. We will."

It became our private joke.

"How are your eggs today?" we'd say.

"Good. How are yours?"

"Good."

We were very conspiratorial and very satisfied with our secret shared knowledge, until Barbara Lynn let it slip to her older brother, who told her mother, who told Mom, who confronted me.

"Gregory," Mom said, and I knew something was wrong. "Mrs. Moores called and she doesn't want you to go up for Barbara Lynn anymore."

"Why not? What's wrong?" I asked, shaken.

"Barbara Lynn told her you and she were taking each other's pants down and then looking at each other's private parts."

As she said this, she tilted her head and looked at me with raised eyebrows. Her voice became very quiet so that the tenants and the neighbours would not possibly overhear it. "Is that right, Greg?"

It had been awhile now since we had checked on each other's eggs and I had almost forgotten about it, but now it returned uneasily to my mind. I was silent.

"Mrs. Moores is very upset and I agree. I didn't know you were doing things like that."

"But we didn't do anything," I protested.

"You *know* that's not right."

I was silent.

"Promise me you won't do anything like that again now, Greg."

"All right. Can I go up with Barbara Lynn again to play?"

"I don't think so."

"Can she come down here?"

"I don't know. Not today, Greg."

This was bad. I suppose I thought I was doing something wrong since I didn't want anyone to know about it but they were acting like we had done something terrible. My dubious status at the Moores' suffered a severe setback. Mrs. Moores had always regarded me with some reserve and was not always happy to see me at the door. I was young and Barbara Lynn could do better. Although she and Mom had gone to Prince of Wales College together, and Mom was smart and a great beauty, Mom had married a Catholic who drove an oil truck, and we had tenants, American tenants, and no car. Mrs. Moores was married to a very proper Protestant. He worked at Furness Withy & Co., a proper English firm, wore a white shirt and a tie to work, and drove a pale green 1952 Dodge with a slope back. And, although Mom was tasteful and kept a clean and tidy house, she had three small boys and could never hope to match the regimentation of the Moores' house, where children from the street were seldom permitted.

One rare day, when Mrs. Moores was not home, Barbara Lynn brought me in to the sacred pantry to look for a snack. This was highly irregular and I couldn't believe how casual she was. The pantry was more tightly controlled than the church sacristy, and Mrs. Moores, as deaconess, never allowed you in to gape and choose. Only she was allowed in the pantry and she would bring you out what snack she allowed. I was, of course, always honoured and grateful for anything.

Only once did I get beyond the kitchen to the hallway and living room. The clean, red floral runners lay straight as an arrow on the shining hall floor. The shellac on the dark wood doors and facings gleamed. The doilies lay perfectly placed under the matching lamps and all was quiet and composed as a tomb, except for the ticking of the large clock on the mantle above the spotless grate. The whole feeling was of a bomb about to explode. I did not linger long for fear I would tip something over, trip the fuse, and be asked to leave. Mostly I waited on the back step and after the fuss died down, I found my way back there.

One morning as Barbara Lynn and I lingered on her back porch, her much older brother came out, arguing through the open door with Mrs. Moores. Robin had a pale, earnest face with freckles, a tall brush cut of light-red hair and a hot temper. Barbara Lynn and I leaned against the rail and did not take the argument as seriously as we should have.

"I don't give a damn about it. I'm not doing it," Robin barked.

"Oh, you said damn," Barbara Lynn chimed in casually, and we laughed.

"Robin is a devil," I intoned after her in a mocking singsong.

Robin looked at his sister then turned on me. In a flash, he flung me down backwards over the steps. I grabbed for the rail, missed and tumbled down the long back steps with a cry. Barbara Lynn screamed and Mrs. Moores came running out and yelled at Robin. She made sure I was all right amid Barbara Lynn's indignant protests, and then made Robin apologize to me. She was very angry with Robin, and even more put out that I should witness such a display of behaviour, and worse still, that she should have to apologize for it, so I made little of it all. It seemed Barbara Lynn's playing doctor with me was not the only thing Mrs. Moores had to worry about, and in time the restrictions on me and Barbara Lynn were forgotten, and we returned to our happy ways.

Kindergarten

I was content with my life at home on the streets, and saw no reason that I should go to school. Mom and I had many long debates on the subject, which I, of course, lost. Wayne had cleared kindergarten, had even cleared grade one, and was now in grade two at St. Bonaventure's College, which was run by the Irish Christian Brothers. It was about a mile from our house, at the end of Merrymeeting Road on Bonaventure Avenue. Before you got to St. Bon's you had to pass St. George's School, a large, plain, pale green clapboard building, where Wayne had gone to kindergarten and where I was destined to follow. St. George's was Protestant. I always felt sending us there was a concession to Mom since she had to agree to have her children raised as Catholics when she married Dad.

One Sunday morning, after an argument of which I was largely unaware, Mom abruptly took me off to Gower Street United Church with her. As we walked over Long's Hill in the pleasant sunshine, I thought of Wayne going off with Dad to St. Patrick's and wondered what this separation might mean.

Did I belong to Mom now and Wayne to Dad? I was as fascinated to go into a United church as I would have been about
going to China. The building was plain inside, like a hall or a
classroom, not like a church, and I could understand everything
they were saying. I even recognized some of the people from
around Town. So this is where they came, I thought. It was
airier, the people a little better dressed, and it felt altogether different and very local compared to the cluttered and distant mys-
teries of St. Patrick's.

But there was no convenient Catholic kindergarten, and so
my brothers' and my first educational inoculation was decid-
edly Protestant. Mom was looking forward to my going to
school, but I was not. Nevertheless, the terrible day came. Mom
and Wayne accompanied me on the bus. We entered school
from a crowded and noisy schoolyard through a large wooden
door that led into the basement and then up the steps to the
classrooms. The smell of bookbag leather, pencils and lunch
boxes made my stomach turn over.

The kindergarten teacher was Miss Snow. She had a clean,
plain face and her hair was pulled back in a neat bun. She wore
a good skirt and a cream, high-necked blouse with a cameo pin,
and sensible brown walking shoes. She smiled at Mom, then
down at me, her grey eyes narrowing slightly.

"I'm sure we won't have any problem here," she said.

I immediately bolted from the room. Mom and Wayne ran
after me and had to half drag me back up the stairs.

"Now, Greg, there's no need to run away. What are you afraid
of?"

"She's a witch."

"Greg!"

"Yes, she is. She's a witch and I don't like her and I don't want
to stay here. Let me go."

"Now, Greg, look, Wayne went here and he didn't mind it.
He liked Miss Snow, didn't you, Wayne? Wayne?"

"It's not that bad, Greg," Wayne offered. "And it'll be over before you know it."

"And Wayne will pick you up after school."

"I will? Do I have to?"

"Yes, Wayne, you do."

"I'm not going."

"Look, now, Greg, you have to go to school today or tomorrow, so it might as well be today."

I cried and wailed and went back to Miss Snow's room. She looked at me with narrower eyes and less affection than before. And so I took my small, hard seat with a row of other miserable, suspicious children under the large capital and small letters and numbers, with cheerful drawings hanging on the walls surrounding us. The door closed and my heart sank.

For several more days I made Mom's and Wayne's mornings miserable, and then just Wayne's. Mom packed me lunches in my new red, square lunch tin with the double handles, but the smell of peanut butter sandwiches mixed with the tin of Jocko chocolate milk made me sick. Finally, when I realized that my tactics were ineffective and no one was going to change their mind about my situation, I gave up. I even co-operated to the point where I was allowed to take the bus to school by myself.

I would catch the West Loop at the top of Mount Royal Avenue on Pennywell Road in front of Walsh's Store, and ride down Pennywell Road, up Adams Avenue, past the Salvation Army Citadel and down Merrymeeting Road to St. George's. Other kids got off at the stop but not me. I stayed on, went on down Parade Street, around the bus terminal, down Long's Hill and along the length of Water Street, past all the department stores. The bus turned just before Murphy's Barber Shop and climbed Casey Street, passed by St. Clare's Hospital and on up St. Clare Avenue to Cashin Avenue, where it finally turned back onto Pennywell Road and stopped at Walsh's Store again. I got off there and walked carefully down along the fences on Mount

Royal Avenue. Hugging our house, I went in the driveway, unseen by Mom in the kitchen window overhead, and went down into the basement, where I stayed all day. I played down there and had my lunch and rarely ventured out. When I saw, through the dirty basement window, the first children returning home, I went out around the front of the house, in through the front door and "came home."

I settled into this routine for a week until Miss Snow finally called to ask Mom how I was.

"Fine," said Mom. "Why? Oh, I see." She hung up the phone. "Gregory, come here, please."

"What, Mommy?"

"Gregory, you've been lying to me about going to school, haven't you? Where have you been all day long? Where? In the basement? You mean to tell me all week while I was up here doing my work, you've been down there the whole time? Cripes Kate, Greg."

With my truancy ended, I returned to the smells of St. George's.

In the back of the class were two large, painted, wooden panel doors, which could slide open to reveal the grade one class beyond. We ate our lunch in the grade two classroom, where I got to know the Kavanagh twins, Frank and Percy. Frank had a lame left hand which stuck out from his arm at a right angle. It was limp and he held it in against himself, covering it with his right hand, and looked out at the world sideways, challenging and belligerent, waiting for someone to make fun of him. He didn't have to wait long at St. George's. There were plenty of children waiting to mock and jeer and taunt the easy targets. Frank seemed surly and suspicious, but the pain of his soft heart was obvious. His twin, Percy, was protective of him, and I felt curious and drawn to them.

"It isn't right for people to make fun of Frank's hand," said Percy. "It isn't Frank's fault. It could happen to anyone."

"Yes, that's right," I agreed. "Did you hurt it in an accident, Frank?"

"None of your business."

"No," said Percy, "it was always like that."

"Does it hurt?"

"No, it doesn't hurt at all. Look. I can even bang it," said Frank.

And he did so to prove how little it bothered him. But it looked painful to me and I couldn't help wincing.

"Can you use it?"

"Of course I can. I can hold lots of things, but I can't do much with it."

And he put his hand back in his pocket. Perhaps I asked too many questions.

I could not warm to Miss Snow. She carried a bright red stick, which she rapped our fingers with if we were not following orders. In class I sat behind another Barbara, not Barbara Lynn. This Barbara had a pretty, pale, freckled face and long, wavy, coal-black hair, which I loved. One day she had it in plaits and I could not resist touching them. I knew that pulling pigtails was the typical bad thing to do. Other kids did it and Miss Snow warned us not to. I had no urge to pull them. I just wanted to reach out and hold one. Miss Snow did not appreciate the distinction, and I felt the crack of the bright red stick on my fingers, and a flash of humiliation and anger. I thought how different her tone was when Mom was present.

I was very fond of this other Barbara for whom I had already suffered, with her lovely American accent, and I visited her large apartment on Cashin Avenue at every opportunity. She was my second love and I was delighted to lavish valentines on both Barbaras.

Mom told me to also bring a valentine to Miss Snow, who lived on Pennywell Road in a very tidy grey house. The front porch had large, clean windows and a perfect fern in a shiny brass pot. I wasn't sure I wanted to give Miss Snow a valentine but I was in the valentine swing and knocked at her door.

"Is Miss Snow in?" I asked.

"Yes, one moment please," said a comely woman with white hair, who lived with Miss Snow.

She was older but seemed younger than Miss Snow, who came to the door wearing a cardigan and taking off her glasses. Her face relaxed into an expression of surprise and pleasure as she took my valentine card and thanked me.

"I wonder what this could be," she said with uncharacteristic playfulness. "I had no idea you were thinking about me."

I wasn't. But I could see right away the favourable light the valentine put me in and began to appreciate Mom's political instincts.

The Best of Times

Little Kerry was such a bright, beautiful and brave-hearted boy that he had many admirers besides Wayne and me, who hardly noticed that our beautiful baby days were now eclipsed, and when our new tenants, Peggy and Paul, saw him, they fell instantly in love with him and he with them.

Peggy and Paul were from Georgia and spoke with a wonderful Southern drawl, which Dad soon began to pick up, to Mom's horror.

"Bill! Paul is going to think you're making fun of him!"

"No," said Dad, for whom admiration meant imitation, and he found lots to admire in the Yanks.

Although they were older than Mom and Dad, the two couples became good friends. Peggy doted on Kerry. She brought him expensive gifts from her trips stateside, and something for me and Wayne, of course. She took him on outings with her and Paul, and kept him upstairs with her more than he was down with us. She even asked Mom about adopting him, an offer which was, of course, warmly rebuffed.

At Christmas a huge stack of presents appeared under the tree for Kerry from Peggy and Paul, among which was a black denim cowboy suit: pants and jacket, with pink piping and snap buttons, a cowboy hat, the very best double-gun-and-holster set and boots, in short, everything that Wayne and I had been dreaming and scheming and pleading for since we knew such things existed. Wayne and I concluded Kerry no longer needed our undying attention and support, and that was it. The honeymoon was over for Kerry.

He had, in any event, been displaced as the youngest by a new brother, Anthony Shane, the Irish tradition still holding. There was no great need to amuse the new baby as he was himself a source of constant entertainment, with his big head of platinum-blond curls and quizzical blue eyes.

"Scully, I believe the milkman brought him," said Uncle Bob.

When Mom first brought him home and was changing him on her bed, he peed right in her mouth, which made us all howl, even Mom. He became the main event at mealtime, putting his bowl of food on his head and laughing so much at the huge mess he made in his high chair Dad said he looked like a bully-boo. We found this very amusing. He was as messy as a barnyard and so we started calling him that, and even sang our own version of the Kool-Aid jingle about him as he threw the food around.

Barnyard, Barnyard, real great
We want Barnyard, can't wait.

With many more messy meals and much repetition, Barnyard became Benyard, and finally Ben, or Beni, a name which seemed to please our happy, egg-headed little brother better than Shane, and to Mom's dismay, it stuck. From then on he was Beni, or Ben, sometimes Barn, but never Shane, except, of course, to Mom, especially if she was mad at him. Everything about little Beni was funny to me and Wayne and Kerry, even his big goose doll with the big yellow beak we found hilarious, and he suffered us to drag him around with us and laugh at him. Barbara

Lynn and I adopted him as our own baby for playing house, and he was rarely out of our hands. Mom saved him from being mauled to death, and so he grew into a willing pawn for many of our games.

✦

With Beni's birth Mom and Dad abandoned all hope of producing the much-longed-for daughter. Uncle Bob and Aunt Mil, now with four girls, decided to keep going for the boy. It was beginning to sound like one of Dad's stories. "There were two best friends. One had four sons, and no daughter, and the other had four daughters and no son," at least not yet.

Although no relation whatsoever, Bob and Mil Murphy were our favourite uncle and aunt, except for Auntie Vera, of course. Uncle Bob and Dad were best friends. Aunt Mil and Mom were friends too, but really Mom did not have friends herself, and never talked on the phone with other women. But she liked Uncle Bob a lot. Bob was classy and handsome, wore a suit and tie, and seemed always to have a tan, which made his friendly blue eyes even brighter. He never criticized us or took Dad's side against us in any arguments, but he always had a word of encouragement, and sometimes a nickel or a dime for us, which made him even more popular.

Before we owned our own car, when Dad got his two weeks of summer holidays, Uncle Bob would come in the big Studebaker with suicide doors, a tester from Adelaide Motors where he was a salesman, and take us all up to the little cabin in Topsail Pond that belonged to his sister, "Aunt" Sheila. There were deserted cabins to investigate, and a perfect woodpecker hole, high up in a tree, that Wayne and I kept a watch on. Uncle Bob and Aunt Mil came out with their girls, Karen, Robin, Tina and Andrea, some evenings and always on the weekends, to go swimming and play horseshoes in the lumpy front yard, and of course, there was food and drink and cards at night. The cabin wasn't on the water, but across the road we had access to the neighbour's wharf, where we would sit, cheering on Mom as she swam leisurely out to the middle of the pond in her sleek, mint-green swimsuit and cap.

"That's too far, you'll never get back," we cried.

"Don't worry about your mother," said Dad admiringly.

For all her glamour and refinement, Mom was never happier than when she and Dad were outdoors in the country, having a "boil-up" on the beach, or camping in the woods. They were our best times, and later when we got our own car we went off for rides whenever we had the chance, to Topsail Beach for a swim in the cold North Atlantic and a picnic on the hot rocks with ham sandwiches and Orange Crush, or to Bowring Park sliding in the winter, or just out for a ride around Town or around the Bay. In August and September, they picked gallons of blueberries on the Tilton Barrens, while we played Cowboys and Indians in the rocky hills.

Uncle Bob and Aunt Mil and their girls often came with us in their car. On one of our late-summer picnics at Powers Court, while hopping stones to cross the river, I fell in. I was soaked and cold and expected a sharp reprimand from Dad, but he was with Uncle Bob, so he was not too annoyed with me. I was immensely pleased when Uncle Bob put his own good plaid shirt around me. It was warm and smelled like Uncle Bob. Any article bestowed on a child by a favoured adult naturally carried with it other blessings. Uncle Bob's protective plaid cloak conferred not only warmth, but safety and acceptance. Then Aunt Mil brought me hot chocolate and I felt very calm and privileged indeed.

Sunday Mornings

Perhaps because my parents' was a mixed marriage, we were not a greatly religious family, and my early Catholic influences were confined to Mass at St. Patrick's Church, where every Sunday Dad and Wayne and I would walk from Mount Royal Avenue. Our route took us across St. Clare Avenue, where we all gasped in admiration one morning at the sight of a dazzling new, salmon-pink and grey '55 Chevy Impala. Without our own car, we continued on foot down the path through the Knights of Columbus field, over Bennett's Brook on wobbly rocks, out onto Lemarchant Road, past the Grace Hospital, down Pleasant Street, and over the top of Power Street, into the old city. Dad said it was the steepest hill in St. John's and he didn't know how they kept pavement on it unless they nailed it on. It was one of the few one-way streets in town. You could only drive down it, not up, for fear the car would have to stop, then stall out and slip back onto Patrick Street. St. Patrick's Church was a tall, stone, neo-Gothic structure with one high, green spire, at the bottom of Patrick Street near Water Street, in the middle of the mostly Irish Catholic working-class neighbour-hoods of the West End.

The men wore their best coats, white shirts, dark ties, and salt-and-pepper caps. They stood up in the back of the church throughout Mass, although there was still space left in the pews. Some even stood outside the door through Mass, until Monsignor Murphy yelled at them from the pulpit that anyone who thought they were fulfilling their Sunday duty standing outside the front door was very much mistaken: they were not, and they might as well stay home and commit mortal sin as stand on the steps of the Church and think they were not. It was an ongoing battle and one hot Sunday morning he stormed down the aisle and slammed the door shut so the slackards couldn't look in and see the consecration, which was technically the only part of the Mass you had to be present for to fulfill your Sunday obligation.

The pulpit was high up and Monsignor Murphy had a loud, deep voice that carried great authority. When he wasn't fighting with the men in the back of the church, challenging them to come up and take a seat, he had his back to us, and I would watch his beautiful green and gold, fiddleback chasuble go back and forth from one side of the altar to the other, his white lace arms went out and up and down. He turned, he genuflected. He intoned incomprehensible Latin words, rocking back and forth on his black brogues, and the altar boys answered back incom-prehensible Latin, on cue. The congregation sat down, stood up, blessed themselves and knelt down on the hard, worn, dirty wooden kneelers. They grabbed the back of the pew in front to stand up again and dusted off the knees of their trousers.

"Don't put your dirty feet on the kneeler. It's not a foot rest."

The children were always a little later than the adults in knowing when to stand, sit and kneel, so the whole event had a gentle, wave-like flow to it.

Dad gave Wayne and me a nickel each to put in the collec-tion. It was the quickest nickel I ever held, and the fact that it passed through my hand was a mere formality to teach us the value of giving up five cents' worth of three-for-a-cent candy once a week to get to heaven for all eternity.

Sitting there in the press of steamy bodies, coughs, gurgles and strange smells, waiting to stand and sit and kneel and give, I always felt half ignorant, half orphan, or perhaps it was half Catholic, half Protestant, since Mom was not here with us like the other children's mothers, who looked more like Catholic mothers than she did. They wore dark, plain coats and bandanas, or dark hats, with little or no makeup, and they whispered endless rosaries through bad dentures and fluttering, closed eyes. Although we were in no way rich, Mom always managed to look glamorous and fashionable, and she liked to be admired. No self-respecting Catholic mother could be seen to want such a thing. Mom lived on the higher levels, in the modern world, near the Mooreses. Dad came from downtown and this was his weekly observance down to the old church and the old people he had come from.

After Mass we went across Deanery Avenue, up Job Street, and over New Gower Street to visit with Dad's parents, whom we called Mommy Lone and Daddy Lone, whom Dad called Skipper. If it was in the late summer and fall, candy season, we would stop in to Power's Store for a special treat of homemade fudge—pink, white or chocolate—or bull's eyes, made of pulled molasses, doled out, piece by piece, by slow-moving Mrs. Power. Power's Store occupied the main floor of a little two-and-a-half storey, saddle-roofed house—which is a house with a high gable roof—in the middle of a long row of identical, saddle-roofed, clapboard houses and stores called Andrew's Range.

Dad's parents' house was a tall, three-storey in another row further east on New Gower Street across from the old Brownsdale Hotel, a green Victorian structure in an overgrown garden of lilac trees and Japanese knotweed on the corner of Brazil Street. On the other corner was Kenny's Fruit Store, where we sometimes got grapes or oranges to bring up to Mommy Lone. T. J. Malone's Grocery, at the corner of Hutchings Lane, was attached on the west side to Casey's Butcher Shop. Skipper and Mr. Casey owned that row of buildings, but recently T. J. Malone's Grocery had closed and stood dusty and vacant except for some barrels and crates. There was a door from the old store into our grandparents' front hall, with its coat stand and long, dark stairs up to the living quarters. Dad would check us over there and warn us to be quiet and behave ourselves, and up we would go.

Mommy Lone was bedridden under a maroon satin eiderdown ever since she lost a leg to diabetes, and they had made up her bedroom on the second floor in the front, next to the parlour. We were taken in and presented. She lay there in the semidarkness, which made it difficult to see she had only one leg. Sometimes her jet-black hair was let out over the pillows. Her forehead was broad and pale and her dark brown eyes flashed as she looked sharply into you.

"Come here," she would say, and, taking my little hand in her damp, fleshy ones, she would press the nickel I had lost in the collection plate only an hour before back into my palm and fold my fingers over it with a squeeze.

"That's for you," she would say.

"Thank you, Mommy Lone."

At the other end of the dark hallway and up two worn steps was the kitchen, a bright room facing south with a large table on the right, covered with an oilcloth, and an oil stove on the left. You could go out a door in the back of the kitchen onto a roof, which had a platform bounded by a picket fence overlooking George Street and the downtown. To the right was the back of the old Salvation Army Citadel on Springdale Street and to the left was George Street United Church with its smooth round tower and long slit windows, looking like a castle in a fairy tale. Below was the old carriage house, where the horse and wagon for deliveries used to be kept. Beyond the rooftops and chimney pots of the houses and stores on Water Street and the Harbour, thick with the masts of ships, lay the South Side Hills.

When Dad was a boy, he would have to fill the wagon with boxes of groceries and drive it up the South Side Hills to the Brow to make deliveries, stopping several times on the way up the steep gravel road to rest the horse. He would throw a block behind the wheels to keep the wagon from rolling back down the hill. Sometimes, if the weather turned bad, he might have to stay overnight before coming back down into the city. One winter he struggled through the deep snow with a box of groceries for an old war veteran who lived in a tarpaper shack not much bigger than an outhouse. He knocked at the door but there was no answer. He forced his way in and there was the vet, dead on his bed, blue from the cold. He had been dead for days, Dad figured, with no one but Dad to find him. There was a lot of poverty there and terrible sights, he said. During the Depression desperate people with nowhere to go put up shacks on the South Side Hills, and tried to get jobs in Town or some food on the dole. Skipper was soft, Dad said, and never collected on half his bills, but told Dad to keep delivering the groceries anyway, which was why they lost all their money in the end, that, and the drink. But it had not started out that way.

✦

Great-aunt Mary Kennedy was Mommy Lone's baby sister and was often at the house on New Gower Street. She had the same dark features and pale face as her oldest sister, Julia. She smoked constantly when I knew her, and had a husky voice with a big laugh and was game for anything. Aunt Mary had a way of suddenly looking at you and fixing you with those sharp, black Kennedy eyes that would penetrate to the back of you and make you confess to anything, whether you'd done it or not. Then her face would light up and she'd laugh with a loud smoker's laugh that ended in a fit of coughing. She was full of stories, which she told with great drama. Her most famous story was that of the Kennedy family being stranded on the coast of the Labrador.

Both the Malone and Kennedy families came from Carbonear, a prosperous fishing town on the other side of Conception Bay, a day's ride from St. John's, where both families had stores on Water Street. Mommy Lone and Great-aunt Mary's father, Captain Nicolas Kennedy IV, was a master mariner with his own schooner and, as was the custom with many Newfoundland fishing families of the time, he went down on the Labrador coast fishing every summer with his wife, Margaret, and their ten children. His brothers Terrence and John, both with their own schooners and large families, set sail with him for Sloop Cove, north of Hamilton Inlet, where the Kennedy clan had fished for generations. There was a large house built long before by the family, a barn for the livestock they brought with them every spring, and a bunkhouse for the sharemen, who fished with the Kennedys for a share of the profits.

May of 1897 found them all settled comfortably into the family compound. It was a happy summer for the thirty Kennedy cousins, playing over the hills and swimming in the warm water of the shallow cove. Aunt Mary was only a girl of five and spent her days playing in her mother's large wooden washtub on the shore, which she called her "boat." The men and the older boys spent the days fishing from dawn to dark, while the women split and dried the fish on flakes for storage. They were the only residents of Sloop Cove, and the only other souls they saw, except for an occasional Inuit hunter, were Captain Dan Pumphrey's sharemen. Captain Pumphrey was fishing north of Sloop Cove, but his sharemen brought their fish in trap skiffs to store on board Captain Nick's schooner with his catch. Captain Nick's schooner, under the command of the first mate, would then leave and arrive home ahead of them, the earlier boats generally

getting a better price for their fish. But with Captain Nick's
schooner filled to capacity with both catches, there would be no
room left for the family, and so, by agreement, Captain
Pumphrey was to stop into Sloop Cove at the end of September
and take the Kennedys on-board his ship for the two-week journey home to Newfoundland.

The season up north comes to a close quickly, with the
shorter days and cooler weather coming on fast, and by the end
of September it was time for John and Terrence to leave with
their families. They implored their older brother to come with
them; they would make room. But Captain Nick was unwilling
to inconvenience his friend Dan Pumphrey and determined to
wait for him as arranged. Nevertheless, it was with a sinking
feeling that Margaret Kennedy watched her in-laws wave goodbye from the decks of their schooners, as they sailed out of the
cove and headed south under grey skies.

The appointed day of Captain Pumphrey's arrival came. The
family was packed and ready. Mrs. Kennedy was in the lookout
when she spied the schooner at full sail. It was five or six miles
offshore and gave no indication of coming into Sloop Cove. She
ran in despair to her disbelieving husband, who climbed the
nearby hill just in time to see the last of Pumphrey's sails disappear under the horizon. It had to be him. There was no other
boat fishing that far north. It was indeed, Captain Pumphrey,
who continued on, firmly convinced that Captain Nick and his
family must have already gone on with the other Kennedy
brothers. And so they were left. By the time Captain Pumphrey
arrived home and discovered his mistake, the ice would be in,
and it would be impossible to send a boat back for the Kennedys
until the following spring. Their situation was grim.

In Sloop Cove the family had only rations for a couple of
weeks, mostly flour and salt fish. There was little fuel. They had
shotguns to hunt game but not enough ammunition for the winter. Most of the bedding and clothes had been packed and sent

on ahead. The big old house, so sunny and secure for so many summers, was now a cold shell and no protection against the brutal advance of the long night. The snow would be coming any day now and the ice would block the cove in. They would surely perish if they stayed, so the decision was quickly made to leave, and try to make it to Emily Harbour, some twelve miles south. There they might winter over with the four Inuit families who comprised the tiny community, if the Inuit would have them, and if the Kennedys could get there.

Travelling overland through the rough bush was out of the question. Thankfully one of the trap skiffs had been left behind. The small children were put on the floor and covered up. The skiff was packed with most of their possessions, but the pots and pans and utensils had to be stowed in Mary's little "boat" and towed behind. Aunt Mary vividly recalled the tantrum she threw, demanding to be put in her little boat, until her father told her to "shut up and lie down." It was a grand laugh to her now. But then, at dawn, as they set out in an icy October wind, it was not.

Captain Nick and the two sharemen rowed, and the older boys spelled them. It took them the full day to make the trip but they arrived safely before dark, and were welcomed and taken in by the Inuit, who gave them one of their small but sturdy dwellings, with a sod roof and an open fireplace. The hunters shared with them whatever game they caught, and in this manner Captain Nick hoped they might survive the deep Labrador winter. Nevertheless, a constant watch was set in case a ship might make it back for them.

After a two-week voyage, Captain Pumphrey arrived safely back in Harbour Grace, where the fish was to be sold, only a few miles from the Kennedy home in Crocker's Cove, Carbonear. On the wharf was His Excellency Bishop Ronald McDonald, anxiously waiting to greet Captain Kennedy and his family. As soon as he understood the calamity, the bishop called up Sir

Robert Bond, who called the British Admiralty, who dispatched a ship to rescue the family, but the slob ice was already too thick for the ship to penetrate, so it was forced to turn back.

Back in Emily Harbour, the situation had become tense. Captain Nick's eldest daughter, Julia, Mommy Lone, had caught the eye of the best hunter in the tiny community, and he wanted to marry her. Mommy Lone was seventeen years old and terrified, knowing how dependent her entire family was on this man for their survival. She was very polite and even honoured, but she insisted he must talk to her father. He did. Captain Nick was diplomatic. It was not their custom to marry so young. He asked the hunter to wait and see, and so they waited a week, but the hunter was not about to take no for an answer. He was a great hunter. They depended on him. Why would Julia not share his bed and keep house for him, he argued? Julia did not wish to answer these questions and stayed close to her mother and out of sight. Her suitor brought gifts of much-needed furs. Captain Nick delicately fended off his advances without angering him, but the situation could not hold for long. The ice was thick in the harbour and though there was little hope now of a rescue, they maintained the lookout. It was now four weeks since their arrival in Emily Harbour.

Meanwhile, in Newfoundland, the plight of the castaway family on the cold Labrador coast was big news, and the story was even picked up by the international press. The SS *Grand Lake* was cruising the mouth of the St. Lawrence River at the time, and Captain Delaney, a friend of Captain Nick's, was convinced that his larger vessel could cut through the ice. He received permission to try and several days later he pushed into Sloop Cove, where a landing party found the note of explanation Captain Nick had left on the kitchen table. The weary, hungry and cold children on the lookout in Emily Harbour could scarcely believe their eyes when they saw the *Grand Lake* steaming into Emily Harbour. Julia ran to the beach and cried freely with relief. Her hunter made one final offer of all his worldly goods, which she kindly declined. Captain Nick was so happy to see his old friend Captain Delaney that he waded out up to his waist in the icy water to greet the landing craft. They were saved.

Needless to say, it was a famous family story, although when Dad told it, the hunter who had sought his mother's hand became a chief.* Never again would the Kennedy family go "down on the Labrador." Only Captain Nick returned for the final time the following summer, after which the family moved to St. John's, where Great-grandmother Margaret Kennedy, who never fully recovered from the strain of the ordeal, died two years later, leaving Julia to stand in as "mother" to her younger siblings, especially Mary and the youngest, little Maudie.

"How we prayed for little Maudie to grow," said Aunt Mary. "She was tiny and Mom had just died, and we were so afraid she wouldn't make it. So we prayed. Well, some prayers are not answered, but this one was. Little Maudie grew up to be six foot four with a voice that could command the Fleet. You know your Aunt Maud. Don't say God doesn't have a sense of humour," laughed Aunt Mary, till she coughed herself into another fit.

Sister Julia was "mother" to many already when she married mild-mannered Thomas Joseph Malone, also from Carbonear, in the year 1903. Was it Tom Malone she had thought of as the great hunter pressed for her hand that winter?

So it was that Julia and Tom's new store on New Gower Street was not only a home to their own growing brood but a hub for Julia's siblings, two of whom, William and Nicholas, were by then master mariners and captained ships for Water

---

*For another version of this story, see my cousin Frank Kennedy's book *A Corner Boy Remembers*.

Street merchants. Uncle Nick and Uncle Will were always at the house, according to Dad, and whenever they got back from a voyage, they always came up to see Mommy Lone.

"One time," said Dad, "Uncle Nick came back from South America somewhere and he had a monkey with him, a live monkey. And he came up to the house with it, but he was afraid of how Mommy Lone was going to take it. So he put the monkey in the parlour and closed the door while he went out to break the great surprise to Julia. Well, he didn't get far. There was a big crash and screeching coming from the parlour. Mommy Lone ran and opened the door. The monkey jumped straight into her arms and sent her right into the fits. The parlour was wrecked. Well, she went wild. She drove Uncle Nick and his monkey out of the house with a walking stick and they were both banished for a week."

"Did the monkey get back in?"

"No, but Uncle Nick did. Mommy Lone had a fierce temper but she thought the world of her brothers. She nearly died herself when they did."

Great-uncle William, Dad's namesake, was killed in the explosion on the SS *Viking* while making the famous film of the same name. Uncle Will was captain navigator of the *Viking* when it was hired by Paramount Pictures for the making of a film originally entitled *White Thunder*. In March of 1931, the Viking was sent back to the ice floes north of Newfoundland to film more shots of the ice breaking up. The director, Varick Frissell, took a large amount of dynamite on board, about which it seems the crew was not properly advised. One night there was an accident, first a small explosion and shortly afterward a much larger one.

"Uncle Will was blown clear out of the ship and landed on the ice with his head split open," by Dad's account. "When he came to he stuck a wool mitt into the gash in his head to keep out the snow and cold. They were tough men," said Dad with feeling.

Will and the cameraman, Harry Sargent, got onto a piece of the wreckage and dragged Uncle Will's friend Clayton King on with them. For two days and nights they were on the icy water exposed to the freezing winds before they were finally rescued by the SS *Sagona*. By then Uncle Will had developed pneumonia and, just before the *Sagona* came through the Narrows into St. John's harbour, he died.

"We only heard that they had been saved," said Dad. "And they had been. But Uncle Will didn't make it, and Mommy Lone never got over it. She certainly loved those brothers."

Uncle Nick died early on as well. He had a colourful career and was captain of the *Terra Nova* when it went to the rescue of the *Florizel*, which went down off Cappahayden in 1918. But his career was cut short by creeping paralysis, a more descriptive name for multiple sclerosis as we now know it, which he bore patiently until his death.

It was Great-aunt Mary who was most in residence at her sister Julia's house on New Gower Street, and it was there she got to know Tom's younger brother Maurice. He was a quiet man like Tom and a perfect match for the boisterous Mary.

"Two brothers married two sisters," Dad said, with some satisfaction.

Mary and Maurice Malone moved to Chicago, where another of the Malone brothers, Faustinus, was a Christian Brother teaching at a large Catholic college. In Chicago, Uncle Maurice managed an A&P store and Aunt Mary worked behind the counter and did the cash.

"I could cut a pound of butter off the slab and never have to go back and add or take off a dab. If a customer didn't believe me, I'd put it on the scales, and they proved me right, every time. I was good, but I had lots of practice," she laughed.

Chicago was a rough town in the 1920s. The store was robbed regularly, and even held up at gunpoint more than once. Finally, when Uncle Maurice was shot in the pocket watch by the mob, they decided to return to St. John's, and bought Leary's farm, twelve acres of meadows and fields on the Oxen Pond Road, on the outskirts of Town. There, in the farmhouse, surrounded by blackcurrant and gooseberry bushes, they lived a quiet life until they moved to Toronto, their final residence, where Great-aunt Mary became a substitute mother for Dad's brother Kit, and grandmother to his family, returning the favour Mommy Lone had done for her when their own mother died so young.

Sunday Mornings, Part Two

Mary and Maurice had no children. Julia and Tom Malone had ten. Most of Julia's children took after her side of the family. The boys were tall and lean with wavy black hair, pale faces with a heavy beard shadow, and strong noses.

"All conk and Adam's apple," said Dad. "The Black Irish."

Molly was the oldest, but there were mostly boys, Eugene, Jim, Tom, Ken, Kit, then Sheila, the favourite, a dark-haired and kind-hearted beauty, whom everyone loved, and finally Dad, Mike and Bren, the youngest. Uncle Bren was a great Nationalist. As a young man at Scout banquets, he voiced the family's political preferences in rousing speeches, at least one of which was printed in the *Daily News*. Being a Catholic from Town, it was hardly possible for Bren to be anything but a Nationalist in 1947 and bitterly opposed to liberal Protestant plans to hand over the country of Newfoundland to the Dominion of Canada. His passions did not move him past rhetoric but he got regular employment every election for his loyalty. The older brothers had the benefit of the more prosperous days on New Gower

Street, but this proved to be of little advantage to them. Uncle Jim even went to University, a rarity in those days.

Uncle Jim was not the first James Joseph Malone. His brother preceding him bore the same name, but died in infancy. The custom of bestowing the name of a dead child on the next sibling in line is, perhaps, not a lucky one. At any rate, Jim's course was crossed. I sometimes saw him at the Gosling Memorial Library, where he spent much of his time reading when he was not drinking and brawling in the many public houses downtown. As a small boy, our cousin Pat saw him on the corner of Adelaide Street and New Gower Street in the middle of one such brawl, his round, wire-rimmed glasses flashing in the fading light as he swung out.

There was a traffic cop at that intersection in those days, as this was where the streetcars turned down onto Water Street. As Pat and his father, Ken, Jim's younger brother, happened on the scene, this policeman was being joined by his replacement for the evening shift.

"We better get in there and break them up, I suppose," said the new arrival.

"Are you joking?" replied the constable on duty. "That's Jim Malone in there. It'd take a half a dozen of us to hold him down. You can go in if you want, but I'm staying here."

So that's Uncle Jim, thought Pat. Neither policeman went in, and that day, and that victory, such as it was, belonged to Jim.

It was hard for me to believe that Uncle Jim was a holy terror. When he appeared one night at our front door, he looked like a dishevelled banker or clerk in his dark overcoat. His glasses were smashed but still on his face, and he leaned slightly into the door jamb. He was, of course, drunk. Mom was upset to see him.

"He's been drinking, I don't want him in here like that, Bill."

"I know. I'll talk to him outside."

"I don't want to start bringing all that up here."

"Calm down, Lovey. I'll handle it," said Dad, and closed the door behind him as he went out into the vestibule.

Jim wanted his glasses fixed. He could not do without his glasses. He could fight well enough without them, but he couldn't read.

Uncle Jim had studied medicine at Dalhousie University in Halifax, but during the summer of the World's Fair, he went to visit his Aunt Mary and Uncle Maurice in Chicago.

"He went to the Fair and started drinking and he didn't stop," complained Great-aunt Mary, who was disgusted at the waste of brains and the lost opportunity.

But Uncle Jim had his demons, as did Uncle Eugene, whom I liked the look of, although I was a little afraid of him. He was quiet and seemed gentle, and even though I knew him to be tough like Jim, I could not decide if he was angry or hurt or both. He too was a great reader and drinker, but it was the smoking that caught up with him at last. Uncle Tom was named after Skipper, Thomas Joseph, and Ken was baptized Nicholas Kennedy Malone, after Julia's dear brother, Captain Nick.

Dad and Mom liked Ken. He was dependable and hard working, like Dad, and generous. Uncle Ken would stop in at our house on Mount Royal Avenue on his way home from Mammy's Bakery with a big bag of baker's scraps, pieces of raisin and apricot squares, and the ends of crinkles and date turnovers, a thrilling variety of rare treats. Naturally we came to look forward to his visits, which were invariably at suppertime, and it happened that, for three visits in a row, we were having beans.

"Oh no, not Ken, and we're having beans again," Mom was mortified. "Bill, he'll think we don't eat anything else."

He never stayed long before continuing his walk home, all the way from the Bakery downtown to the old farmhouse on Oxen Pond Road, in the back of Town, which he and his wife, Pat, and their large family rented from Great-aunt Mary. It was still surrounded by blackcurrant bushes and Leary's Brook still ran freely through the grassy fields, but newer streets of bungalows, like Hatcher Street, were cutting in to the old farm.

Uncle Ken and Uncle Kit, just two years older than Dad, were part of Dad's crowd. Handsome and charming like Dad, and a swell with the girls, Kit was a bit like Dad and Ken, and a bit like Jim and Eugene. He had worked and held down a good job in Toronto at McDonnell Douglas, but he drank, and it was the drink that won in the sorrowful end. Like Eugene, there was some injury, some sorrow or grudge from which he could not break free. What happened to that family with so many fine boys gone to drink? Tom and Bren and Mike also struggled with it like the older boys did, and like them, came off the worse. Only Dad and Ken, two out of eight boys, survived the scourge.

"Mommy Lone," said Dad, in a rare moment of exasperation with her, "was too stern, too strict with the boys. They couldn't do anything right for her, so they stopped trying and did what they wanted, I suppose. She was a great character and she was very funny, but too hard. And Mommy Lone was the law. No good to go to Skipper, and then the boys didn't respect Skipper. I don't know what happened, but it wasn't a happy house, and I stayed away as much as I could."

Dad didn't get an education like his older brothers did. He was kicked out of Holy Cross School, kicked out of St. Pat's, and finally settled at St. Bon's. At Holy Cross he pulled Brother Egan off his younger brother Mike. Brother Egan was a bully, he said, and always picking on Mike, so Dad challenged him. For his interference he was strapped on both hands until they turned red and swollen, in which condition he went home for dinner hiding his hands under his arms.

"What's wrong with your hands?" asked Skipper. "Let me see them." Dad showed his father his swollen hands.

"Who did that to you?" asked Skipper.

"Brother Egan," said Dad.

"What for?" said Skipper.

"I stopped him from beating up Mike."

"Come with me," said Skipper.

He took Dad and they both went over to Holy Cross together.

"Skipper was very quiet and hadn't really noticed me or interfered much in my life before that," said Dad, "so I was very nervous and didn't know what to expect when we got to Brother Egan's class."

Skipper went in with Dad up to the front of the class to Brother Egan and grabbed him by the front of his cassock.

"Don't you ever lay a hand on my son again," he said. "And if I ever hear you have, I swear to God I'll come back over here and give you such a beating you'll never stand up again, do you hear?"

When Dad told us this story his lip trembled and his eyes misted over. "I never knew until then that Skipper cared about me. Brother Egan never touched me or Mike again."

After grade eight, Dad left school to help Skipper run the store. Every house on New Gower Street had a still in those days, and the greatest achievement of any young man was to hold his liquor. Dad's older brothers were a great success in that department and would then come into the store and take money from the till. They fought with Skipper, which Dad could not understand, and when he came between them and tried to defend Skipper, they would fight with him, beat him up and laugh at him. He was very bitter about those days in the store and his older brothers, but he found diversion and his own business opportunity with his good friend Chrissy Andrews. The Andrews family was Lebanese and lived across the street. Chrissy and Dad had an old dory tied on down in the Harbour. In the evening they would row around the docks collecting scrap metal, especially copper, even relieving some ships of their copper fittings, when scrap was scarce. They sold these valuables to old Mr. Taylor, the scrap man, and did so well for themselves that when Skipper was going through a hard time and in need of some extra money Dad offered to lend him $100, a small fortune in those days.

"Where are you getting that kind of money, my son?" Skipper wanted to know.

So the story came out. Skipper was horrified and gave Dad a good beating, but he took the money anyway and got out of his jam.

Skipper Tom was generally content to leave the running of the household and the disciplining of the children to his high-spirited and domineering wife, Julia Germaine, while he ran the family business, T. J. Malone's, downstairs. He was fair haired and mild mannered and spoke little, unless he was on a bender with Mr. Casey. Friday nights were often a problem, and Julia was known to station two of the older boys outside the front door with baseball bats and instructions to beat Skipper back in if he tried to leave the house. She was both terrified and mortified that Skipper would get drunk, climb to the top of the mast of one of the schooners on a dare and dive into the Harbour. They fell out over Skipper's benders, but those days were long past and now he mostly drank warm water and sat in a semi-trance in his low, slope-back leather chair in the dining room, where he smoked his pipe and worried over Julia. I cannot ever remember him speaking to me or anyone else. We would sit with him by the window, looking down into the yard of George Street United Church and up New Gower Street, watching people in their Sunday best go in and out of the Brownsdale Hotel and Kenny's Fruit Store.

The dining room was the main room on the second floor. We never went into the front parlour, except on Christmas to see the dark tree with its old silver and red decorations. The foil bunting stretched from each corner of the room and met in the centre at the old brass chandelier, from which dangled a large, red, tissue-paper bell. The walls were covered in dark purple and taupe paper and dark-framed pictures. The Victorian settee and chairs were the same blue-grey purple with gold piping, and it seemed to me as though no one had ever used the room, except for the monkey, of course, and the priest when he came.

In the dining room, the large oak table was always taken up with an almost-completed jigsaw puzzle. Romantic views of European cities were cut into thousands of tiny, irregular pieces. The puzzles were the ongoing work of Uncle Tom and the stacks of comic books on the piano were his as well. Uncle Tom's wife had died and his daughter, Mary Lou, was living with her mother's people. Tom had moved back home to take care of Skipper Tom and Mommy Lone.

As we went up the worn steps into the warm, steamy kitchen, it was Uncle Tom who turned to us from the big pot of salt beef, vegetables and pease pudding boiling on the stove. He was an incongruous sight, with his white store apron on over his good pinstripe shirt and wide, dark-red satin tie with the big diamond pattern on it, and his brown suit trousers with the thick suspenders. Tom was tall with watery blue eyes and his nose was the strongest of all with a large wart on the left side. He was named after Skipper and had run the store with him till the end. Like his father, he was gentle and fond of his drink, but unlike Skipper, he was more affable and much more talkative. He wiped his large red hands on his apron and greeted us.

"There you all are. Come in, come in. Just from Mass, are you? How are you, Andy?"

"Good, Andy, how are you?"

"I can't complain," replied Tom.

Dad and his brothers called each other "Andy" though none of them bore that name. It was a joke born of an unreliable memory for names, which ran in the family. One simple "Andy" for all saved Dad from stumbling through Jim, Gene, Ken, Kit, Bren, Mike and Tom till he got to the "Andy" in front of him.

"Did you see Mother?" asked Tom.

"Yes. She looks good. How is Skipper?"

"Not too well this morning. I think he's nodded off in there. We won't disturb him now, and maybe he will have some appetite for his dinner when he wakes up. You boys sit down and visit with me. Sit in there now, Wayne, and this must be the lover boy, what? You're the boy with all the girlfriends, I hear," he said with a watery wink at Dad.

I was shocked that anyone had noticed me, let alone my girlfriends.

"Boy, I wish I had one of your girlfriends. I don't have one girlfriend. Do you think I could have one of yours?"

What could I say? "No" was not polite but I couldn't say "Yes."

"I don't know," I said.

"No," said Tom, "They probably wouldn't want me anyway. I'm too old. It's you they're all after. What have you got that makes them all chase after you, I wonder. I wish I knew."

"Yes, he likes the girls," said Dad, proudly. "Don't you, Greg?"

"Yes."

"I suppose he does," said Tom. "And you're getting an early start in. Ha ha."

Wink, wink.

"Don't let us hold you up now, Andy," said Dad.

"Not at all, Bill. Why don't you take this cup of tea down to Mother? She's waiting for it."

"All right. No sugar, right?"

"No. No sugar any more, and she hates that."

Dad left.

"I'm going to pour off a bit of this," he said, taking two cup towels and gently tipping the big, steaming pot till a noisy stream of pale liquid came gushing out into a bowl.

"There. That's a whole meal there in that pot liquor," said Tom. "You don't want to waste that. Would you boys like some?"

he asked as he poured some of the hot broth over a slice of white bread in a bowl.

"No thanks, Uncle Tom," we said.

The thick smells and steam of the kitchen mixed with the puffy, wet bread made us queasy.

"Oh, you don't know what you're missing," he said, as he shook some pepper over the swollen bread and raised a dripping piece of it up to his lips with a large spoon, blowing on it several times before he sucked it in with great satisfaction.

Our Sunday visits to Mommy Lone and Daddy Lone's were regular but brief. Sometimes we saw Uncle Jim's boys there. David was blond and soft-spoken, with cotton batting in his ears because of his constant earaches. His brother, Kevin, wore his windbreaker with the zipper half down and the shirt collar open, summer and winter. He never wore a cap, even on the coldest days, but preferred to wear large amounts of Brylcreem in his high, brown, wavy hair. They were downtown boys and grew up on Flower Hill behind the Brownsdale Hotel. Uncle Jim was not much of a family man. Mommy Lone had warned Aunt Mer not to marry him, that he would break her heart with drink and never amount to anything, but Aunt Mer was besotted and married him anyway, and lived to rue the day. She worked her whole life to bring up her family.

David and Kevin did chores for Skipper and Tom. They filled the coal bucket, ran messages, cleaned up and got an allowance for their work. They were older than Wayne and me. David smiled at us and was always polite. Kevin gave us a hard look and told us about the latest guy he'd beat up. I was fascinated by them and liked them both a lot, but I am not sure they liked us, or were perhaps shy of us because of the advantage Dad's sobriety and hard work gave us over them. But they seemed to belong there in that house with Skipper and Tom much more than I did, and I envied them their familiar ways. I always felt like an observer, an outsider, an uplander from the higher levels. After we left they stayed and helped ease the last days of life on New Gower Street.

Wayne went down to visit Kevin once on Flower Hill and Kevin came up once with Wayne on the bus. But Wayne threw up over himself on the bus and had to walk backwards down Mount Royal Avenue to avoid being seen and jeered at by Don Piercey, and that was it for Kevin.

Later, when Mommy Lone died, Dad would bring Skipper up to our house on Friday nights to watch wrestling on television. They both admired Whipper Billy Watson. Skipper sat almost motionless in the armchair with a glass of warm salt water resting on a doily on the wide, green arm. He smoked his pipe quietly, while Dad sat next to him, puffing proudly on an unfamiliar cigar, happy to have him there in the home he had provided. When Mom served him his supper, his tired blue eyes lit up and followed her out of the room. He died within a year of his wife and left everything to Tom, who sold the old house and store and went on a holiday to New York. Before he left, Tom and Bren, who were both still living at the New Gower Street house, invited Dad and Ken down to have their pick of the furniture.

Dad was very hurt and upset that Skipper had left the house just to Tom and that Tom had disposed of it so quickly, and so this magnanimous gesture from Tom and Bren pleased him greatly. He and Ken were looking forward to getting together with them at the old place for one last time to share memories and what little remained. On his way, he met Ken coming back up Casey Street fuming.

According to Ken, there was nothing left in the house. It was already all gone. Dad was flabbergasted. Nevertheless, they both went back down to New Gower Street. Ken was quite right. The settees and chairs from the parlour, Mommy Lone's secretary desk and the dining room furniture were all gone. The house was empty. Where was everything?

"Well," said Tom, "I didn't think anyone wanted all that old furniture. Too many memories."

And their cousin Neil Kennedy was very interested in it, so Tom and Bren had struck a deal with him. Dad and Ken knew Neil, of course. He ran the Bond Store, which controlled the all-important dispensation of liquor, and he was only too happy to swing a few cases of rum Tom and Bren's way for their generosity.

"Would you and Ken like a bottle to take home?"

No, they would not. Dad and Ken had no trouble believing Tom and Bren would do such a thing. They simply could not accept it and they fell to arguing.

"I can't believe you sold it all for a bloody drink! You bums! If Mommy Lone was still here you'd sell her for a drink too, I suppose."

"Hold on, hold on now, the two of you. You don't know what it's like. We were the ones stayed home, remember, and took care of Skipper."

"You took care of yourself, the star boarder. Free room and board, and you took everything you could get your hands on and drank it away."

"We did what we thought best, now, that's all."

"You never thought of nothing or no one but yourselves. You're no good, you never were any good and you never will be any good."

"Now you sound like Mommy Lone," pronounced Bren.

"Now, now, there's no need for all that now, boys, that's all the past. Come on now, sure, have a drink and forget about that old stuff," slurred Tom.

They might have come to fisticuffs but Tom and Bren were already too drunk for any satisfaction.

And so there they stood: the two sides of the family, so different in sensibility, and a great chasm opened up between them. It was the last time my father expected his brothers might turn around and do the right thing. It was the end of calling each other "Andy." It would be Tom and Bren, Bill and Ken, after that day. It was the end of trying to act like they were some kind of family who kept in touch and cared about each other. They did care, of course, in their own way, the way they were Catholic and went to church every Sunday. That was all taken for granted, and so there was little action in that direction. But they were paralyzed by their own unresolved tragedies, which required their constant attention. There was nothing now and no one to return to. What remained of the past had been bartered away for a case of rum. Skipper, worn out and depressed, and slowly dying of grief for his beloved Julia, had not the interest to remember Dad or Ken or any of them, and had simply left the house and all in it to the last one left home.

Dad was angry with Tom and Bren, but he was devastated by Skipper. He would now have to be content with the memory of Skipper coming to his rescue and defending him against Brother Egan as the greatest proof of his father's love.

On the Street

The first day of summer holidays after kindergarten, I came out of our house on Mount Royal Avenue in the stillness of the early morning, anxious to enjoy every minute. The street was empty but the sun was already beginning to warm it and the sky was blue overhead. I stood in the middle of the street, looking down over the Knights of Columbus field to the rest of the city and the South Side Hills beyond. The curve of the hill, as it sloped away, made me feel as if I were standing on top of the world and the summer stretched before me without schedule, a warm and sunny eternity.

We lived on the Higher Levels, as the ridge that ran along the top of Town was called. The houses on Mount Royal Avenue were not particularly bigger than downtown but there was more space between them and more trees and gardens. It was a small street that ran between Pennywell Road in the north and St. Clare Avenue in the south.

Ours was the only duplex on the street. The whole building was painted dark green, and Wayne and I watched in amazement as Dad mixed cans of bright blue and yellow paint and came out with cans of green. We lived at number 18 and the Martins, an old English couple with chintz covers on their chairs and vases of flowers, lived on the other side at number 20. They had a blue '49 Chevy and an ancient English setter, which Mr. Martin loved and we were all very sad when the dog died. Mrs. Martin was pleasant and looked like the Queen Mother. Their children were grown up and gone, and Mr. Martin did not like us walking on top of the fence that separated their backyard from ours, so he put up barbed wire on the divider between our galleries. One afternoon, when Mr. and Mrs. Martin were out back, Dad said to us in a loud voice, "You know, I don't like that barbed wire. Someone could get hurt on that. It's not very friendly."

He paused and added with great dignity.

"And it's certainly not very English"

The barbed wire disappeared after that and Dad had a seesaw and swings made up at the Plant on the South Side and installed in the backyard to help contain us.

Mom wanted a garden, so Dad fenced off a small area between the front of the house and the sidewalk, and planted dahlias and gladiolas in a bed under the living room window. He also installed a small square of lawn in the backyard, which had been just gravel. In those early days, children did not play indoors. You were sent out in all but the worst weather.

"Stay out and play," was heard almost daily, till the sky grew dark.

I put the outdoors to good use, but I had a passion for clubhouses. There was an old cupboard out on the back verandah, just big enough to fit two small children. I took out the shelves, lined it with cardboard, and sat in it with Barbara Lynn until the rain came through and soaked us. But the basement never got wet, and it was filled with treasures for playing house, and no one ever bothered us down there. As our playhouse became more elaborate, I cleared away more space, and even dug away at the mound of dirt in the front part of the basement, which was only partly excavated. I lined the new rooms with old bricks and rocks, and scavenged boxes to use as furniture and other treasures to decorate our new "house." Barbara Lynn would stay home cooking in the alcove by the chimney, while I went to work on the mound, developing new territory. What joy!

Barbara Lynn liked all the improvements. Dad did not. But I had no idea of this until I walked into the kitchen.

"What are you doing down there, digging up the damn basement for!"

He had never been mad like this before.

"We were just playing house down there," I stammered.

"I told you to stay out of it, for the last time," he thundered. "Do you hear me?"

"Yes."

"And it's all piles of dirt everywhere. I'm telling you if you go down there again, I'll give you something to remember," he threatened.

Was he going to hit me?

"Wait now, Bill," suggested Mom. "What were you digging for, Greg?"

"It doesn't matter what he was digging for. I don't care if he was digging for buried treasure. He was told not to go down there."

"Tell me now, Greg, what is all the digging for?"

"We were playing house and we needed more rooms," I faltered.

"More rooms!" exclaimed Mom. "Good grief, you don't need to go that far, Greg."

"You can find somewhere else to play for all that!" burst out Dad.

"But that's the best place," I somehow dared.

"I don't care! Look," he snarled, "You're down there in the dark. There's paint and kerosene and things I got put away, and who's down there with you?"

"Barbara Lynn, I suppose," said Mom.

"Yes, and her mother will be down here complaining to us next."

"We're careful," I ventured.

"You're not careful. You got the place tore up, and you're at it with the pick. You could have taken someone's eye out. Don't ever do it again. Do you hear me?"

"Can I just go in when it's raining if I don't use the pick?"

"No! No! No! You shouldn't be down there anyway. You should be outside with the other boys."

There was no way to get him to agree without getting him angrier, so I stopped. He had been irritated with me before but not like this. What was so valuable in the basement? I reluctantly left our newly renovated playhouse and returned to the open safety of the backyard and the sidewalk before it too became off limits.

At the top of the street were the Waddens, and I lived in fear of them. Mrs. Wadden had a broad, pale forehead, unsmiling, dark eyes and curly brown hair, and you didn't knock on her door. Jimmy Wadden, "Hot Dog," was my age, and he had an older brother named "Hamburger." Wayne said Hamburger wasn't too bad, but Jimmy was forever threatening me, stopping me from going up the street or down the street. I complained to Wayne about him but Wayne told me I could take care of him myself.

One day while Barbara Lynn and I were playing, Jimmy threatened to beat us up if we didn't let him play too.

"Okay, come on, Jimmy. You can be the son. I'll be the father."

"I don't want to be the son. I want to be the father."

"Okay, you be the father, and you have to go to work."

"Where do I work?"

"On the verandah. That's your office."

"I don't want to work. I want to stay here. I want to have a gun."

"No, Jimmy. It's not that kind of game."

"I don't care. I'm having guns. Watch out. Bang. Bang."

It was impossible to keep house in such conditions.

Just down from the Waddens' was a pleasant, pale green, shingled house with people we never saw. They were probably hiding from the Waddens and the Yetmans, who lived on the other side of them. Bobby Yetman was older than me, Jimmy's age, and they sometimes formed an uneasy alliance against us. Bobby was a great spitter and landed a gob on any article that displeased him, like Mr. Martin's brand new '54 Chevy. It could not be proved that the bubbly, gelatinous pool that appeared one sunny morning on Mr. Martin's new front seat was actually Bobby's, but when his calling card appeared on Baby Kerry in his carriage, the jig was up. Mom did not take it at all well. There was pause, and talk of the cycle of revenge, but something had to be done, and Mom did it. She and Mrs. Yetman had a good talk. There was no real damage to Kerry, but I'm not so sure about poor Bobby.

Mrs. Yetman was a tall, fierce English woman, with sharp, dark eyes. Her curly black hair was pulled back tight on the sides but was full and loose in the front, 1940s style, and she wore short-sleeved, printed dresses, which were open at the neck, and sometimes a cardigan with the sleeves pushed up. The painted yellow nails of her large, pale feet showed through the toes of her white sandals as she stood on the front step calling out for Bobby or his sister, Gwenny, with her strong accent and her loud voice which went up at the end. "Bob-BY, Gwen-NY." They had a brother, a little older than Wayne, who got his foreskin stuck in his zipper and had to go to the hospital to have it detached. The whole street felt that. Bobby was part of the larger gang and played most games, but he was never fussy about rules and he was no good at all to play house, and besides, his sister Gwenny wouldn't have him anyway.

Next to the Yetmans lived a large, quiet policeman and his large, well-groomed wife in their perfectly kept house, which always stayed the same. They could not have children and were very religious. Then there was the Clearys' house, which was called Clearys' even after they left. A Chinese family tried to buy their house, which we thought very mysterious, but some neighbour took grave exception to this novelty and got up a petition to pressure the real estate company not to sell them the house. No one knew exactly who signed and who didn't. Dad and Mom did not sign and disapproved of the entire exercise. How could it be allowed and was it legal? Who on the street could have initiated such a thing? Not the Waddens or the Yetmans, it wasn't their style, nor the Basteaus or Tizzards. Dr. Giovanetti was dying, and even if Mr. London, the retired carpenter in the house next door, or Mrs. Cyril, further down, had signed the petition, they were not likely to have launched it. Dad discovered the truth from the author himself, our own neighbour, the proud Mr. Martin, who could not help boasting of his success. The Chinese family did not get their house. It stood vacant for a time and then went from family to family and seemed no kind of home in the end. Dad, accustomed to the polite ways of his father-in-law, was shocked that an educated Englishman would exert himself to such a thing, and for a time we all lived in the shadow of the street's shame.

Don Piercey, Wayne's best friend and a constant torment to me, lived directly across the street from us with his older brother, a pharmacist, their widowed mother, and his large, overfed beagle. Don made my life a misery with that dog. He would sic him on me. Then he and Wayne would laugh as the big, barking beagle chased me, and I ran, crying, for safety. One day as I walked home down the gravel sidewalk from a message at the store with my hands full, the beagle took off after me. I dropped the bags and scrambled up the high fence in front of Keats' Mattress Factory and clung desperately to the narrow top, with the crazy dog snapping and clawing below. Luckily, it was Saturday and Dad was there in the driveway to see it all. He ran out and kicked that beagle so hard it let out a great yelp and ran off, never to cross the street again. Don emerged and protested wildly, but Dad said if the dog ever came after me again he would kill it. I was saved and satisfied, and even proud that Dad had seen fit to exert himself with such energy on my behalf. Both the beagle and Don backed off after that for the most part.

The Braces lived in the house below Don's, but you could not see them. The house they rented was built onto the back of the house that faced onto the street, making two houses attached back to back. You had to walk in a long, dark, narrow lane to a small backyard and their only entrance. I never went into the Braces'. No one really went into the Braces'. It was too full of Braces. They were large, high-strung, slow-moving people, with big features, and little Wayne Brace had to contend with the taunt of "Tubby" more than once. His brother Calvin was slim, quiet and quick, the exact opposite of Wayne and everyone else in the family. As you came near the door, Mrs. Brace would loom large and upset from the gloom, yelling at Wayne if she wasn't fighting with Lorna or Calvin.

"Go on out. Don't bring anyone in here. There's nothing for anyone in here. I can't feed the street. Close the door, I said. No room in here to come in playing."

Wayne often came out sulking. Once he came out content, with a slice of baker's bread covered with margarine and sugar.

"What's that?" I asked.

With both hands, Wayne held the sparkling slice of bread aloft like a priest with the wafer.

"It's a sugar sandwich."

Wayne could be very dramatic. He took a large, perfect bite and relaxed in the evening sunshine.

"A sugar sandwich?"

"Didn't you ever hear of a sugar sandwich before?"

"No."

"I have them all the time. They're my favourite," he said, his voice muffled by sweet, masticated dough.

I had never tasted a sugar sandwich before and I didn't then.

Wayne Brace was my best friend and a Protestant, so it was only natural, sitting on the concrete steps in our little front yard, with the late summer dahlias Dad had planted for Mom, that I should try to save his soul, by persuading him of the superiority of Roman Catholicism. I boasted about the richness and splendour of the Basilica of St. John the Baptist, the statues, candles, altars, the gilt, the gold, all surely signs of preferment from God, as opposed to the plain brick and plaster of Gower Street United Church. I was persuasive, and if it had been up to me, Wayne Brace might be papist today. But he was firmly under the thumb of his powerful older sister, Lorna, with her large, pale, round face and long, wavy, black hair and demanding eyes. Lorna was as loud as she needed to be.

One winter night on the snow-packed street, when it seemed that the whole street was out playing after dark, Lorna suggested that someone, that I, in fact, should slide down Mount Royal Avenue, over the hill at the bottom, and across St. Clare Avenue into the Knights of Columbus field, as a test to see if it was safe. My brother Wayne spoke up.

"No, Lorna. Why not volunteer your little brother Wayne to slide over the hill first, or are you afraid he might get hit by a car?"

"No, I am not. Why don't you go over the hill?"

"You go over the hill, Lorna, if you want someone to go so bad!"

"Shut up, Wayne Malone," yelled Lorna. "You're a bully."

"Look at Lorna. Gonna have a fit."

"Shut up," she shrieked.

It was understood that Lorna liked my big brother, Wayne, a lot.

Brace and I managed better alone. The other member of our little gang of three was Lionel "Lioney" Churchill, who also lived in a house attached to the back of another house. You entered their house from a side walkway, and their house was offset in the back just enough to allow for a doorway facing the street. Lioney's grandparents lived in the front house, behind thick white lace, and in the mornings high loaves of pale, Protestant bread sat cooling on the railing of the front verandah. Oh, the smell was sweet, but I could never wrangle a slice, and was only inside the Churchills' once, for Lioney's birthday, a rare and short visit. We never played in Churchills' backyard because Lioney's father kept beagles, which he took with him when he went hunting and fishing on vacation in his lovely brown and cream '54 Ford hardtop. Lioney stayed on the street all summer and boasted about his father's guns and hunting skills. He had an older brother, Spencer, and two older sisters, Allie and Sandra, who was called Wow, and was a favourite with everyone.

Boisterous Bruce Tizzard would play with us sometimes, or troublesome Bobby Yetman and Jimmy "Hot Dog" Wadden, but mainly it was us three. Lioney was small and wiry and cautious. Brace was big and emotional and quick to laugh or cry. He had a good sense of humour, though, and a great double take, so it was hard to stay mad at him, and besides he hated hockey and baseball but, like me, delighted in all the games of our own invention: Pirates, Robots, Cars and Trucks, and even Cowboys and Indians. It was not hard to cajole either of them into most adventures: raiding Mrs. Cyril's overgrown garden for pea shooters or Mr. Frost's garden on St. Clare Avenue for crabapples, or just trespassing in Mr. Pope's long, long garden on Golf Avenue for the fun of it, but at the critical moment, on top of the fence, you might look behind and find them gone. Loyalty was a major issue and many promises were made and broken.

Lioney came to my door to get me one afternoon. Wow had given him money and he wanted me to go up to Hodder's Store with him to spend it. One of the Hodder girls, with a lime-green voile scarf over her curlers, came through the curtain from the living room on fluffy, knit slippers, took her place behind the counter and waited. Lioney ordered up five cents' worth of cherry candy. They were three for a cent. He also ordered banana candy at two for a cent. He ordered fifteen cents' worth of the best, no jawbreakers, and not one hard candy in the larger-than-usual paper bag. We went out the corner door, across the intersection of Golf Avenue and Mount Royal Avenue and walked slowly down the gravel sidewalk, along Dr. Giovanetti's picket fence in the warm afternoon sun. The shades were drawn in Dr. Giovanetti's large house, as usual. He was retired and now lay dying inside with only his housekeeper to care for him. He was in there so many years I began to think you could live a long time dying. Lioney was enjoying his candy thoroughly, especially the cherry candy. He bit one in half to examine it and showed me the white centre and thick red walls. Then he sucked one white. I thought he must be enjoying them so much, he'd forgotten to offer me one. After all, I thought, why else did he ask me to go to the store with him?

"Can I have one?" I asked.

Lioney chewed hard and swallowed a mouthful.

"Too good b'y," he said and reached into the bag again.

I was flabbergasted. We walked on, and when we got to my house, I said casually, "See you later then."

Lioney swallowed again, twisted the paper bag closed and put the rest of the candy away for later.

"Come on, let's go play Cowboys."

"No, not now."

He would never have gotten away with that from Brace, who would have demanded his share and had a fit till he got it, and I suppose I could have too. But I was too stunned. I had to see how far he would go. All the way. "Too good b'y." The phrase lodged in my mind, a slogan and motto for the modern age.

Lioney's mom was a small woman, wiry like Lioney, with curly, close-cut, light brown hair. She had a sharp nose and a thin face. Mrs. Churchill was a no-nonsense, no-frills woman and wore slacks. "Don't come in here. I just cleaned up. Stay in the porch. I'll pass it out to you."

She could quickly take the illusion out of any game. "What are you supposed to be dressed up as? Cowboys? You don't look much like cowboys. You wasted your money on that gun. That won't last a day."

But I liked her. I felt she took care of a lot.

It was considered poor to be "on the street" all summer. Every respectable Townie got out into the woods at some point. Even working-class Townies of modest means had a cabin on a pond somewhere, or access to one, or at least a tent for camping, or relatives around the Bay to visit. Fortunately for us, we had Murphys' cabin in Topsail Pond again that year, which I had blurted out to Brace and Lioney before thinking.

"My dad's got to work all summer, so we can't go anywhere," said Brace.

"I'm going with my dad on a big hunting trip this summer," boasted Lioney.

"No, you're not. You always say that," said Brace.

"I do not."

"He won't let you go. You're too small."

"He said this time for sure I could go. He said when I was big enough to hold the gun I could go, and I can hold it now."

"You said that before. He won't take you."

"Yes, he will. He's better than your dad. You dad never takes you anywhere.'

"He can't," defended Brace.

"Why not?" Lioney wanted to know.

"He has to go to university to get his degree, so he can teach and get more money. And it costs a lot of money to get a degree, and he has to work all summer on the train to pay for it. So he can't take any holidays either, until he gets his degree, and then we're moving out of here and getting a car and having a holiday."

"Yeah. Well, I'm going this summer."

"I bet you don't."

In the end Brace was right. But he didn't rub it in too much when Mr. Churchill left for his hunting trip without Lioney, who returned to us red-eyed with a large sandwich, and we all felt very bad indeed.

In a small yellow bungalow in a large yard across from the Churchills lived the Tizzards. Our friends Bruce and Bonnie Tizzard were twins and had big brothers and sisters and a baby sister, Nancy, who had Down's syndrome. Mrs. Tizzard was talkative and excitable, with big brown eyes, and loved to grow flowers and vegetables. Mr. Tizzard, in his suit and overcoat, walked every day to Bowring's Department Store, where he worked as a floor walker. They never had a car, were very late to get a television, and Bruce wore a pair of purple corduroy pants his mother had made over for him. He hated them, but for me they only added to his appeal.

"Beautiful" Bruce was good natured, and we were glad if he played with us, but he was a little older and preferred the challenges of hockey and softball to our odd games, and was just as likely to try and thwart my more ambitious designs for his own amusement, as happened one hot afternoon after I had finally finished the great labour of constructing two fully functional cardboard robot suits for myself and Lioney, in homage to *The*

Copperhead television series. I was delighted with the visual results, but they were hot and hard to navigate out the driveway and up the gravel sidewalks because you couldn't look down at the uneven ground. Bruce spied us and immediately stood in our way, laughing and pulling and pushing at us until Lioney fell over. After constant warnings to leave us alone, I exploded and swung at him with a homemade wooden rifle, which split the back of his head open. I had never lost my temper and hit someone like that before and I did not mean to then. But from inside the cardboard costume I could not see what I was doing. Mrs. Tizzard was very upset and called Mom. Mom demanded I say I was sorry but I wouldn't. Bruce had pushed us and I had warned him. Mom said I would stay in the back porch until Dad came home to punish me if I didn't apologize. I didn't. Mom was shocked. I was shocked and ashamed I had hit him and was digging in to prove he must have deserved it. But I was careful to relent before Dad came home. I knew better by now the danger of adding to his burden.

Bruce's sister Bonnie had wavy brown hair and big brown eyes like Bruce and big white teeth. She was tall and beautiful and wore a plaid dress with crinolines.

> *Down in the valley where the green grass grows*
> *There sat Bonnie as pretty as a rose . . .*

Bonnie was the authority on the rules of all street games, counting-out rhymes and skipping games, especially French skipping and Double Dutch. Barbara Lynn was also highly knowledgeable.

> *My mother and your mother were hanging out clothes.*
> *My mother gave your mother a punch in the nose.*
> *Guess what colour blood came out.*
> *Red Blue Red Blue . . .*

For Double Dutch you needed two kids to get the two lengths of rope swinging and keep them going long enough for everyone waiting in the line to jump in. If someone got tripped and stopped the ropes, that person had to turn the rope for the rest of us, or go to the back of the line. To keep the game going as long as possible was the greatest thrill. It was always a challenge to find enough of the right kids to set the game up.

"Come on lardy pants," Bonnie said to Brace. "We're going skipping."

But Brace was not a good skipper.

"I don't want to play skipping."

"Come on. You can turn the ropes for us then."

"What will you give me?"

Lioney was a fair skipper but reluctant to play a "girls'" game. It might reflect badly on his image as a hunter. I was always happy to jump in with Sharon, Gwenny, Barbara Lynn and Bonnie, to perfect my skipping skills, with whoever would play. It was a rare occasion when the other boys joined in, unless we set up a big game of Double Dutch. That was the best but it required a lot of negotiation, and if Bruce or my brother Wayne agreed to a game, you might even have to promise to play softball in return.

In the long summer evenings, on special nights, the whole street would join forces, with an even split of big and little kids on each team, for a big game of Hoist Your Sails and Run, which some called Hoist Your Tails and Run. One team would scatter into the gloom of Basteaus' driveway, and into the backyards and bushes of the fields beyond. The team leader returned to draw elaborate maps in the gravel sidewalk under the pole light for the pursuers. Shirley Basteau's brother had just returned from France with a new, pale-yellow and silver Citroen, which was the nearest thing to a spaceship we had ever seen. It had pneumatic suspension, and we never tired of pushing it down and watching it rise slowly back up. It was an irresistible choice for "gouloes" or home base, and so he was forced to find a garage for it shortly afterwards.

"Ink Pink Pudding Stink Lassie Fingers Out."

My brother Wayne hoped that Ronnie Sparkes, who had just moved into the large bungalow up from Basteaus', would make a good addition to his gang, but Ronnie was just too odd. Ronnie wore his dark brown winter coat and peaked wool cap all summer in the heat, and he rode his beautiful, maroon pedal car with its white trim up and down in his own driveway, where he would not have to give turns on it to rowdies. When Ronnie moved out, two old ladies moved in, one tall and sociable, the other bent and taciturn. The bent one walked in the middle of the street, swinging her purse at any noisy children who came too close. Every Christmas, Dad would bring two plates of Christmas dinner with all the trimmings over to them. I went once and the little bent-over lady took the dinners at the door. The dark brown and pink skin around her eyes was wet with tears, and she thanked Dad warmly. Everyone thought the tall one took care of the bent one, but it was the other way around, as we discovered after the tall one died and the bent one appeared in a brand-new red coat and matching hat and a most unexpected smile.

From the new picture window in our kitchen we looked out at their bungalow and the large front yard of Keats' Mattress Factory between us, the only business front on the street. The tall wooden fence along the street was almost as high as the low-slung building where Fred Keats and his brother George made straw and cotton mattresses. All around the factory were bales of hay and cotton, and rolls of striped mattress fabric, and the whole place was covered in straw and cotton dust. Barbara Lynn and I ran messages for Fred and George, up to Hodder's Store to get an Orange Crush and a raisin square for their break. But Kerry was Fred's favourite, and as soon as he was old enough to go up the street by himself, all the messages were his.

"Where's Kerry?" Fred would ask us. "I promised him I'd let him go to the store for me today."

On the weekends and after work, when the Keats brothers weren't around, we played Stretch and May I and Statues in their long, overgrown front yard.

✦

As soon as they could afford it, Mom and Dad put up a wall along the stairs and divided the house into separate apartments, with two French doors in the vestibule. They opened up our living room to the hall with a big archway, put a bathtub in the little bathroom under the stairs, and an extension on the back, with two bedrooms, one for them and one for us, with Hopalong Cassidy wallpaper featuring Hoppy on his horse and a fence and cacti. There was a little vent in the wall next to the kitchen that allowed heat in and allowed us to listen in on our parents' conversations at night around the kitchen table with Auntie Vera talking darkly about the problems between her husband, Ron, and their son, Buddy, or with Uncle Bob and the latest news from Adelaide Motors.

Mr. Layman did the renovations. The house was "in slings," as Mom put it, for weeks, but there were few activities which cheered her up or gave her as much satisfaction as renovating and decorating. Dad was no carpenter, but he and Mom did all the clean-up and painting and wallpapering, with much exasperation over the lumpy paste and determination to make the cacti and the fence match up. Under the extension was the best part. It was closed in with a short door, child-sized, and made a perfect little playhouse, even though Mom and Dad did not want us down there anymore than they wanted us in the basement, but everyone always played in our backyard.

The back gallery was our stage. We did not play to the gallery but from it. We turned it into a ship, sailing over the square of lawn below. If you hit the lawn, you drowned. There was a lot of death at sea in our play and our little lawn was often strewn with bodies. The gravel driveway was divided up for games of cars and trucks. Roads were built in the dirt and boards laid across the lawn for highways. Territory was claimed and fought over endlessly. Then the Martins put down fine crushed gravel, perfect for playing cars and trucks, on the sidewalk in front of their house.

But the Martins did not want "their" sidewalk divided into roads and highways and estates, so we stopped and then started again, then stopped, then started, until Mr. and Mrs. Martin warned Dad and Mom the games had to stop. Dad warned us in no uncertain terms, and for a while we did stop. But one sunny afternoon we found our way, working feverishly, around the corner into Martin territory again. We'd fix it later, before anyone saw it, we thought, but we forgot, and Mr. Martin called up and complained. I watched Dad go into the house when he got home, and come bursting out the front door again. I didn't need to ask what he wanted. I flew up the street and Dad flew after me. He was a fast runner and still held the Newfoundland indoor record for the quarter-mile sprint. But he didn't catch me that day, though he chased me across the street, between parked cars, back down the street and finally into the lane between Martins' and McGraths'. There was a fence at the end but I didn't stop. I sailed over it. I don't believe I touched it, except for maybe a glancing foot. Dad stopped at the fence. I think he was surprised I could clear it and he uttered a warning after me.

"When I get hold of you, you'll be sorry," and he turned back.

I was learning about Dad's temper. It was like a volcano. You didn't wait around for the blast to hit you. But the heat of his anger was quickly spent, and if you could avoid the first fifteen minutes, the worst might pass. I waited out the first eruption and when the air had cooled I slunk back and hovered in the porch until I was noticed. I got a tongue-lashing and left Martins' sidewalk alone after that, for the most part.

The only other house that we were allowed in was McGraths', where we watched *Hopalong Cassidy* after school. Mrs. McGrath didn't mind having kids in sometimes. They were Catholic and had four kids: Liz, Leo, Patsy and Sharon, the youngest, who was my age. Mr. McGrath worked for Browning Harvey, which bottled Coca-Cola, and when Patsy got pregnant and left high school to marry her handsome, taciturn boyfriend, Mr. McGrath got him a job driving a Coke truck, and he moved in with the family. I presumed I would have to marry Sharon when we grew up because she was Catholic too, even though I would rather have married Barbara Lynn.

Beside the McGraths were the Osmonds, a handsome professional couple who lived with old Mrs. Osmond in her pale grey house. They bought a beautiful new Buick every year, which we all looked forward to seeing with great anticipation.

"I wish we could get a new Buick every year like the Osmonds."

"It's all right for the Osmonds, they don't have any children."

"I'd rather have the Buick," Wayne said quickly and I agreed.

"Yes, and how would you boys like it if your dad and I decided to have a new car every year instead of you fellas?"

Case closed.

There were five stores at the top of the street. Wells' Grocery occupied the corner of Mount Royal Avenue and Golf Avenue, and opposite was Hodder's Store. Beyond that, Mount Royal Avenue ended at Pennywell Road and Walsh's Store. There was also old Mr. Penny's store and Howell's Store at the top of Morris Avenue, but they didn't want children in looking for two cents' worth of three-for-a-cent candy. Walsh's did, and had comics too, but we only went to Walsh's Store as a last resort. Victor and Ritchie Walsh were older than us and had brothers even older. The Walshes were tough, tougher than the Waddens or the Yetmans. Pennywell Road lay along the top of the ridge of land that was one of the highest points in Town. In the winter, snow would drift in up to two storeys high or more. One winter the road filled in so much, it was closed for days. Victor and Ritchie dug a veritable catacomb of tunnels and caves on several levels in the huge bank that had formed in front of their store. They put up a flag and charged admission to crawl through their great winter wonderland. If they wanted our money, they probably wouldn't beat us up, we reasoned. So we paid our pennies and took the grand tour. It was an amazing amount of digging they had done. There were tunnels going up inclines to different levels, and slides and caves. But these dangerous bullies had very strict rules for going in and out, which they enforced rigidly.

"Time's up or pay again."

It struck me as odd that these toughs would follow convention as strictly as our kindergarten teacher, Miss Snow. There were threats and near-fights when people lingered too long in the more spacious caves, but like Miss Snow and her red stick, Victor and Ritchie quickly got the malingerers moving. When the snow blower finally got through it could not reach the top of the drift, and left a long curved overhang above the smooth white wall, which now looked like a Swiss cheese of sliced tunnels and caves.

Behind Walsh's Store, stretching down over the ridge to Freshwater Road and Empire Valley, was Walsh's Field, a wild terrain where we would ride our bikes like horses or play games of softball when the Walshes allowed it or weren't around. I don't know if the Walshes actually owned the field but I don't think the municipal council would have challenged their control over it.

Their store carried mostly cigarettes, pop, chips, squares, candy and comics. One spring evening I ventured in to look for the new Superman comic. Mrs. Walsh, in her rouge and lipstick, stood impassive, with her hands on the counter, staring intently at a man, whom I slowly realized must be drunk.

"I want a package of Export 'A'," he slurred.

Mrs. Walsh looked him straight in the eye.

"Show me your money first," she said.

The man lurched forward and smacked her hard across the cheek.

"Give me the fuckin' cigarettes," he yelled.

Mrs. Walsh looked coldly at him. Without turning, she reached behind and calmly passed him a package of Export 'A'. I froze to the comic stand.

"Now give me some matches," he growled, grabbing at her sweater.

She put a box of Eddy's on the counter. He let her go, picked up the matches and staggered out. Mrs. Walsh didn't flinch. I put my new DC issue of Superman on the counter with my ten cents.

"Thank you, Mrs. Walsh," I said as politely as I could.

"That's terrible," said a customer, who suddenly materialized from the corner.

"Don't worry," said Mrs. Walsh. "He won't do that again."

No, I supposed he wouldn't do that again or much of anything else after Victor and Ritchie got him, or perhaps their grown-up brothers would take care of that situation. I began to pity the foolish drunk.

Walsh's Store marked the boundary of our little territory, the guardhouse of the north, and if they were tough on us, they were tougher on intruders. There was a tough crowd down on St. Clare Avenue too, but they rarely made the effort to come up the hill. To the west was Mundy Pond, the toughest of all, a whole neighbourhood of toughs, while access to the more cultivated and prosperous east was controlled by the Dillons on Franklin Avenue, who took their duties very seriously. Jerome Dillon was very angry and vicious all the time, and would stop me and Wayne going to and from school on Pennywell Road so often we had to use Merrymeeting Road and bypass him altogether.

Jerome was older than Wayne and had two German shepherd dogs, but Wayne was taller, and Jerome really didn't like that. He didn't like much.

"Hey, Bean Pole. Think you're somethin', do ya? I'll kick the shit outta ya."

We hadn't seen him come up behind us as we waited at the bus stop to go back to school one afternoon. Jerome attacked Wayne like a madman, but Wayne got away from him and fled in panic, and Jerome tore off after him. I could see the bus coming so I stayed and got on. The bus passed Jerome chasing Wayne, then it passed Wayne. I tried to get the bus driver to stop to let Wayne on, but he wouldn't. At the next stop, I stood in the open door and made him wait until Wayne caught up and jumped on. The door closed and we left Jerome panting on the sidewalk. Wayne was heaving and greatly relieved, and I was very pleased to be able to help him out. This was a real-life "assist" and I'd scored valuable points that I would surely need later.

There was simply no direction I could take from our little house that did not have its perils. It was an innocent world full of danger.

St. Bon's

E very school morning, Mom and Dad both struggled with the laces of Wayne's and my itchy breeks, which laced up along our calves, then on with grey knee socks over that, white shirts, blue-and-gold ties and navy wool blazers. No wonder I couldn't sit still. When you took off the breeks after school, the print of the laces and lace holes would stay on your skin until you scratched them red. All our clothes were carefully laid out in the kitchen the night before and we dressed there in the warmth of the oil stove. At first I kissed Mom and Dad goodbye every morning and then just mom, as Dad decided I was getting too big for kisses.

Dad went down over the hill to work, and Wayne and I got the bus up on Pennywell Road to St. Bon's. I watched the boys cry and protest on the first day of grade one. I knew it was hopeless and looked on dry eyed and vaguely grateful to have gone through that at St. George's the year before in kinder-garten. For the first time in my life I felt older. It was a massive class of almost fifty, in a massive room, with two massive double-hung windows looking out over the massive campus, which we could not see because the massive window ledge was over our heads.

St. Bonaventure's College was so grand and imposing a structure that it took many years for me to take in fully the extent of its architectural offerings. The old school, a four-storey, granite, Georgian structure was built in the 1850s and served as a monastery for the Irish Christian Brothers, with a large dining room for them and the boarders, as well as the school library and two extra classrooms. The main school building was a sprawling structure with pillars and porticos, attached to the north side of the monastery. Both looked out over a large, oval-shaped field, which was called the "campus," where track and field and football were practised and Sports Day was held every June. The campus was bordered by a paved path and was the setting for many walks and talks at recess time. Beyond the campus stretched a line of chestnut and maple trees that marked the boundary with Bonaventure Avenue. There was a grotto with statues of St. Bonaventure and Our Lady, and gravel tennis courts on the north end of the campus. Perhaps the most popular feature was the indoor hockey rink at the back of the school. This feature ensured the dominance of the senior boys' hockey team, which won the coveted Boyle trophy so often it came to be considered their own.

There were hockey, basketball and football teams, cadets, Scouts, religious clubs, and a debating club, the Vesper choir, which sang at the basilica, and a large glee club, which every year combined with the drama club to produce lavish musical productions like Gilbert and Sullivan's *The Pirates of Penzance* and *H.M.S. Pinafore*. Senior boys like John O'Mara and John Doyle played the female parts in flaxen wigs and pink-and-blue satin gowns, opposite their school chums dressed in the finest naval uniforms with gold brocade and feathered hats. The deck of the *Pinafore* projected out past the proscenium with canvas sails and ropes and a poop deck. The effect was splendid and completely dazzling to my grade one mind. All of these triumphs were dutifully recorded and photographed by the yearbook staff and the camera club, and presented at year's end in the *Adelphian*. St. Bon's had students from grade one to grade twelve. Many of the high school students were boarders from the outports around Newfoundland. They slept in the sprawling dormitory on the third floor and washed at rows of oval sinks in the attic behind the large circular window in the main gable.

Next to the boarders' dormitory, at the top of the building, was a large and beautiful chapel with stained glass windows where Monsignor Fyme, who had come as a missionary from Holland to St. Anthony on the Great Northern Peninsula, now served out his retirement. To the south the monastery was attached to the archbishop's library, underneath which, on the ground level, was a tunnel through to the stables, which had been converted into garages. The archbishop's library was attached to his palace and the palace to the Basilica of St. John the Baptist, a tall Romanesque structure with two towers, where, standing on the front steps, you could look through the great stone archway of St. John the Baptist, over the roofs of the buildings downtown, and out through the Narrows to the open sea. This impressive maze of buildings was a world unto itself, an almost exclusively male world.

"I don't like grade one much," I said to Mom.

"Why, what's wrong? Did something happen?"

"No."

"Then why?"

"I don't have any friends," I said, starting to cry.

"Oh, Gregory."

"I can't make any friends."

"Why not?"

"They already have friends and no one likes me."

"Don't say that. You'll make friends. I was like that for a while in school. It feels terribly lonely, I know. But, you'll see, you'll meet someone soon."

"I don't think so."

Brother French, our grade one teacher, was strict, but after Christmas he let us choose where we wanted to sit. I had met Steve MacDonald, whose father owned MacDonald's Fruit Stores. He was older than me, and taller, with black hair, and he was very good looking. He had a reputation for being tough, but I found him friendly and thought he must have better friends than me, but since he was sitting alone in the back of the class, I went and asked if I could sit with him. He smiled at me. Brother French scowled.

"Be careful, Mr. Malone, how you choose your friends. Well, I'll let you stay down there for now, as long as your work doesn't suffer."

"Yes, Br," I replied using the familiar diminutive employed by all the boys and pronounced "Burr".

I felt badly for Steve, but he seemed used to the suspicion. I liked him. He was kind to me, like my brother Wayne, and he gave me tips on how not to get caught cheating, which I couldn't use, and I tried to help him with his arithmetic, for which I got into trouble.

"You worry about your own work, Mr. Malone."

The class was so full I felt in danger of being lost and was anxious to distinguish myself from the pack. Sports Day was overwhelming. Troops of senior boys with gold stripes down the side of their grey flannels marched in formation around the campus swinging blue and gold batons and wands in synchronized routines to the rhythms of the Mount Cashel Boys Band. There was every kind of race and relay to entertain the crowd. When our moment arrived, dozens of grade ones crowded at the starting line for the race. We were so piled up that when the whistle blew there was a stampede of boys shoving, pushing and some falling over. As I rushed forward, I felt myself being pushed back, and in a panic reached out and grabbed the shirt of another boy who was ahead of me, pulling him aside. It was little Sean Power, who let out a low moan as I raced on ahead.

In spite of the mangled start, I managed to finish in the top five and a harried official took my name at the end, which pleased me. But the thin taste of that victory did not linger nearly as long as the thick knot of regret. It was a brutal world, this school, and I had already succumbed to its brutality. I had won the race but failed the test. I was troubled and ashamed to have pulled poor Sean back, and wished I'd had the courage to let myself be pulled back into honourable obscurity. I would have to be more careful not to panic and behave badly, yet still survive, and if possible, even be noticed.

✦

Our grade two class was in the little room behind the chapel and our teacher was Brother Clancy. When we had settled into our double desks on that first day, he said to us, "Look down the aisles."

No one moved or quite understood his command.

"Look down the aisles," he demanded again.

And so we turned, confused, and gazed back and forth at the bare wooden floor and the iron legs of the desks that marked out the narrow aisles.

"Now," he announced, "these aisles will be running with blood before this year is out. Do you understand that?"

I could not think what he meant by it, but no one asked him for an explanation. I watched him from my seat in the front row. Suddenly he was right in front of my desk, staring down at me.

"Don't look at me with those eyes like that. It's like you're looking right through me," he said, almost surprised but without anger.

I was shocked and struggled to rearrange my face, but before I could look away he gave me a smile, which I attempted to return as best I could.

✦

We had our own car by grade two, a pale green, two-door, Chevy sedan, which we quickly named Nellybelle, after Pat Brady's jeep on *The Roy Rogers Show,* and every chance we got, we went for rides. During the winter Dad drove us to St. Bon's in the mornings, and he and Wayne would listen to VOCM, cheering and groaning at the hockey scores.

"The Leafs blanked Boston in Toronto last night."

"Ooh!"

"And the Habs snatched victory from New York with a hat trick late in the third period by the mighty 'Rocket' Richard."

"Yeah!"

"Go, Rocket, go," cheered Dad.

I endured their enthusiasm and even pretended some of my own when Dad turned to me in excitement. Dad could never understand my lack of interest in sports. In fact, he forgot it regularly as he pushed me to play hockey and try out for soccer and basketball. I evaded this advice as politely as possible.

Dad dropped us off by 8:30 so he could make it to work on time, and I would spend the extra half hour waiting outside the chapel to go through to our class. The double doors to the boarders' dormitory were across the hall. Andy Jones found himself there early in the mornings too. We became friends and waylaid the boarders, who were senior boys and almost grown-ups to us, on their way out. We rarely saw them during the school day but here they were captive. Our good friend was a tall, slim fellow with a ducktail and curls down over his forehead. He called himself Tex but he had an accent from the Burin Peninsula. He and his friend Dusty patiently answered our endless questions with endless lies about their life on their ranch out West.

"Why does he call you Tex?"

"That's my name."

"What's your real name?"

"That's it, Tex."

"Sure, he sings cowboy songs and everything," added Dusty.

"You don't."

"Yep."

"Sing us one then."

"Yes, sing us a song," agreed Andy.

"You sing me one first."

"We don't know any."

"Well, I don't have my guitar with me now."

"Right. You don't really have a guitar."

"Yes, he does," said Dusty. "Just look in the door over there. See down that row of beds by the wall, there leaning up against the last bed. That's his guitar."

They mixed enough truth in with the lies to drive us mad.

"Wow, okay, so you sing songs. But you're not really a cowboy."

"I sing songs and I am really a cowboy," and it was not hard to believe as he spun out his cowboy philosophy, and we found ourselves in many deep conversations.

They never did tell us their real names though, so we looked them up in the *Adelphian* at the end of the year. I loved talking with the boarders so much that I sometimes failed to notice the approach of the ancient Monsignor Fyme, shuffling down the hall to open the chapel. This was a mistake. He used a large cane and, if you were within striking distance, would quickly hook you around the neck and pull you in for a hard look. Or, if you were close enough, he would give you a playful knock over the head with his wooden knuckles, leaving you dazed and confused. But the price of this loss of vigilance was worth it.

In fact, Andy and I were having such a good time we were shut down. We hadn't done anything wrong, so we couldn't rightly be beaten, but the fun and gaiety, especially first thing in the morning, must stop, and we were forbidden to congregate in the upstairs hall anymore. Now there was just class.

Who Is God?

E arly one morning in our little class behind the chapel, high up above the handball alleys, we were wrestling with the most profound theological consideration that had been posed to us the day before by our catechism book.

"Who is God?" it asked.

Some of the grade twos were cool, high up on that grey morning. Other grade twos were sweating. All of us felt slightly sick. Brother Clancy was over six feet tall and athletically built, a young American with lots of energy on the basketball court, in the handball alleys, and in the chemistry lab, which was his domain. But this overwrought twenty-two-year-old celibate was not at his best in grade two—in the morning or in the afternoon.

But it was a slow morning and tempers were tight and Freddie Gladney had no idea who God was. His name? His description? No, he simply could not fathom it. And there was no question of Freddie remembering it, none at all. All the grade twos knew this. Only Brother Clancy seemed not to remember it. The class strained silently and earnestly to communicate this thought to Brother Clancy. However, he was too agitated to pick up such etheric signals. He strode vigorously up and down the aisle, his legs pumping, his cassock swishing and brushing, bristling for a reply.

"Who is God, Mr. Gladney?"

By now Mr. Gladney had shrunk so low in his seat that his small black head looked like a raisin on a ruler. Our minds fled to the page in the catechism where the answer lay. Who is God? I could see the question clearly and the shaft of light breaking through a cumulus cloud above it. But I could not see the answer to the question. It was blocked out by Brother Clancy's thick forefinger, which kept the catechism wedged open while the rest of his large hand held it aloft, over Freddie's head, over the row, over the whole class. All else was utter silence except for cassock swish and heartbeats.

"Who is God?" repeated Brother Clancy.

Dear God, I beseeched, please stand up and identify yourself. He did not. Freddie's head moved.

"I don't know, Br," he mouthed.

There was simply no air left in him.

"You don't know!" boomed the basketball star.

He now seemed taller than his six feet two inches, and redder. He yanked the sash of his cassock around to the side and tugged at his collar. The room had become quite hot all of a sudden. The reflection of the electric lights on their long chains blazed in Brother Clancy's flesh-coloured glasses and his round blue eyes flared behind them, bubbles appeared at the edges of his perfect American teeth, and then, and this was later independently verified by several present in class that day, it was as if Brother Clancy's strawberry blond brush cut physically lifted off the top of his flaming scalp, right in front of our unbelieving eyes—an actual ghastly miracle. Brother Clancy rose to meet the miraculous brush cut, his face twisted and his full cheeks horribly blotched. Strange noises began bursting out of him.

"You don't know who God is? I'll tell you who he is," promised the voice from Brooklyn, and a great spray of spittle descended on the front two rows.

It was coming. Good, I thought, at least he is not going to hang Freddie out the window three storeys above the handball alleys to trigger his memory. Perhaps because it had not worked before. Brother Clancy thrust the catechism out in front of himself. It no longer looked like a book. It was twisted into a thick paper bludgeon. He raised it aloft and thundered. "God is Love, Mr. Gladney. That's who God is. God is . . ."

The bludgeon-book came down on Freddie's raisin head.

"L."

Smack.

"O."

Smack.

"V."

Smack.

"E."

Smack.

"Love."

Smack.

It was over. Brother Clancy, pale and spent, withdrew with a great swoosh to his perch at the top of the class. The room was hushed with theological implications.

No one moved a muscle or dared breathe except for the most necessary and shallow breaths. Even our blood had stopped moving, which was good because it would prevent an involuntary spasm from re-igniting the inferno. Existence must be reduced to the lowest possible point. I am not here. You do not see me. And then I saw it, the second miracle: Freddie Gladney had vanished. He was gone completely. Well, his coat was still there, sitting up at his desk, but his head had disappeared totally and never did return to that classroom again.

We heard later that it had reappeared, along with the rest of him, at Mary Queen of the World School run by the nuns and even some laity. Freddie must have had good parents, by which I mean they must have believed him, were horrified, and never returned him to be terrorized again, which was unusual, as it was not common Catholic practice or custom to blame a viable adult for something that could readily be fixed on a dumbfounded child.

When the time finally came to leave the class that day, and we were released, we found that we could move without blood, find our way without eyes, and eat a complete lunch without tasting anything—the third miracle. And from that day all knew the answer to the question "Who is God?" but as to what Love might be, that was now more of a mystery than ever.

The Accident

Frank Graham was an executive with Imperial Oil in the main office, well-educated and witty, and an excellent writer, especially of sports stories. Frank always drove a sports car and wore good suits and silk ties, a dapper dresser. Frank was a big supporter of Dad's when Dad had been captain of the championship St. Bon's basketball team and now that he was coach of the victorious Esso team in the commercial league. He was fond of Mom and Dad, but I had never seen him at our door before. Mom was pale, her lips tight, as she turned back into the house with him.

"What kind of accident? What are you saying, Frank? How is Bill? Is he all right?"

"He's alive. They don't know yet how he is. I'll take you to the hospital now."

The next day the *Daily News* was filled with the terrible pictures. An oil truck had rolled over the South Side Hills and crashed on the wharf.

It had been snowy and slippery when Dad and the other drivers left the plant with their tanks full and started up the road for deliveries. The South Side Road runs along the lower part of the South Side Hills, with several exits to the wharves and buildings below. Eric Burt, in the lead truck, and the other drivers continued on into Town unaware that Dad was no longer part of the convoy. When Dad reached the high point of the road, the brakes on his truck failed, it slipped back and broke through the guardrail and began to roll back down over the rocky hill. Dad was thrown out of the cab but got caught between the cab and the tank as the truck crashed over the rocks, through some water pipes and finally into a building on the wharf, which stopped it from plunging into the Harbour. From the dramatic pictures in the paper, you would not imagine that anyone could have survived the calamity, but my father did.

Before very long he was home, though he was on his back, at first on the floor, and then on a board on the chesterfield. He looked the same and had no visible signs of injury but his back had been hurt, so he had to sleep on a board and not get up or walk around, and the doctors were worried. In 1956 the Workmen's Compensation Board had just been established but they had yet to release any cheques. Mom went there every day to state her case and ask for the cheque but to no avail. One thing was clear: Dad would not be able to return to his job. It was tense and serious at the house for a long time as we wondered what turn our lives might now take.

One gloomy evening as Dad lay on his back in the living room and Mom was in the kitchen, I found a pair of hair clippers in a box in their closet. They weren't electric. You could work them like scissors, and I went right up the side of my head with them. I clipped my sideburns and kept going, and then made another cut up next to it. They worked all right. My head now had two clean, even, bare patches up one side.

"What are you doing there, Greg? What are you doing with the clippers? What have you got done?" said Mom with increasing anxiety as I tried to turn away.

"Let me see it. Oh! For Heaven's sake, Gregory, what did you do that for?"

"I don't know."

"What's going on out there?" came Dad's strained voice.

"Come on in and show your father what you've done. Come on . . ."

"No."

"Yes. Come on."

I trailed in.

"Now, show your father what you did with the clippers."

"Jesus Christ. What the hell did you do that for?" yelled Dad. "Come here. Come over here," he demanded from the couch.

I edged a little closer, and he turned on his side and swung out at me. I felt the iron tips of his fingers clip my head as I pulled back. Dad let out a groan and sank back on the board.

"Be careful now, Bill!"

"My son, you're some lucky I'm here on my back because if I could get at you now, I'd give you some crack."

"My God, Greg, what are we going to do with that? It's too late to go to the barber. Look, you've clipped it right up the side."

"Let me see. Let me see," demanded Dad.

"You can't go to school like that," said Mom.

"He'll have to go to school like it then," said Dad, "and look like an idiot. There's nothing you can do with that now. You're gonna have to wait for it to grow out."

"Cripes Kate, Greg, how could you, how could you do this now, with your father sick and on his back and everything?"

In the end, Mom evened it off as best she could. She also managed finally to get the first cheque out of the Workmen's Compensation Board, with the help of Harry Roberts, their doctor. And Frank Graham was able to help Dad get a new job at Imperial Oil, as a commission salesman, signing up home-owners, businesses, schools and churches to buy their furnace oil from Esso. He was good at it, but he had to wear a back brace, and he installed a special hard seat made of wooden slats in Nellybelle.

He was also completely deaf now in his bad ear and the doctor said if he got water in that ear he would black out. He would know what you were saying if he could see your face, even from across the street. But if you were back on to him, he couldn't hear you anymore. The doctors said his hearing would get worse and we all had to say special prayers for Dad's ears so he wouldn't go totally deaf. And he didn't. Whether it was the St. Anne's Oil or our prayers that were the deciding factor, Dad's hearing did get better and better. In fact, it got so good you had to be careful what you said around him again. The doctors were amazed. Dad was back in just about full form and our belief in his indestructibility was confirmed, and now with his new job and the better opportunities, it was generally agreed that the accident was the best thing that ever happened to Scully since he met Ada.

✦

"I know where babies come from," I said to Mom confidently one afternoon.

"Do you?" asked Mom, her interest engaged.

"Yes, Barbara Lynn told me. They come out of the mother."

Mom paused for an instant.

"Yes, that's right," she admitted, smiling.

"Good, because that means I'm part of you and not part of Dad, right?"

"Well, no, now Greg, it doesn't mean that. He's your father. Why don't you want to be part of your father?"

"He doesn't like me."

"Yes, he does."

"He's always mad at me."

"He might get mad at you sometimes, but he loves you boys."

When Dad came home, Mom called him in to tell him what I had said. I didn't realize she would tell him. I felt betrayed and it threw me into a panic. Now he'd really be angry with me.

"No, Mom, don't tell him. I just said that to you."

"Now, Greg, I have to tell your father. Don't worry. It'll be all right. Bill, Greg thinks you don't like him."

I cringed at Dad's display of shock and surprise edged with impatience.

"What's all this about now, Greg?"

"Nothing."

"No, he feels that you're mad at him all the time."

"I only get mad when you do something wrong, Greg. You know that."

"I know."

"Well, I guess Greg doesn't feel like that."

"Sure, now you know I like you. You're my son."

"Your father does a lot for you, you know, Greg. He thinks a lot about you boys."

"I know."

I agreed to everything. What else could I say? What else could he say? But now what?

Dad was determined not to be slowed down by the accident, and, in fact, he was so much better now that he and another man dug out more of the dirt in the front of the basement and installed a big, frightening floor furnace, which stung your nose and puffed out your clothes when you stood over big grill in the floor of the downstairs hall. The newly dug basement, so full of ancient artifacts like Dad's yellow Arctic sleeping bag from his days surveying the west coast with the Newfoundland Rangers, tennis rackets and skis from the Mount Pearl days, and old trophies and tools, drew me in again, and I found myself down there one day with the pick, just levelling off the floor. But I lost control of the pick and put it through four storm windows, which were stacked against the wall. My heart stopped. I certainly had been warned before and here I was again. I would have to brave the blast without excuses or hope. I told Mom and waited the rest of the day in grim expectation. I saw Dad come home from work and go in the house. I waited but he did not come flashing back out the door after me and I finally decided to go in and face him. But Dad was very philosophical and understanding, and I was amazed to the point of disbelief.

"Well, these things happen. Don't worry too much about it."

Perhaps he was happy to be back on his feet again, and perhaps he took this opportunity to prove he wasn't always mad at me. I concluded it was the latter, and I thought it a very good proof, and so we were back on neutral ground.

The Austin

When Mr. Moores traded in the old slope-backed Dodge for a large, new, self-satisfied, jade-green Austin from England, Mrs. Moores decided to take Barbara Lynn and me with them for a drive and a picnic one Sunday afternoon. This was the first time I was ever offered entrance to the Moores family car. The Dodge was in showroom condition when it was traded in, and the new Austin was supernaturally clean, and the prize possession of the family. I could tell Mr. and Mrs. Moores were immensely pleased with it. It was a new era, and their pleasure had spilled over in this new-found generosity towards me.

This was not merely a ride in a car, I realized. On a deeper, more important level, it was an initiation, a ceremony, a journey of acceptance into the inner world of the Mooreses. I was aware of it, and Barbara Lynn's extra delight told me I was not mistaken. Mom even took time to wash and dress me in clean play clothes. Mrs. Moores instructed us in the rules of appropriate behaviour in the Austin. We were not to make a mess in the back seat, although I could not imagine what we could make a mess with as there was absolutely no question of food in the Austin. We were to leave the red plaid car rug folded on the back window shelf, sit properly in the seat and not stand up.

Mr. Moores drove. Mrs. Moores sat comfortably in the front and occasionally turned to check our position. I sat directly behind her and Barbara Lynn was next to me in the middle. Our feet did not reach the new-smelling carpeted floor, which looked as though it had never been stepped on. The Austin purred quietly as we glided past the new bungalows on Elizabeth Avenue.

"We can go out along Windsor Lake and stop there," said Mrs. Moores.

"Yes," said Mr. Moores. "It's a paved road all the way."

They settled back. It was silent in the car with the windows closed, and the thick aroma of the new leather upholstery, carpet and polished briar filled the interior. Barbara Lynn fidgeted and made faces at me. I looked back at her blankly, as the car gently rolled and weaved. I felt slightly giddy. I took a deep breath of leather and polish to steady myself and immediately threw up a pool of orange vomit on the untouched carpet, and that was it. It was all over. I had tripped the switch. The bomb had gone off.

"Oh no. Greg is sick," said Barbara Lynn.

"Oh dear. Stop the car," said Mrs. Moores.

"Oh my," said Mr. Moores, as he pulled over to the side of the road.

"You should have told us you were going to be sick," said Mrs. Moores, as she got out and opened my door.

"I didn't know," I whispered.

"Oh, what a mess. Well, you'd better get out in case you get sick again, and let me clean this up."

I hunched over on the side of the road, shivering in the warm sunlight next to the offended Austin.

"What am I going to do with that?" said Mrs. Moores, as Mr. Moores slowly got out, opened the boot of the Austin and produced some newspapers.

I turned away as Mrs. Moores wiped out the mess and covered the violated carpet.

"Are you better now?" asked Barbara Lynn.

"Do you think you're going to be sick again?" Mrs. Moores inquired in a worried voice.

"No," I said.

"Oh my. Well, you'd better get back in then, but tell us right away if you feel sick again, won't you?"

We all climbed back in. Barbara Lynn looked anxiously at me.

"Well, there's not much point going for the picnic now if you're sick like that," her mother said. "We'd better take you back home."

The Austin wheeled around and headed back to Mount Royal Avenue.

"I'm sorry I got sick," I said, as I got out in front of our house.

"That's all right, now, you'd better go in."

The door closed. The Austin drove off. I was never again to smell its leather and briar interior. I was back out in the fresh air, on the back step for good.

The Dentist

It was a cold day and Wayne and I were kept home from school in the afternoon but not because of the weather. One other stormy morning we were bundled off to school, but by the time Wayne and I had struggled to the top of Mount Royal Avenue, swirling snow overcame us and the high wind took our breath away so we turned back home. Mom had greeted us with a suspicious look but let us stay home, which was a good thing because the schools were closed.

But today Mom kept us home because she had made an appointment with the dentist for us to have some rotten baby teeth pulled. She promised us it would not hurt and that we would have a party afterwards and she would make our favourite peanut butter and banana sandwiches, cut into triangles the way we liked. So off we went.

Dr. Hogan was Mom's old boss. She had worked as his receptionist before she got married and for a while after until Wayne was born. He had an office near the Court House on Duckworth Street in a row of red brick buildings called Lawyers'

Row. The waiting room was small and dim with an overhead glass globe on a chain. There were *Reader's Digest* and *Life* magazines and a bright Norman Rockwell print on the dark green wall. I went in first.

In the middle of Dr. Hogan's office stood a large black machine with gold letters. It had a round body with arms and black tubes and wires running off it, a big light and mirror, and seemed like a giant robotic sewing machine. Dr. Hogan was a thin man with a deep voice, thick glasses and a bush of white hair. He wore a neat white smock over his shirt and tie and his sleeves were rolled up showing two strong, hairy forearms.

I was asked to lie on a narrow table under the big sewing machine. Dr. Hogan looked in my mouth and made some deep bass grunts. His assistant, an unconcerned young woman, looked on with Mom.

"Don't worry. This won't hurt now," said Dr. Hogan.

There was a hissing sound as he took a big black mask, which looked like a plunger on a hose, and put it over my face, leaving just my eyes showing. The stench of rubber and gas terrified me and I couldn't breathe. I thought I would suffocate. I didn't think this could be right.

"No, No," I said, "take it off," and turned my head away from the mask.

"That's all right now," the dentist said, holding me in place.

I was panicked.

"No. No. I can't breathe."

I struggled to get the mask off, but Dr. Hogan only pressed it harder and held my arm down. His assistant held my other arm as I squirmed and fought to get free with everything I had. My heart was racing out of my chest. Then Mom held down my legs so I didn't kick the dentist and nurse. It took the three of them to keep me down. I held my breath as long as I could, but finally I had to gasp for air. I got none. A wave of foul rubber and poison gas flooded into my body, which slowly let go.

I held off a bit, then took another breath, and my whole body was filled with a strange, tingling feeling. I seemed to rise up to the ceiling and then come back down slowly. I heard voices around me as if I were under water as I descended but could not understand what was said. I had the sensation and sight of something being pulled, stretching, stretching like gum and then finally letting go. Again the garbled voices. Again the stretching.

Suddenly I was back on the table, sick. My mouth was thick and full of blood.

"Just spit it out here."

I did and rolled off the table, stupid, humiliated and angry.

"How are you now?" said the nurse.

I gave her a look filled with daggers. I wanted her to see what I thought of them. But they only smiled at each other.

"You'll be all right," she said.

She and Mom reached out to give me a hand but I pulled away from them angrily. They finally reacted to me.

"Oh my!"

"Don't worry. He'll be fine."

But it was not true. Nothing they said had been true and neither was this. I went out holding my raw, bloody mouth, and Wayne went in, but I could not warn him properly.

We returned home in the cold afternoon gloom. The wind took the storm door and banged it into our faces. We moaned and went inside, took the bloody tissues out of our mouths, put in fresh ones and lay down, convinced we were permanently scarred.

"Would anyone like some peanut butter and banana sandwiches?" asked Mom.

"No," we gagged.

"How about I cut the crusts off the way you like so it will be softer to chew?"

"No, no. Not now," we pleaded.

"That's just the gas making you sick. When that wears off you'll feel better. That's all right. We can have them tomorrow."

We weren't interested in sandwiches. We felt sick and dizzy, and couldn't imagine chewing on anything again. And we were angry and uncertain, not about the sandwiches, the bloody mouth, or even oddly enough, about the gas. We felt we had been tricked by our mother into a situation where we believed we might die, as we were bound and slipped into unconsciousness. Of course, my violent reaction to this surprise became the reason for not telling me about it, and many other unpleasant surprises. But Wayne and I agreed on the cause of our disappointment.

The next year I had to go to the dentist again. I refused, but Mom promised me it would not be like the last time, and they would not give me gas. This was just a check-up. I was not happy about it but finally I relented. The same dark waiting room, the same *Reader's Digest* and *Life* magazines, the same bright Norman Rockwell print. I went in. The machine stood there, arms outstretched as before, and Dr. Hogan, with his sleeves rolled up, was ready for me.

"Now this won't take a minute, young man. Just hop up here."

I lay on the table as before.

"What are you going to do?" I asked.

"Don't worry, now," he said.

I heard the hiss of gas but before I could bolt the assistant flung a heavy khaki canvas sheet over me. It covered me from my neck to my feet and had three leather belts sewn onto it, which they quickly pulled tight, strapping me down. I struggled desperately but I was bound and helpless. Then Dr. Hogan took the gas mask and gently put it over my face and I lost control again. The tingling sensation filled my body again and filled the room. Again the voices outside. Again the manipulation. Again the deception.

A few years later, after we took over the upstairs from the tenants and we had the big, upstairs bathroom, Wayne and I would play a "game" with our little brothers, usually Beni, the

youngest and weakest. We would chase him, catch him and tie
him up. Then we lowered him, with great drama, into the empty
bathtub. He screamed and squirmed and tried to get out, but I
kept him in the tub and Wayne slowly turned the water on,
humming his own threatening soundtrack. We waited coolly as
the water inched towards Beni's feet and Beni screamed and
struggled helplessly. We knew that the water would not hurt
him and that his childish distress was needless. We were in total
control and always, at the crucial moment, we would turn off
the water and let him out. But this "game" set the house in a
minor uproar. Beni and Kerry complained to Mom, who got
angry at us.

"Just having fun, Mom. Okay, we went too far. Gosh. We
won't do it again."

And we didn't. Next time we tied him up and left him bal-
ancing on a narrow ledge at the top of the stairs and warned
him not to squirm or call out or he might fall off. Bondage, and
a certain detachment from resultant distress, began to figure in
my games and fantasies. That was later, but perhaps closer in
time to the dentist's office, and the canvas and leather restraints,
than the years and the hormones might suggest.

Shifting Ground

I became convinced my parents were trying to kill me. Even though grown-ups were generally very friendly, I knew they could be unpredictable, especially to children. I was not sure of their reasons for wanting me gone but I was in little doubt of it. Perhaps I was too much trouble, asked too many questions or was not exactly what they wanted, at least not what Dad wanted, and they were often surprised or irritated by my games. I kept an eye out for hints and signs of sudden change, but it was still a profound shock to have my suspicions confirmed so suddenly one lunchtime.

We rarely came home for lunch because it took over twenty minutes to walk home and another twenty back, leaving only twenty minutes to eat lunch, which was in those days still called dinner, but today the weather was fine and walking home was no great hardship and Mom had prepared a full-course dinner, complete with salt beef and vegetables. Soon after I began to eat, I bit into a potato that was chalky and dry inside and totally unlike any potato I'd ever eaten. I dropped my fork and knife, and, trembling, took the piece of chalk out of my mouth. I'd barely saved myself. If I hadn't noticed, if I'd swallowed it, I might now be dead.

"What's the matter?" asked Mom pleasantly.

"There's something wrong with this potato," I said quietly.

"What? Let me see. Oh, that's just a dry bit in the centre. That's just a bad potato. I'll get you another one."

"No, thanks," I replied, concealing my panic, and toyed uncharacteristically with the rest of my food.

I left the table shaken and washed my mouth out in case any of the poison chalk still remained.

"What's wrong with you?" Wayne asked as we left the house to walk back to school.

"Nothing."

"Yes, there is. You haven't said a word since dinner."

"Yes, well, it was bad. It could have poisoned me."

"Poison? What do you mean? The potato! Ha ha! You think Mom is trying to poison you? Yes, you do, don't you?"

"I don't know."

"That's why you're so upset. Yes, boy. Greg, Mom could be trying to poison you. You are a lot of trouble."

"Very funny."

"No, really. Watch out for supper tonight. If she didn't get you at dinnertime, she might try again tonight," and he laughed.

Had my dear mother actually tried to poison me? If so, she was very cool about it all, a master criminal. But there were no surprises in supper and everyone was so casual that I was eventually persuaded to relax my guard a little, and sure enough, I found myself alive for school the next day.

✦

Although September was wearing on, it was still warm and sunny when Dad got home from work, and we all went out to

Bowring Park and had a picnic for supper and a swim. We set up on the north bank of the Waterford River, which had been dammed up, forming a long pool, which was shallow upstream and deep by the dam. There were concrete sides and several sets of steps descending into the green water. The shadows were long but the evening was still warm and peaceful. Wayne and I could not swim but luckily Nellybelle, like every other car of her generation travelling over rough roads, had many flat tires and left a stack of patched inner tubes in her wake, two of which Dad produced for Wayne and me to float on in the pool.

We were almost the only ones left there that evening. Mom had her swim and was back with Kerry and Baby Beni on the blanket, while Wayne and I spun around in our inner tubes.

"Now, you fellas, don't go through the barrier into the deep end. Stay up here close to us."

I wanted to, but the tube did not. The current took me easily under the flimsy rope barrier and I began to float briskly down to the deep end.

"He's going, Bill!" Mom shouted in alarm. "We better get him."

"I'll get him," said Dad, jumping up.

"No, Bill, you might get water in your ears. I'll go."

But Dad was already underway. He ran through the shallow water and down along the broad bank but he could not reach out far enough to grab me. I was now gliding in deep water and coming up to the dam. I decided I'd better do something on my own behalf and struggled to slow my speed by paddling, but my hands only grazed the water and the tube spun around.

"Don't let him go over, Bill. Be careful," called Mom.

I could see Dad almost alongside me now and I slipped my feet through the centre of the tube intending to kick towards him but slid right through the wet rubber and out of his sight just a few feet from the dam. As I sank under the warm water, I had only a moment to consider my situation before I felt Dad grab me, and in an instant I was back up on the shore. He didn't get water in his ears or black out. He carried me back to Mom and put a towel around me.

"Did you swallow any water?"

"Not much."

"You gave us some fright."

"That tube is too big for them, Bill."

"Are you all right?"

"Yes, I'm fine. Thanks," I said, as I sat there shivering.

But I was in shock. I couldn't believe Dad had saved me. I felt the strength in his arms. He really does care about me, I thought. Then I felt a little ashamed, and surprised, to have had such a thought. But there it was. Surely the fearful notion that my parents were trying to kill me would lose some credence now after this heroic display of the opposite. I was baffled.

★

Brother Brennan was only a young man but he seemed to be nearly worn out. His pale, thin face was the most continuously unhappy one I had seen in my eight years. This naturally gave rise to concern for him and curiosity about what tragedies might have kindled such early grief and despair. But Brother Brennan was as unaware of his own unhappiness as he was of ours or us. He lived in a distant land we could not reach and we had not the language to make ourselves understood. So any budding concerns or caring quickly withered and died.

Brother Brennan had no pets, only peeves. He was not particularly mean nor was he particularly forgiving. He ruled, sullenly, by the book, and administered the standard discipline regularly, but without energy. He employed a flimsy and totally ineffectual rubber knife as his strap, a mere toy. Even to cowed grade threes, this was a joke. Most days, after the inevitable offences at recess, the pirate's play knife came out of the drawer and Brother Brennan would go through the rituals of disappointment and anger. His pale forehead was broad and his brown hair exceedingly recessed for so young a man. The narrow band that remained in the middle, although so well combed and trained to the side that it seemed artificial, slid frequently over his wide brow and onto his thick glasses as he worked the useless rubber knife up and down, sending it flapping painlessly over the happy hands of some of the most hardened grade threes in the city.

Brother Brennan never cracked, although we sometimes did. Behind the thick lenses of his glasses, his despairing blue eyes remained dull, half-closed, committed to some great inner injustice that we could never hope to redress, no matter how hard the spongy blade came down on us. He even worked up a sweat, strapping delinquents, pushing his equally disobedient hair back out of his sad eyes again and again, but there was no real passion, merely an exhausted and peevish impatience at the necessity of rousing himself from the sadness that had already engulfed his youth.

Grade three was tedious. More catechism tests. More of God's laws. More cumulus clouds. More Divine condemnation. How could I ever commit a mortal sin? I'm not going to rob a bank. I imagined the horror of actually taking an Oh Henry! bar, a large ten-cent one, from Puddister's Store on Pennywell Road, the halfway point on the way home from school, and a convenient place to drop in and pick up a snack. But who ever had the money, and to steal one? No, I could never steal a bar, let alone rob a bank. Ha ha, I am never going to hell. I'm definitely going to Heaven.

Jimmy Beehan lived in a roomy detached house across from Puddister's Store and so we sometimes walked home together, complaining about the weight of homework and the daily, dull catechism tests. I wrangled a visit to his house once, but only once. The Beehans were serious, even suspicious, and not given to displays of hospitality. Even Jimmy regarded me with a jaundiced eye. He disapproved of all fancy and fantasy, and was quick to correct any exaggerations in my exuberant musings. With the look of an older uncle, eyes wide, head cocked to the side, then bowed in a quick, disapproving shake, "Skipper" Jim strove to instill in me a greater fear of the world.

But I failed to take adequate note of his warnings. We shared a double desk, and the occasional rolled eye at Brother Brennan's rubber knife, but the gap between us was a large one, in fact exactly the space on the seat between us where, one morning I brazenly placed my open catechism book to read the answers to a question I had failed to memorize the night before. The endless questions and quizzes were so monotonous, what difference could it make to copy one? I had never considered it before though I knew other boys did it. After all, who could be afraid of the rubber knife? Jimmy Beehan gave me a look, raised his eyebrows, looked at the book, and then gave me the look again. I ignored him. He looked at the book again and raised his hand.

"Yes, Jimmy?" Brother Brennan answered him.

"Br, he's cheating on the test."

"What?" said Brother Brennan.

"Yes, he's got his catechism book out," Jimmy explained calmly.

I quietly imploded as Brother Brennan picked up the book. The rubber knife, of course, was nothing, especially if you were strapped with several others. But alone—and for cheating . . . I had not yet felt the indignity of that. Now the other guys might think I was stupid, too stupid to pass a stupid catechism quiz. This was all too much for my pride and I never resorted to such strategies again. Our relationship having flowered and achieved its purpose, I saw little of Jimmy Beehan after that. The dark, unpleasant angel sent to keep me on the straight and narrow seemed to vanish back into the class.

I had to consider as well that if it was possible to cheat on a test, it was possible to steal an Oh Henry! bar. If it was possible to steal an Oh Henry! bar, might it then be possible to even go to Hell? No. Cheating, especially on a religion test, would not do. I must be good so that my prayers for Mom's conversion would be heard and answered.

From the moment she had signed the marriage contract, the prayers for Mom's conversion to Catholicism were ongoing. Each of us, as we were baptized, made our First Confession and Communion and were confirmed, were instructed to pray cease-lessly for the conversion of any non-Catholic parents so that they might have a chance of going to Heaven with their Catholic families, and of avoiding the eternal banality of limbo, the unfortunate destination of all other good Christians.

Wayne and I discussed the importance of Mom's conversion and included it regularly on our list of Heaven-bound requests, which was awkward for Mom and us, but she endured it with grace. We had Protestants at St. Bon's of course, like Richard Seary, who was allowed to read in the library during religion class. His conversion was prayed for, but no great point was made of it. It was hoped our pious example would be sufficient to persuade him of the natural rightness of the true faith. To this end, he was treated with respect by the teachers, though with the student body he would have to take his chances like the rest of us.

By now I could count Billy Cooper, Gus Lilly and Andy Jones as friends. Bill was tall and funny with a head of thick blond curls and I called him Billy Goat, which annoyed him. His friend Kevin Whittle defended him and they would both chase me up into the old tennis courts and hold onto me until I promised not to say it again. It was a promise I broke often and Kevin Whittle was mystified when Bill and I became best friends by year's end. I was gratified not to be alone during recess. Of course, the ground could shift quickly and I knew this pleasant situation could easily change and I could end up like the Mercy girls.

As I walked out the main door of St. Bon's on my way home one dark Friday evening I saw a crowd of boys gathered together at the edge of the campus, shoving someone and shouting.

"Go on with your brother," shouted an older boy as he pushed another boy onto the ground.

"Look at the little girls crying," said another.

"The Mercy girls, look."

Girls, I thought, from Mercy Convent, here at St. Bon's?

"Who is it?" I asked.

"It's the Mercy girls, look, the Mercy girls are crying."

The circle of torment parted and I saw Jim Murray and his twin brother, Paul, crumpled together on the ground. They were not fighting back. Their eyes were closed and they cried freely as the blows and taunts rained down on them. Some even kicked them.

"Look at the Mercy girls crying."

"What did they do?" I asked.

"Nothin'. They're Mercy girls."

"What do you mean?"

My literal mind could not grasp how they could be girls. They were boys, weren't they?

"They're Mercy girls. You don't even have to hit them to make them cry."

But he hit them anyway.

"You shouldn't do that," I ventured.

"Oh, you want to be a Mercy girl?"

"No."

"Then shut up."

I certainly did not want to be a Mercy girl if this is what it meant. Did this mean the Murray brothers weren't boys now? I was confused and alarmed. The figure of a Brother approaching from the main entrance sent the brave crowd into retreat, leaving the rumpled figures of Jim and Paul on the ground facing each other, crouched in a fetal position. They did not look like boys anymore. How awful. They had literally been turned into Mercy girls. This could happen? Were they physically different like girls? They did look a little different. They were both a year older than me, and I thought I would like to know them. I would have that opportunity later.

✦

On Saturday, Dad took Wayne and me down to Murphy's Barber Shop on Water Street for our haircut. He would chat all about the news in the West End with Mr. Murphy and his assistant, a tall, thin man with a pleasant face and a thick thatch of white hair which reminded me of a shaving brush. They both wore clean white smocks and were very professional. It was not possible for me to stay still in the booster seat for the whole operation, and once when I turned to check on the person next to me, Mr. Murphy stopped cutting my hair and exclaimed, "Now look what you've done, moving around. You made me slip with the scissors and you got a cowlick now, right in front. Look."

"I didn't move that much," I argued.

"It doesn't take much," he rejoined.

"Will it go away?"

"No, you'll have that for good now."

He squinted and laughed at Dad. It seemed a great punishment for squirming, I thought, with a vague sense of unease.

"Now don't move again or I might accidentally cut your ear off."

Mr. Murphy seemed very entertained by the thought. I didn't like him and tried to arrange it so that when my turn came I fell into the hands of his quiet assistant.

Dad stopped taking us when Wayne was big enough to take me with him, and soon I took the long walk downtown alone to be shorn with another unexciting crew cut and to fend off

Mr. Murphy's hectoring jokes. I walked guardedly into his comfortable shop among the lines of brushes, combs, scissors, razors, tweezers and bottles of talc and lotions, another specimen to be examined, clipped and labelled by these bogus barbers in their lab whites.

Mr. Murphy squinted down at me, half laughing, half serious, with the familiar expression adults wore, which told me that I knew nothing of the world but that it was very amusing to watch me act as if I did. Outside afterwards on the sidewalk, with the cool wind breezing around my naked ears, I looked with dismay into the large picture window of the hardware store next to Murphy's Barber Shop.

The profusion of articles was overwhelming, from the bunches of tin kettles hanging from the ceiling on lines, to the tools, nails, nuts, bolts, saws and myriad other items of whose use I had no idea. What an elaborate display, I thought, and how much trouble they have taken to trick me. I was utterly convinced that as soon as I left everything would return to its original state, part of an alien world whose ways were secret and hidden from my gaze. I walked around the corner onto Waldegrave Street, then ran back as quickly as I could and looked in the window to see if I could catch everything returning to its real appearance and see the world as it really was. But I was never quick enough.

The lines of shiny kettles still hung on their hooks. The man standing inside the hardware store caught my eye and gave me an understanding smile. He knew he had fooled me and that there was no tell-tale seam of the truth showing to betray their elaborate deception. I wondered if they could read my mind and anticipate my moves. I continued on up Waldegrave in some dejection, carefully watching my surroundings for signs of anything out of place.

At the bottom of Casey Street I stopped to look at the big old brass lion ceaselessly spewing out white water onto a grate.

A small, dirty girl struggled to hold a bucket steady underneath the stream. When she opened the worn-out door to her crooked house and stepped over the thin threshold with her bucket, her bare feet hit the same black ground as outside. The house had a dirt floor and the little girl was bare and dirty under her ragged shirt. She was real. How could she live there? How was life possible in such a place? I gaped in disbelief at the wretched scene until the little girl saw me staring at her and frowned. I looked away. The lion continued to roar water as I started the long climb up Casey Street, altogether exhausted with vigilance.

★

Saturday was a grey and damp winter's day, but I thought I would brighten it up with a visit to Barbara Lynn. We had been going together for five years now and our relationship was very well known to all. Little Beni had hardly been out of our hands all that summer. We dressed him and undressed him, pushed him to the top of the street and back a dozen times a day, and fed him food he didn't always want to eat at picnics on our square of lawn in the backyard. Since school started, I had seen less of Barbara Lynn. A new family had moved in next to the Moores, and they had a boy our age named Carl. Barbara Lynn was not down on Mount Royal Avenue as much. As I walked down the snowy driveway I could hear them playing in the backyard.

"Hi, Barbara Lynn."

"Hi, Greg. You're just in time."

"Hi, Carl."

"Hi."

"We're making some snowmen and we need you to help us, right, Carl?"

"Yeah," said Carl indifferently.

"This big ball of snow is too big for Carl to roll to make our snowman. But you're so strong. I'm sure you can roll it."

"Okay," I said, flattered. "I'll try." I did not want to fail and be classed back with Carl, and so with all my might and main I rolled the big ball into place.

"Yay!" cheered Barbara Lynn, "he did it. He's like Samson. Come on, Samson, roll the other one over now."

"Okay," I said, cheered by her praise, and I pushed the other giant snow ball until it rested next to the first one.

"Yay, Samson did it again! Come on, Samson, let's put it on top of the other one and start the snowman," said Barbara Lynn. "I've got a hat for him."

"I'll get some rocks for teeth," I said.

"No, we've already got his teeth. Me and Carl will make the snowman. You have to roll another big snow ball over here."

"What for?"

"Because he needs a friend. We're making a snowman and a snow woman."

"Okay," I said, and started on the third large ball, which I could hardly budge.

"I can't make it move anymore," I panted.

"Come on, Samson," they cried. "You can do it."

But I could not.

"You two come and help me," I said. "I can't do this one by myself."

"No, that's your job, Samson." She laughed.

"Yeah, Samson, you have to roll the balls," Carl laughed.

"Come on, Samson," she taunted, as she put the wool hat on the big snowman, to Carl's approval.

"I don't want to roll any more snow balls. I want to make the snowman too."

"No, you can't. That's mine and Carl's job. We're doing that."

"That's not fair."

"Well, that's the rules. Come on, Samson, we need another snow ball," she demanded.

I stopped, hot and sweaty inside my wool duffle coat, and a

chill ran through my heart. This is it, I thought. She's taking Carl's side against me. Me! Carl regarded me with smug confidence.

"I'm not doing this anymore if I can't make the snowman too," I said.

"Come on, Samson," Barbara Lynn chanted.

"No," I said.

"Well, you can go if you're going to be like that. We don't need you anyway."

We? I shrivelled at the word, and that was it. It was over. I walked miserably down Mount Royal Avenue. How could she be so cruel to me? What had I done? Had I been mean, selfish, inattentive? I knew I could be all three, but I could not believe these were the real reasons. Carl was older, of course, and Protestant. Perhaps he was more like her, not as wild as the crowd down on Mount Royal. Well, she'd better be happy with her pale choice because that was it for me. I would not humiliate myself again. She was not going to take advantage of me. Yes, now I could see this had been coming. This was just the flat and mortifying end. I never thought our love could die. Now I was alone.

"You'll see her again, Greg," Mom said. "She'll probably be down for you tomorrow."

"No, she won't, and I'm not going back there again, either."

"I can't believe that, Greg."

But it was true. The great romance was over. Now it looked like I'd definitely be marrying Sharon McGrath after all.

✸

Mom dropped the receiver of our new wall telephone, distraught and agitated.

"What is it, Lovey?" asked Dad, jumping up.

"Oh my God, no, Bill."

"What? What?"

"It's Len. And Yvonne."

"What? What happened?"

"Yvonne's dead and I think the baby is too," she broke down sobbing.

"What happened?"

But Mom could not relate the terrible story.

Uncle Len had married pretty, gentle Yvonne Warren from Buchans, a mining town in the centre of the Island, and they had been driving back there to visit her family, with their daughter Rhoda, who was Kerry's age, her little brother, Stephen, and the new baby, Lenore. It was dark and snowy on the gravel road and Rhoda wanted to sit in the front with her mother, but Yvonne had the baby in her arms, so Rhoda and Stephen had to sit in the back, and she wasn't happy about it. The family continued on, tired and testy, until they approached a bridge on a bend in the road. Uncle Len could not see that ice had formed on the surface and as soon as he turned onto the bridge, he lost control of the car, which careened violently into the concrete railings. Yvonne and Lenore were killed instantly. The others were saved.

Mom and Auntie Vera, ashen and grim, boarded the train on Water Street for the long, miserable journey to Buchans, and we awaited their return.

"It was terrible," Mom said. "Poor Len could hardly stand. Vera and I had to hold onto him. And when the baby's little white coffin came out, well, everyone in the church just broke down. It was terrible," she repeated, "terrible."

Uncle Len was not well afterwards. Nanny and Pop rented out Charlton Street and took a bigger house with a yard on Blackmarsh Road, and Len and Rhoda and little Stephen moved in with them. Nanny took care of the children while Len recovered, and we visited them there. Nanny was very protective of Rhoda and warned us not to be too rough. Our little cousin was quiet and pretty, and Wayne and I, and even Kerry, did our best to amuse her and make her laugh. We played with her whenever her nose was not bleeding, which seemed to happen a lot, and Nanny would rush in and hold her nose, and shoo us off to go and have some fruitcake.

Trail's End

D ad was at his best in the Boy Scouts. When Dad spoke of E. B. Foran, his devoted scoutmaster, his eyes misted and his lips trembled, brimming over with respect and love for the man who provided the guidance he lacked at home.

The Scouts had been a saviour for Dad and so it seemed only natural to him that they should be a saviour for me and Wayne as well. Being in grade three and eight years old, I naturally found it difficult to part with ten cents for dues at our weekly Cub and Boy Scout meetings. It didn't seem right to pay ten cents for something I didn't want when there was so much else I did not have the funds for. More good money was spent on the itchiest knee socks in the Commonwealth, held tight with itchy elastic garters, creating almost exactly the sensation of standing at attention up to your knees in a barrel of black ants.

But socks were not the most important part of the Cub Scout uniform. They just had the greatest sensory impact. Next came the itchy, green wool jersey, held at bay by a cotton T-shirt, except for the uncovered itchy arms. A thick, thankfully cotton, neckerchief, the pale green colour of the troop, went around your neck and was held together in front by the woggle. The woggle, a sort of ring, could be of varying size and shape. Senior Scouts and troop leaders never wore an ordinary, store-bought woggle. They spent hours carving bone and ivory woggles with eagle heads, or making fur woggles with braided leather edging, brass woggles with turquoise stones, and silver woggles fashioned out of old spoons. You could tell a Scout by his woggle. It showed his skill, his devotion, his ingenuity and his narrow grip on sanity. Thus would a senior Scout distinguish himself from the pack.

Mine was a standard brown leather woggle with a gold wolf's head stamped on the front, but I longed for something more exotic. The regulation short navy blue pants were also blessedly made of cotton, which left only the itchy green wool cap. In short, while in uniform, all your extremities, legs, arms and head, itched continually so that you never forgot for a moment that you had legs, arms and a head, and perhaps that was the point. The wool felt alive, bristling with continuous woollen commands. The socks were better Cub Scouts than I would ever be. They would keep me standing to attention should my own legs falter. But while the extremities flamed, the torso, protected by cotton, remained relatively unmolested, a neutral zone where the nervous system might withdraw for momentary relief.

"Malone, what are you doing there? Pull up your socks and put on your cap for inspection."

We shuffled dumbly into line on the dusty auditorium floor.

The First St. John's Scout Troop and Cub Pack were not affiliated with St. Bon's College, or any particular school or with any particular parents or adults as far as I could tell. It was an old troop whose glory days were in the past, Dad's past. The leaders of the Cub pack, Mr. Kelly and Mr. Wells, were senior Scouts. Ron Kelly was a St. Bon's boy and would go on to become a priest. Years later, when a Royal Commission revealed shocking stories of sexual and physical abuse of orphans and altar boys by Christian Brothers and priests, Ron Kelly's name would come up. He would be charged and convicted for sexually abusing young boys, and quietly depart the priesthood at the height of the Mount Cashel Orphanage scandal.

Mr. Kelly and Mr. Wells laughed loudly at each other as they strode over to our little patrol then abruptly snapped to seriousness as they turned to face us.

"Attention."

We stiffened. Bedecked in badges, woggles of bone and silver, and with coloured braids of cord through the epaulettes of their enviable cool, green cotton Scout shirts, they looked down at the uneven line of Cubs before them. Mr. Kelly's straight blond hair was almost white and his strong, pale face almost handsome. His busy blue eyes danced over us, looked at me, past me.

"Straighten up . . . you . . . what's your name?"

"Higgins."

"Higgins, sir!"

"Higgins, sir."

"Those shoes are not shined. One point. Woggles must be tight, Mr. Malone, and the corner points of your neckerchief must match up, Mr. Benson, is it?"

"Yes sir."

"What's this? Take that off, Mr. Benson. I'll show how you fold a neckerchief."

His voice was loud and confident as he spread out the neckerchief and folded it over into a perfect triangle, rolled it up with a few deft flicks, wrapped it around Mr. Benson's neck and tightened it briskly with Mr. Benson's common, store-bought woggle.

"There. That's better, Benson."

"Yes sir," squeaked Benson.

"Neckerchief: one point, Mr. Wells."

"Yes sir."

Mr. Wells recorded our inadequacies on his clipboard. We had done badly but others might do worse, our hope. We chanted.

A-Ke-La. We'll do our best.

Our best? Of course we would. It was at once a promise and a threat.

We'll dib dib dib. We'll dub dub dub.

I felt confident I could both dib and dub when the time came, but what did it mean? Whose secret language was it? To whom were we swearing allegiance? These uncertainties swam around me as I attempted to penetrate the distant lines from Kipling. Someone had given us a quick run-through of the story and one day it would sink in, but now the verses lay cold on my lips as I crouched like Mowgli (and wished I were dressed like Mowgli) and sang about Shere Khan.

Mowgli's hunting, Mowgli's hunting
Killed Shere Khan, Killed Shere Khan
Killed the cattle eater

Cattle eater . . . Why kill the cattle eater if that's what he was?

Killed Shere Khan

We sang on. No time to pause or reflect.

There were beans, beans, as big as submarines.

Really?

In the store, in the store
There were beans, beans,
As big as submarines
In the quartermaster's store.

Only a quarter master? Not yet a full master?

In the store, in the store.

I felt a slight cramp as we sat cross-legged on the cold floor singing.

My gal's a corker,
She's a New Yorker.

Our voices swayed uncertainly around the lopsided circle in the dim light of the electric campfire. In the centre, red crepe paper poked out through a small stack of never-burning logs. At one corner, the red paper did not quite meet the logs and the light bulb could be clearly seen inside. We stared into the faux fire, an ignorant urban tribe, generations from our roots, singing other people's songs, hoping, with our clumsy props and home-made amulets, to recreate some distant, primal event when the Great Scouting Spirit, called forth by the wild faces of that first tribe around a roaring fire, had entered the dancing circle and breathed into them the first rules of Scouting, weaving them into the ways of the woods, giving them meaning and purpose.

A-Ke-La. We'll do our best.

The First St. John's Troop had problems with meeting rooms so we moved. There were absent troop leaders so meetings were cancelled, still we trooped on and even went swimming at the King George V Institute. I did not know there was an indoor swimming pool in St. John's, let alone in this dark, red brick building. Yet there it was, not fifty feet from the centre of Water Street, a pool of warm, dancing water, reflecting light onto the shiny white tiles in the dim and din of the steamy inner sanctum. You entered naked. No swimming trunks were allowed, as the dye might pollute the water. You showered and swam naked with the other boys, or you did not, if you so chose.

I went in cautiously at the shallow end. At the deep end, one of the senior boys strode up to the diving board. His thick thatch of brown pubic hair shocked me. He was tall with a pale, serious face and one eye half closed, which gave him an appearance slightly reminiscent of Frankenstein's monster by whom I had only recently been scared out of my wits. He lurched onto the board and, as he bounced and sprang into the air, his long white penis swung around before he crashed into the flashing water with a great splash. It took all my courage to get in after him. The pool was small and the room echoed with the shouts and yelps of skylarking boys. It was an overwhelming and riveting experience to which I would have returned, but the First St. John's had more scheduling problems and that was the last I saw of the warm pool and the naked monster.

Damp, snowy spring turned into summer. School ended and our weekly meetings in the dusty auditoriums were overtaken with plans for the main event of the year—summer camp. Whether you were a Scout or a Cub, Scouting meant camping. Two weeks away from home seemed like a long time to me and I didn't really know the other Cubs well. But I arrived in front of St. Bon's one sunny Sunday morning with my duffle bag and sleeping bag and my uncertainty fortified by a pocket full of spending money Mom and Dad had given me to buy bars and drinks at the canteen.

One of the O'Keefe boys did not have a proper sleeping bag.

There were a lot of O'Keefe boys. Their father was a strict, rough-and-ready ex-Scout and true believer like Dad, and none of his boys would miss summer camp for lack of a fancy sleeping bag or spending money. So, instead of a sleeping bag, Terry had a bed roll, several blankets folded over and pinned together down one side with large kilt pins, then rolled up like a sleeping bag, but not enough like a sleeping bag for those in the happy possession of a real one.

"Hey, boys. Look at O'Keefe's crazy sleeping bag."

"Don't stick yourself with a pin in the middle of the night, Terry."

"Watch out the ants don't get you, O'Keefe."

Terry's freckled face flushed the colour of his blasty red curls and I filled with indignation for him. But he managed to smile and joke back.

"Watch out now, Wadden, or I'll stick *you*."

He bore it far better than I would have and I began to worry that my own sleeping bag might not qualify as normal either and soon come under fire. It was Dad's old Arctic sleeping bag. The ribbed, cream-coloured, down-filled body was covered with a yellow waterproof outer shell. It had arms and a head and tapered in at the legs creating the effect of a mummy. Inside, with your arms in the sleeves, you could reach down and zip the whole thing together up past your chin, pull down the blue-coloured visor to protect your face, and you were sealed and self-contained and ready to face the permafrost. Luckily, it proved to be a popular novelty.

We crowded onto the bus and headed for Trail's End, the first St. John's campgrounds, several miles northeast of Town on the Indian Meal Line, just past Torbay. The camp was set in rolling hills among thick black-spruce and fir woods with grassy trails between small meadows, which were laid out with tan-coloured army bell tents. At the end of the trail on the shore of the pond was a brown-stained lodge with large windows looking over the water. It had a large stone fireplace and served as canteen and meeting place in bad weather and as sleeping quarters for some of the troop leaders.

In the hot morning sun we stood to attention in full itch. There was inspection every day but here at least it made more sense. There were grounds to clean, clothes and gear to be organized, tents to tend to. Only the uniform seemed to serve no purpose, except that its removal immediately after inspection created perhaps the happiest moment of the day.

The thick green spruce trees skirted the path and tapered to a V of vague grey sky. The air was close as I walked along with Gordon Bailey. He was a year older than me, wore glasses that were brown on top, clear plastic on bottom, and his expression was serious and intense as he warned me about the various perils of camp. We came to a clearing where two more boys emerged from another path. Gordon looked at them, looked at me, then punched me in the stomach for all he was worth. I crumpled to the ground as Gordon ran off with the other boys.

"That's for nothing, and don't try and follow us," he shouted.

I didn't. I lay wheezing in the grass. What did he mean, follow them? Why would I? Gordon hadn't warned me about the biggest danger so far—himself. But he had taught me a valuable lesson. Beware of random acts of Scouting aggression. Luckily, there were no more.

I enjoyed buying unfamiliar bars at the canteen, and the foreign songs of camaraderie were more at home here in the woods around a real fire.

And as I go, I love to sing,
My knapsack on my back.
Val-deri, Val-dera.
My knapsack on my back.

The val-deri was still a mystery, but I felt its meaning would be revealed somewhere here in the woods. I avoided Gordon. He glared at me, or perhaps it was his normal look. When he caught my eye, I quickly walked in another direction to signal to him clearly there was no danger whatever of my following him.

I was happy to demonstrate the Arctic sleeping bag for the rest of my patrol. I stuck my arms in the puffy, down sleeves and zipped the body shut for the night. I even put up the hood. But it was too warm for the tinted visor and too dark. I fell quickly to sleep and woke suddenly in the middle of the night in a state of panic. I could not breathe or move my body. My head felt as though it would explode. My heart raced up behind my tongue and choked off speech. I felt it was only seconds before I would lose consciousness. With enormous effort, I swung my padded arm up, grabbed the zipper and pulled down as hard as I could. A knife of cool air sliced down the centre of my stewed body. I struggled out of the hermetic seal of the Arctic bag onto the cool ground in the night air.

The popular Arctic sleeping bag had almost killed me. The others all lay deep asleep, unaware of my life-and-death struggle. The paths were dark and empty. The stars shone distantly overhead. My heart began to slow. The night was not cool at all. It was warm but I had been at cooking temperature. After all it was an Arctic sleeping bag and best used above the Arctic circle, not here on the balmy Avalon Peninsula in July. I crawled cautiously back in on top of the steaming bag. Pulling one side half over me, I kept one leg outside on top of the mummy sack in case it should spontaneously fold over and entomb me during the remainder of the night. I lay there keenly alive and amazed at my own consciousness and near unconsciousness.

I saw little of Mr. Kelly and Mr. Wells. They were busy with their own amusements, but the telling of ghost stories that frightened small Cubs into early, surly maturity was one duty to which they brought genuine enthusiasm. "The Bloody Hand" was a favourite at Trail's End and had been told to so many troops that it was now taken as historical fact, at least that's how Mr. Kelly told it:

"Many years ago, around this time of year, three robbers were rowing across the pond one evening, with a sack of stolen silver and jewellery, which they were going to hide in the woods. Two were brothers and the third man owned the boat. But the brothers, emboldened by the success of their crime, became greedy and decided to kill the other man and keep all the treasure for themselves.

"The owner of the boat was rowing, and when they got out near the middle of the pond, the older brother, sitting in the stern of the boat, stabbed him in the back. The brothers threw the heavy body overboard into the pond. But the man was not dead. He came up to the surface and grabbed onto the side of the boat, pulling it down into the water. Frantically, the brothers tried to push him off. They hit at him with the oars and tried to pry his hands off the boat. They pulled his right hand off but could not loosen the grip of the left hand. Finally the older brother took an axe and, with a great blow, he chopped off the left hand. The victim's mouth opened in a silent scream, his eyes widened as he looked up at the older brother and then he sank noiselessly beneath the gently lapping waves.

"The brothers stood dumb for a moment then tore at the left hand, still clinging to the side of the boat. It took both their efforts to pull it free. The older brother flung it far into the gathering darkness at the centre of the pond. Exhausted and rattled, they put the boat into the little wharf at Trail's End, broke into the old Scout Lodge and, after several restless hours, finally fell asleep. But their sleep was not peaceful and in the early morning, just before dawn, they awoke to the sound of scratching. The older brother said it was a rat but the scratching moved closer and seemed to be coming from overhead. He fumbled in his jacket for a match and struck it. In its small light, above them on the open rafters was, not a rat, but the mutilated and bloody hand he had cut off only hours before.

"There could be no doubt. It scrambled along the beam, dripping blood onto their upturned faces. They could not move or utter a sound. Suddenly the hand dropped down straight from the beam onto the older brother's bare throat. His match flickered and died. He did not scream but began to choke and struggle in the semi-darkness. In the sickly, pre-dawn light, his younger brother watched as he writhed and twisted, trying to free himself from the death grip of the wounded hand. He could see the terror in his brother's eyes as they looked frantically at him for help. The younger brother staggered to the fireplace. He stumbled over the bloody axe and picked it up. With one desperate effort he swung at the hand, but it had already relaxed its grip and dropped away, and the axe cleanly sliced off the lifeless head of his older brother.

"At this, the younger brother let out a low, strangled moan. Shaking violently, he dropped the axe and fell out into the dark woods and ran and ran and ran. Days later he was found babbling feverishly about a hand that had killed his brother and chased him for days and nights. He died years later in the mental asylum where they took him that very day. At first he was not believed, but slowly stories began to emerge about people rowing on the pond who had seen a strange object on the surface of the water, not a fish or a muskrat, but something different, and of people camping who had seen just such an object crawl out of the water onto the shore and disappear into the woods. And sometimes in the early hours of the morning, just before dawn, as their eyes struggled to make out the shapes in the gloom, Scouts sleeping in the old lodge swore they could hear the sound of scratching up in the old rafters. But that hasn't happened in a long time, at least not since last summer."

Mr. Kelly stopped and looked intently at the Cubs, frozen to the floor in front of him. He picked up a junk of birch and threw it on the dying embers in the stone fireplace. It crackled and flared up brightly, sending shadows jumping up behind them, then slowly the room returned to the deep silence of the woods. Mr. Kelly turned back to the Cubs. He leaned back and his gaze fixed on the rafters above. It was impossible to look up. It was impossible *not* to look up. So, painfully, one by one, our heads tipped back until we all peered up into the quivering shadows above. As we did so, Mr. Kelly suddenly scratched his hand along the floor into the middle of the tense group of Cubs. Screaming and shrieking, arms and legs flying, we scrambled and tumbled over each other, tearing our way to the door. Mr. Wells blew his whistle to restore order then blew it again and again. It took several blasts and finally Mr. Kelly's commanding voice to avert a stampede.

"All right, Cubs, it's just a story. Settle down now. Okay, it's late now. It's time to go back to your tents and hit the sack. And don't worry. If you feel something grabbing your ankle on the way, it's more likely to be a lynx or a bear than a bloody hand."

Mr. Kelly seemed immensely pleased with himself. We marched miserably up the centre of the dark path to our tents. There were muffled cries and murmurs as hyper-sensitized Cubs accidentally brushed against each other. But mostly there was dead silence as we strained to hear the sound of scratching among the branches rustling in the wind.

The Cubs zipped their sleeping bags up over their heads. Terry O'Keefe clutched at the gaps between the pins of his bed roll. I had to choose between suffocation and strangulation. I chose strangulation and lay on the surface of sleep waiting for the hand in the dark that never came though I felt it many times.

"Come on, you Cubs, out of your fart sacks and get this place in shape. This is your last inspection. Let's make it a good one."

This had been, indeed, the last camp of the First St. John's Cub Pack. The unorthodox antics of the troop leaders attracted the displeasure of Dad, Mr. O'Keefe, Mr. O'Dea, Dr. Higgins and some of the other old Scouts. Mr. Kelly and Mr. Wells had failed to live up to the standards of E. B. Foran, and with those venerable days in mind, Dad and the others took it upon themselves, with the blessing of St. Bonaventure's College, to form the First St. Bon's Boy Scout Troop, in which they took a very active hand.

Sean Power

Grade four was in the same classroom as grade two, and with the same teacher. We did not look forward to this return. The big class from grade three had been divided into Four A and Four B, which was changed the next year to Five Blue and Five Gold in an attempt to avoid any implication of worth. The endless catechism quizzes continued unabated from grade three, but now the stakes were much higher. We knew what to expect from Brother Clancy and we braced ourselves.

Sean Power got strapped every morning. He was the smallest boy in our grade four class. With short brown hair and a tanned face, he was cute like a little monkey. Sean never did his homework. Neither did Andy Squires, the second smallest. He was strapped every day as well.

Few of us could comprehend this though we had witnessed it all before in grade two with Brother Clancy: the same room, the same boys, the same strapping, the same sick fear. Sheer terror drove me to homework every night. There may have been other healthy reasons to want to do homework, but I was unaware of them. I drew the margins perfectly with a ruler. I put J. M. J., Jesus, Mary and Joseph, the motto of the Christian Brothers, on the top of every page. I underlined it. I underlined it twice. As the year wore on, I framed it and decorated it with filigrees and curlicues, until it dominated the page like an elaborate baroque altar. Finally Brother Clancy told me to stop. A simple J. M. J. would do. I could underline it only once. How would he know I cared . . . too much?

One morning I got all of my multiplication wrong. My heart sank. The blood drained from my face and my mouth dried out. What punishment would I suffer? Every question wrong. I had forgotten to carry over. My terror neared tears. Brother Clancy leaned over my desk, pointed out my error and asked me if I understood. Yes. Yes. Then he smiled and moved casually on. That was it? Perhaps he had noticed my bloodless face and shaking body and decided I had suffered enough. It took the rest of the morning for the molten terror that filled my body to ebb away.

I had good reason to fear. The blackboard still bore the marks of last week's multiplication disaster. Ricky Bidgood had not been able to remember the product of 3 x 3. Brother Clancy took him through 1 x 3 and 2 x 3 twice already, but he still stalled out at 3 x 3. Having primed Ricky for the answer several times, Brother Clancy was now wound up to an explosive pitch, and at Ricky's final failure, he flung the arithmetic book away, rushed up to the front, put his hands on the blackboard and banged his head off it nine times, sending clouds of chalk dust out of the seams and into the classroom. As he banged his head, he counted to nine loudly and then spun around and screamed.

"Nine! Nine! Nine!"

And then, in letters almost as tall as the board itself, he engraved the word NINE, spelling it aloud as he went. He cut so deeply into the board that the word could not be erased. I stared at the clear traces of it now, grateful that my own ignorance had not been similarly memorialized.

Sometimes Brother Clancy smiled at Sean Power and Andy Squires. Some days the religious giant would pick up tiny Sean and, laughing, throw him up in the air and sit him on top of the classroom door. Sean the monkey would cling on with a nervous smile: Br likes me now.

"Will I leave you up there all day?"

Yes, Br. No, Br. What was the right answer?

"No, Br."

Right answer.

"Come down then. Do you have your homework done today, Sean?"

"No, Br."

Wrong answer, Sean, we silently screamed.

"Why not?'

"Don't know, Br."

For God's sake, why not, Sean, we almost cried.

"You know what happens when you don't do your home-work, Sean?"

We do, Br. Isn't that enough?

"I suppose so," answered Sean.

"You suppose so?"

"Yes, Br."

"Class, do you know what happens when you don't do your homework?"

We knew. Oh yes. Brother Clancy moved to his desk, opened the middle drawer and removed a long strap made of several pieces of black leather stitched together.

"Come up here, Sean, to the front of the room. I'm going to have to strap you."

Do you really have to? we silently begged.

"No, Br," said Sean.

"Yes, Sean, come up here," said Brother Clancy.

Sean shifted up.

"Raise your hand, Sean . . . higher, Sean."

Sean needed to raise his hand very high because Brother Clancy was such a tall man. It was a long way to come down to hit Sean. When Sean's hand had finally reached the desired height, Brother Clancy raised his arm and the strap came down very quickly on Sean's hand, with a sharp smack.

"Ow, Br! That hurts."

"I know it hurts, Sean. That's why you should do your homework. Again."

"No, Br."

"Yes, Sean."

"Ow! Ow! Ow!"

One. Two. Three. Four. Five times, Sean put that hand back up there.

"No, Br."

"Yes, Sean."

The tension in the class was extreme. Not a muscle moved among us. All were rigid.

"Keep it up there, Sean. Don't move it or you'll make me mad."

Yes, Br. No, Br. What was the right answer? Six. Seven. Eight. Nine. Ten. Thank God, it's over. Sean was crying softly now and returned to his desk. The scene of tension, terror and pain had a narcotic, numbing and subversively stimulating effect. Brother Clancy returned the strap to the middle drawer.

"Now, that's over. Let's all forget about it. Open your catechism books to the Corporal Works of Mercy."

Who could think of them? Surely Sean would not forget his homework again. Surely tomorrow morning he would . . . No. The next morning Sean still did not have his homework done and Andy Squires also did not have his homework done. There was a lineup for the strap. This morning there was no playful bouncing Sean up onto the door.

"Sean, why didn't you do your homework?"

"I don't know, Br."

"You must know, Sean."

"No, Br."

"Andy, why didn't you do your homework?"

"I was watching television, Br."

Good God, Andy, no! Don't say that. Lie! Say anything, but not television.

That was it. That was enough. Andy would be the first. He had answered with the honesty of a saint, and now he would suffer like one.

"Now, Mr. Squires, I'm going to strap you ten times on each hand. And I want you to keep count as I strap you. Hold that hand high, Mr. Squires."

"Yes, Br."

Swoosh. Brother Clancy's hand came down hard and hit his own leg with the strap. Andy had pulled his hand away at the last minute. Brother Clancy turned red.

"Mr. Squires, hold that hand up. Give me that hand."

Brother Clancy held Andy's small hand up.

"Oh no," whimpered Andy.

"Oh yes," roared Brother Clancy and down the strap came. This time it made contact. Andy's eyes filled up.

"Count, Mr. Squires."

"One. Two. Three," Andy counted

"Don't move, Mr. Squires."

"No, Br."

He released Andy's hand.

"Four. Five."

Swish, Andy pulled away and Brother Clancy hit himself again. There was the slightest gasp from the class.

"Put that hand back up, Mr. Squires."

"Yes, Br."

"Don't move it."

"No, Br."

"All right."

Brother Clancy swung his arm high over his head and came down hard.

"Seven," whimpered Andy.

"No, Mr. Squires, that's not seven. It's six."

"No, Br. It's seven."

"No, Mr. Squires, it's six."

"No, Br."

Brother Clancy paused.

"All right, Mr. Squires, we'll start again."

"No, Br, please, Br, no, Br."

"Yes, Mr. Squires, give me your hand."

"One. Two. Three."

Andy cried and screeched and sobbed. I could hardly hear it. My heart was pounding, my head was drumming, my face was hot. Finally, years later, Andy walked back down the aisle past us sobbing and holding his hands under his arms, and Brother Clancy started in on Sean, who was already crying.

If only there was something we could do to help. Distract Brother Clancy. Appease him. We all thought hard. We strained but could think of nothing, and so we sat.

"Hold up your hand, Mr. Power."

"Yes, Br."

"Don't move it, Mr. Power."

"No, Br."

One. Two. Slap. Slap. Slap. At last it was finally over but it seemed to go on and fill the whole morning like an echo. I sat numb in my seat. Helpless. Ineffectual. It seemed impossible to think of spelling after this, to recall the words.

"Mr. Malone, spell 'broken.'"

"Broken. B-R-O-K-E-N. Broken."

Brother Clancy seemed satisfied but somehow I felt I had let Sean and Andy down.

"Mr. Squires, spell 'window' for us."

My God, no, Br. Please.

"What, Br? I didn't hear you."

Brother Clancy paused again.

"Spell 'window.'"

"Window. W-E-N-O . . ."

"No, Mr. Squires. Mr. Harrington, can you spell 'window'?"

Of course Mr. Harrington could spell window.

"Window. W-I-N-D-O-W. Window," came the immediate response.

Brother Clancy seemed pleased.

"Now, Mr. Squires, I want you to write out 'window' twenty times tonight along with your regular homework. Do you understand?"

"Yes, Br."

No, no, Br. Don't do it, please. You know, we all know, Andy will never do it and it will just all be worse.

"Don't forget, Mr. Squires."

"No, Br."

But Mr. Squires did forget and was strapped again. Eventually Mr. Squires' brother George was brought into the class. George always did his homework. Perhaps he could explain to Brother Clancy why Andy didn't. George said his mother was busy with the little kids and the baby and George was busy too. Sometimes he reminded Andy but Andy liked to watch *Hopalong Cassidy* and *I Love Lucy* on television. Yes, George would remind Andy more often and make sure he did his homework.

"Now, Mr. Power, where is your homework?"

"I don't have it, Br."

George's heart was not in his new task. He didn't want to be in our grade four class, explaining why his brother didn't do his homework. And so the next morning Andy and Sean got strapped again.

Brother Clancy was getting mad at "having" to give the strap to Andy and Sean every morning. Now it was like Brother Clancy was failing. He told us he was talking to the grade two teacher, Mrs. Firth, about the problem. One morning Mrs. Firth took the time to come into the classroom and talk to us about how important it was to be responsible and write down our homework assignments so we wouldn't forget to do them. Yes, yes, we could not agree more. What did Andy think?

"Yes, Br. Yes, Mrs. Firth."

Brother Clancy was in a good mood now. He swung Andy up in the air and stood him on his own desk. Mrs. Firth had something special just for Andy. What could it be?

"Now, Andy, this is a special present for you to help you remember. I know you want to do better and Brother Clancy and I believe you can do better."

She opened her large bag and took out a beautiful little book with a colourful cloth cover. On the front was a loop, which held a pen the same colour as the book.

"This is a special book, Andy, with all the days of the week listed, and it is especially for writing down your homework assignments. So then you won't forget them."

There was a pause.

"Well, Andy, do you see how many people care about you and are worried about you? I think it's very generous of Mrs. Firth to spend her own money on such a beautiful present for you. What have you got to say to Mrs. Firth?"

"Thank you, Mrs. Firth."

"You're very welcome, Andy," said Mrs. Firth. "I hope that from now on you will have no more trouble remembering your homework, will you?"

"No, Mrs. Firth."

"Well, thank you very much, Mrs. Firth, for taking the time to come in here today and help us all out. Class, let's all show Mrs. Firth how much we appreciate her help."

Brother Clancy started to clap and we all quickly joined in, clapping as hard as we could. Mrs. Firth smiled a big smile. She had a small round nose and big brown eyes and big white teeth which seemed to push forward when her lipsticked lips stretched over them. Brother Clancy smiled too. They shook hands. They were very happy and relieved that the problem was solved. Andy held his special new book and looked up with a strange half smile. We all hoped the problem was solved but were not convinced, and were very sorry when we were proved right, and Brother Clancy and Mrs. Firth were wrong.

"Andy, I can't believe you didn't do your homework again after all that Mrs. Firth and I have done for you. I can't believe you could be so ungrateful to Mrs. Firth and everyone else who cares so much about you. I'm going to have to increase the number of straps from ten to fifteen. Come up to the front of the classroom, Mr. Squires."

The Strap

Brother Clancy was not always angry. Sometimes the giant was friendly, like the day he accidentally stapled his own finger with his stapler. He yelped and squeezed out several drops of blood, which he licked up, laughing like we were all friends.

"Now don't go home and tell your parents that Brother Clancy stapled his own finger or they'll think I'm too stupid to be in charge of you."

His fears were groundless. We would not dream of telling our parents any such thing.

Brother Clancy wanted pets, and he brought in hamsters, which I could not relate to. But I could not blame the hamsters. They seemed as nervous and puzzled as we were. They were popular with many of the "inmates" though and featured in our class picture in the *Adelphian*. He also wanted to do a play, which I could relate to, one with a holy theme about the apparition of Our Lady to the peasant girl Bernadette Soubirou at Lourdes, and I was thrilled to be one of the chosen performers, along with Michael Harrington, Peter Jardine, Jimmy Duggan, Bobby Tilley, David Stamp and Danny Williams.

We had rehearsals and gathered costumes. The core cast of Mike and Danny and I decided, at my enthusiastic instigation, to have a dress rehearsal, which Danny didn't really want, but which he graciously agreed to host in the attic of his grandmother's house, a tall Victorian duplex, on the corner of Patrick Street and Hamilton Avenue.

Danny was small, but fierce, and not at all plesased about wearing a dress, which he made sure we all understood. Mike then followed with a poor show of not wanting to put his dress on either. I was more than comfortable with the prospect, but restrained my glee and waxed philosophical as best I could, assuring Danny that we knew he didn't want to wear the dress, and that it wasn't his idea, but for now, for the sake of the play, devotion and duty required a good show in full costume, which in this case meant dresses. And Danny was playing Bernadette, the Saint herself. He would have to set the tone. There was no point in me, as Bernadette's chatty sister, appearing in a full-length dress with smock stitching, a lovely white shawl and bandana, however authentic and attractive I might look, if my little sister, the Saint, was in a plaid shirt and pants. He would have to think of his faith, if not his fans, and let devotion trump ego for the sake of appearances. He finally relented, but struck a hard bargain. He would wear the dress but not the bandana at the rehearsals and the full outfit for the performance only. Mike followed suit while I chose to illustrate the full effect. But we had a good run-through, after which Mrs. Williams served us refreshments, which I thought very civilized.

The play was a huge success. Everyone knew their lines. Danny forgot about his female attire and rose to the occasion, while I, swept along happily in my skirt, gave every bit of feeling I could and then some. Our classmates clapped their hearty approval, and Mrs. Firth, who had been invited to witness our efforts, was entirely complimentary. The momentary ecstasies and glories of these budding theatrics now over, we took off our women's robes and returned to our regular schedule.

In a culture where discipline meant corporal punishment, it was hardly possible to avoid the strap, however careful you might be. The reasons could be unimportant or even irrelevant. It might be a whim, even a personal goal of a particularly dedicated brother that no child should escape the strap, in which case reasons enough could be found. Sometimes you were aware you were committing infractions, and sometimes you were not, like poor Larry Connors.

"Now, Mr. Connors, since your pen is broken, I will lend you my own pen to finish the assignment."

"Thank you, Br."

Brother Clancy was being tolerant and generous, giving Larry his pen, and showing us a good example.

"This is my favourite pen, so be careful with it and don't break it."

"No, Br."

Larry was not the only one who borrowed Brother Clancy's pen, which appeared on his desk at the end of the week covered in ink, which might as well have been blood.

"Who broke my pen?" asked a hurt and offended Brother Clancy.

There was no response.

"All right," he demanded, "who borrowed my pen this week?"

Richard Simms, in an excess of honesty and innocence, and unaware of the coming storm, put up his hand and was immediately called to the front of the class. Two other suspects were weeded out.

"And you, Mr. Connors, you used it too."

Larry went to the front of the class.

"I didn't break it, Br."

"I didn't ask if you broke it. I asked if you used it."

"Yes, Br, but—"

Larry did not have time to finish his excuse. Brother Clancy had already passed judgement and without warning he turned and punched Larry so hard in the stomach that he flew down the aisle and landed at the foot of Andy Jones's desk. The class pulled back in panic as though to escape. How far would he go? Larry staggered to his feet, as white as paper, and Brother Clancy backed off. He'd had it in for Larry ever since Larry and Austin "Autie" Thorn had climbed out of the window at the back of the class, around the post over fifty feet above the pavement below, and then back in the next window, a perilous prank for which they were both strapped. But Brother Clancy, it seems, had not been satisfied.

The punch lingered in our minds and conversations and shook the commonly held opinion that school was safer now than in the days when Dad had fought off Brother Egan. The strap was, after all, only painful and humiliating, but not a life-threatening event, like the time Andy Jones's uncle Jack was thrown down three flights of stairs for dropping an orange on Brother Buckingham's head. Yes, perhaps things were better now, and although almost everyone knew how the strap felt, should there be any who through some oversight had missed its persuasive touch, they would eventually be corralled on those occasions when the whole class was strapped for failing to act as one obedient body. That day came when we trailed back from recess late, for the third time.

Recess was a greatly anticipated and much-needed psychological break in the morning's tension. Boys could give chase, or be chased around, on the slimmest pretext. Gangs could be improvised for great, stampeding battles. Our grade four geography book was an inspiration of romantic watercolour paintings and stories of Bunga in his little village in the jungle, and Suvan in his fantastic yurt on the steppes, and Roberto on the vast pampas. For us, the campus was the pampas, and on spring days we managed to convince enough boys to create rival tribes to line up on opposite ends, and with a great yell, we'd charge at each other, meeting in the middle in a great dusty cloud. It was a thrill and a great spectacle, even when running in the middle of the dusty horde, and a great release for pent up energy. The stampede over, no one knew quite what to do when the two armies met in the middle. We couldn't really do much fighting with our uniforms on, although we tried, for which effort the spectacle was soon banned by the brothers, and we returned to tamer pastimes.

With the grade three class divided, recess was still a challenge as far as friends went. My situation was much improved from the loneliness of grade one, but Billy Cooper was in the other grade four class. I didn't call him Billy Goat much anymore and we were both disappointed to be parted. I was pleasantly surprised when Andy Jones and I quickly became good friends. We did a great deal of talking and laughing and even signaling in class, at least on my part.

One day the noise level in the classroom somehow rose to the point where Brother Clancy warned us that the next person who spoke would get the strap.

Before class, I had been entertaining Andy with the lyrics from an old Irish tune Dad had quoted to me in the car on the way to school in response to my growing complaints about our teacher.

Clancy, Clancy,
Tickle me fancy,
Oh me charmin' Billy boy

Dad chanted, letting his Irish accent loose in the car for our amusement.

After Brother Clancy's threat, even in spite of it, I actually turned around to Andy, who was, of course, sitting perfectly well behaved at his desk, trying to avoid me, and mouthed the silly phrase again, until he finally gestured me to turn around. Brother Clancy, who failed to see me twisting around in the front, immediately picked up on Andy's reacting in the back.

"Mr. Jones, I warned everyone about talking in class. Come up to the front please."

Oh no, I had really gone too far and now Andy was going to get the strap for it.

"Bend over, Mr. Jones."

Oh no, how humiliating. He bent over and Brother Clancy administered one strap to his grey flannel posterior. Andy walked with great dignity back to his seat, narrowing his eyes only slightly as he passed me by. Oh no, now I've probably lost my new friend as quickly as I got him.

"Don't talk to me," were his first words outside class.

But I could tell by the even narrower burn of his eyes, which made me laugh, that all was not lost, and I kept up a steady stream of apologies and enough groans of commiserating agony to appease him and our friendship was saved.

I was lucky with Andy and some of his friends from the East End, like Billy Chafe, the joker, easygoing Eddie Taylor, and chatty Mike Harrington. Sometimes Billy Cooper was out there with the phantom grade four, which sometimes appeared and sometimes did not. And then there was Johnny Violette, who came from Maryland, late in the year, in a pair of brown corduroys and a red plaid shirt, which he wore daily instead of the regulation uniform to our great disbelief. But there were "extenuating circumstances" and the red plaid didn't seem to bother Brother Clancy who, delighted at the arrival of a compatriot, hung the Rebel flag on the wall over Johnny's desk, and gave us a glimpse into the divisions in that great land. But Johnny was not that sort of hero. Pretty, pale and thin, with dishevelled brown hair, he was more than languid with his Southern drawl. He was, in fact, half asleep. His family had recently arrived from the States, at least he, his mother, his older brother and baby brothers had arrived, and moved into a vacant store on Feild Street. I walked home with him sometimes, and through the big window of the little old store I got a glimpse of the "extenuating circumstances."

Looking into the jumble, I thought he must sleep in his clothes, if he slept at all, and I could understand why he came to school with the pungent aroma of his unchanged little brothers on him, at least I presumed it was the baby brothers. It was painful to see him defend himself against the inevitable comments on this aromatic feature, which was gaily linked to his name. It was enough to keep most boys at bay, but not Andy or me. Johnny was very resilient and playful. In his tired, laughing way, he would "fall asleep" on Andy's shoulder, and Andy would give him a punch in the arm to get him off. This became a regular, amusing routine between Johnny and Andy, with me on the sidelines shoving Johnny back to Andy after Andy had thrown him off, and gradually developed into Andy giving Johnny some pretty hefty shots in the arm, which Johnny willingly absorbed, staggering back too close to Andy again in a strange ritual of self-sacrifice.

I was amazed to see this tough-guy character emerge from Andy to deal with this laconic, sleepy Southern sissy. What did Johnny mean by it? I knew Andy alternately liked and didn't like the game and that no real violence was meant against the Violette. Andy scrupulously avoided hostilities, even when he enjoyed superior strength, and I hadn't seen him in this light before. Andy was naturally serious and studious, after all, and I was naturally not. This arrangement suited us quite comfortably, except when I got us, or just him, into trouble. And so it was a great surprise to hear that the voice suddenly calling out for restraint was my own.

"Andy, what are you doing hitting Johnny?"

"I don't know. I just have to hit him."

"That's not like you."

"Yes, it is. He makes me hit him."

"You could say something to him."

"That doesn't do any good. Don't! Don't come any closer. Johnny! See what I mean? Look: This is the privacy zone. Don't come any closer than that. If you cross the privacy zone, I will have to hit you. I don't want to hit you, but I will have to hit you."

"Why?"

"It's the rules."

"Oh no, I'm so tired. Just let me rest for one minute."

"No! No, Johnny, you see, that's too close."

"That's too close, Johnny," I agreed. "He's gonna have to hit you."

"Oh no," moaned Johnny, and collapsed on Andy's shoulder again, where he got another solid jab to the arm.

"Oh no, that's too hard!" moaned Johnny.

"Yes, I agree. Andy, that's too hard."

"It's not me, it's him."

"What are you saying? What's happening to you?"

"Okay, okay, I'm sorry, Johnny. Johnny?"

"What?"

"I'm sorry."

"No, you're not."

"Yes, I am. I'm sorry I hit you too hard."

"Come on, let's walk around the campus," I suggested.

"That's too far," complained Johnny.

"Well, you stay here, Violette, and rest while we walk around."

"No, I'll come too."

"Oh all right, come along. But don't fall asleep."

"I'll try."

"You see what I mean?"

And in fairness it must be said of Andy that, though he cared little about Johnny's arm, he was careful not to bruise his feelings, and could, in that sense, be said to be cruel only to be kind. Exactly where Johnny's feelings lay I could only guess. He had wisely not attached them to his physical circumstances.

Recess was a complex affair, and now the class was late getting back again for the third time. It must be said in our collective defence that our classroom was the highest in the building. We had to exit through the chapel, genuflecting on one knee to the altar if the Holy Sacrament was present in the tabernacle, then out along the corridor to the staircase and down the four flights on our short legs, double-file into the washroom for a pee at the wall urinals, which were taller than we were, and finally out the front door and down the front steps, fleetingly free for the moment. In this manner fully half the recess time could be consumed, and more especially when you consider our lack of enthusiasm for climbing back up the four flights to Brother Clancy's class. We were late again for the third time and Brother Clancy, true to his promise, as always, lined up the entire class to receive one strap on each hand. One strap was nothing for old strap hands like Sean Power and Andy Squires, but there were those among us who had never felt its sting, like me, and Johnny Sullivan and Danny Williams, both of whom were not only the youngest and smallest in the class, but also among the smartest and were great favourites of Brother Clancy, especially Danny.

I could tell Johnny Sullivan was surprised by the depth of the sting in just one strap. He had a very fine and expressive face and had not been hit yet that year. Neither had I, but I returned to my desk in stinging amazement after just one blow and developed a new respect for the regulars like Sean Power and Andy Squires. I looked up to see Brother Clancy towering over Danny Williams with his arm raised high. It seemed impossible that he would hit him, and he didn't, for as Danny raised his hand into the air in front of him, his eyes rolled back in his head, and with a short groan he crumpled to the floor in a dead faint.

Afterwards it was hotly debated whether he had really fainted or had merely pretended. If he had indeed fainted, it was lucky but weak. If, however, he had feigned the faint, it was a dramatic master stroke and heads above his performance as Bernadette Soubirou in our little play. That was how it impressed me, a bold performance, but my opinion was irrelevant. I was not the intended audience. Brother Clancy was and he was utterly captivated by the show. He dropped the strap in alarm, fell to his knees with a gasp and swept the crumpled form up off the floor. Brother Clancy was deadly earnest as he brushed everything off his desk and laid the limp body on top. He blew on Danny's face, patted his hand, sent for water and he prayed. Finally, but only after he had smacked Danny across the face, his prayers were answered. And what a sigh of relief there was from Brother Clancy at last as Danny revived under his ministrations.

The strap, which had caused so much distress, was not mentioned again that day, perhaps for fear it might bring on a relapse. The remainder in the lineup could only be grateful for this turn of events, and so Danny avoided not only the strap but also much of the taunting and hazing that should rightly follow such a convenient escape.

Jim Murray, like Sean Power and Andy Squires, could not understand what all the fuss was about. Jim had been kept back a grade and ended up with us. When I saw him and his brother, Paul, I was always reminded of that terrible evening outside school when they were curled up on the ground with a crowd of boys beating them up and yelling, "Look at the Mercy girls." Although Jim had gone through grade four already, he was still at a loss about it all, and came in for his share of leather from Brother Clancy. I decided to befriend him, and as he was delighted to have me as his new best friend, he insisted on taking me home with him, so I accepted.

He lived down on Lime Street, in a row of shabby houses on the hill. His family did not own the house but rented a room on the second floor. There was a double bed in one corner. The kitchen table and a small stove were in another corner and there was a low old couch. Jim's brother, Paul, on the double bed in his uniform, was clearly not pleased to see me and did his best to ignore me. His little sister was friendly and his father did not say much. It was dark when his attractive mother arrived home from work and gave me a suspicious look. There was no, "Now who's this little fellow?" or "What's your name, young man?"

"What's he doing here?" she inquired unhappily.

Beaming up at me, Jim announced that I was his best friend and that I was staying for supper. This was as much a shock to me as to his mother.

"I don't know if we got enough for us tonight," she said, turning away.

"That's all right. I'm not hungry. He can have mine."

"No, that's all right, Jim," I said. "I should go home to supper anyway."

"No, no," said Jim, "you're not going, you're staying."

"We'll see," said his mom.

"You're definitely staying, don't worry."

I was worried, but not about staying. Mrs. Murray seemed to have a lot on her mind and was a lot more unhappy than my mom. She wearily set aside her purse, took off her coat and busied herself in the kitchen. Paul stayed on the bed, turned in to the wall. Jim's little sister demanded my attention as I sat at the table with Jim looking at me. Enough fish sticks and potatoes were found to feed all of us around the table where we sat and slowly began to discuss our day. Mrs. Murray hadn't had her job long and wasn't sure how much longer she would have it. Mr. Murray was looking for work and when he got it they were getting out of this place. Her own worries let loose, Mrs. Murray asked us about our day, and eventually even Paul relaxed and talked a little.

I returned home in shock at the Murrays' living arrangements. Did they really live in that one room? Yes, they did and it was not easy. Our simple frame house on Mount Royal suddenly expanded into a roomy mansion in my mind, and what had once seemed ordinary now appeared as luxury. I would have to return Jim's hospitality and bring him home to supper with me, but before I got a chance to properly prepare Mom for this unexpected guest, Jim happily invited himself home with me after school, and I had no choice but to ask him to supper.

"You don't need to invite him to stay for supper, Greg. I'm sure he's got his own home to go to."

"I had to invite him, Mom. He asked me over to his place last week."

"Yes, that's all very well, and I understand that, Greg, but you should have asked me first."

"I was going to but he just came home with me."

"I'm not even sure if I've got enough tonight."

"I'm not hungry. He can have mine."

"All right, Greg, all right. I'll manage something, but don't do this again without at least telling me first."

"Yes, I promise. Thank you."

This delicate discussion was carried on with Jim in another room, but I'm sure he understood exactly what was going on. At his house this discussion was held altogether in one room because there was only the one room and there was something appealing about the openness of such dealings, where even children could hear what was really going on. Even so, I was glad to spare Jim Mom's reluctance, and in the end there was no great difference between the fish sticks and potatoes at the Murrays' and the pork chops and potatoes at the Malones'.

This, as it turns out, was the high point of our relationship. I could not possibly live up to Jim's expectations and there was nothing of mutual interest between us except the desire for such an interest and so we soon gravitated back to our accustomed spheres.

Dominic Savio

The classroom lights had been turned on long before school was over at four o'clock. The frosted globes hung, pale yellow, against the gathering gloom of late January. They shone and winked in the rippled black glass of the windows, which shuddered as the icy winds drove into the seams of the sashes and down onto the small rounded backs of the pupils at their desks. A fat, gilded radiator hissed in its mission to convert the Arctic blasts to warmer waves.

Sitting comfortably on the side of his desk at the front of the class, Brother Clancy concluded his account of the single-minded determination and sacrifice that was the remarkable life of St. Ignatius Loyola. From under the classroom door that opened into the chapel, the last traces of incense and candle wax from the lunchtime Communion service were drawn in to mingle with the cool draughts and warm waves, producing an almost hypnotic effect on the tired pupils.

For the past several weeks Brother Clancy had been reading to us from *Lives of the Saints*—St. John Bosco, St. Dominic

Savio, St. Ignatius Loyola. With the help of visiting brothers and priests, we, as well as the grade fours from St. Patrick's Hall across the street, and the girls from Presentation and Mercy Convents, were being prepared to receive the Sacrament of Confirmation.

On that day, in our best Sports Day school uniforms, white pants, navy blazers and school ties decorated with red and gold satin ribbons, we would be confirmed in the Roman Catholic faith of our ancestors by His Grace, the Reverend P. J. Skinner, CJMDD, Archbishop of St. John's, in an impressive, elaborate ceremony under the nave of the Basilica of St. John the Baptist, on top of the hill in the city that bore his name. There, shepherded by brothers and nuns, we would all kneel in turn before the archbishop, his deacons and priests to renounce Satan and all his works and pomps. He would anoint our foreheads with sacred oil and call us by our new Confirmation names, the name of the saint or martyr we chose as our model and mentor. And that was it. There would be no turning aside then if the Chinese Communist hordes burst into the classroom and threatened to machine-gun every last grade four student unless we renounced Christ and the Virgin Mother. We would if not long for, at least choose the machine gun. We prepared now to confirm that choice, and the patron saint whose name we chose would give us the courage to do so.

St. Ignatius was not a Christian Brother like Brother Clancy. Quite the contrary, he wasn't a brother at all but a priest, and the founder of the Jesuit order. St. Ignatius was the captain of the rival team, like St. Pat's was to St. Bon's. And that team, Brother Clancy implied, in the most tolerant of terms, could on occasion go too far, even operate outside Church law, in their zeal to win souls for Christ. The powerful weapons of knowledge and intellect must be yoked in humility and obedience to Holy Mother Church and the will of the Vicar of Christ on Earth, the Supreme Pontiff and Servant of Servants of God, His

Holiness Pope Pius XII. It was, hinted Brother Clancy, only the direct control of the pope that kept the highly strung and war-like Jesuits under control at all. But St. Ignatius, being himself a saint, was beyond any such reproach.

The captain of our team, Brother Edmund Rice, the founder of the Irish Christian Brothers, was not a saint—yet. But this embarrassment in Rome was only temporary. He was not that long dead, not as long as St. Ignatius, and major efforts were underway to have him canonized. The process of declaring a person a saint was, however, far stricter now than in St. Ignatius's time. Otherwise Brother Rice's residency in Paradise would have been declared a fact long ago. But the canonization process was very complex indeed. There was, for instance, a Devil's Advocate, who did everything possible to prove Brother Edmund was not a saint. Because of the high degree of cunning involved in being the Devil's Advocate, this unwanted but powerful position usually went to a Jesuit. But long before I knew of the conspiracy by the Jesuits to keep Brother Rice out of Heaven, I had decided against their brilliant founder as my patron saint. The cold commitment and rigid life of the ascetic Spaniard was no match for the love of the peasant boy from Italy.

The story of the frail and fearless life of Dominic Savio drew me in and possessed me completely. His suffering in the damp, cramped house in the narrow dirty streets of nineteenth-century Italy, where a crust of bread was a meal, a meal given to others, always given to others, the crushing poverty, his sickness, the feverish joy of his faith, and finally his meek and powerful death, stunned me. We were obliged to read the life story of at least one saint in preparation for choosing our Confirmation name. I had already choked and sobbed my way through the life of Dominic Savio, and now I stayed behind after class to borrow his biography again. If only I could have known him, helped him, fed him! If only I could have been his friend. Now

I must pray to him, keep him close to my heart. He would be my guide.

There were others in the class, I knew, who might take the name of Dominic as well. I didn't care. They did not know him as I knew him or love him as I loved him. He was mine and I was his. I would make myself worthy of him. How he had suffered, his tender young soul purified, burned white by his struggle, the struggle of the helpless and true against the powerful and cruel, the brutal triumph of the greedy over the needy. I considered my warm and well-fed life. How could I suffer? There was suffering around me. I could see that now everywhere: the boys with the same shirt all week with the dirty white collar, the boys with little or no lunch, the boys who were picked on and bullied like the Murray boys. The world of Dominic Savio was a different world.

I decided to give up my lunch, a predictable affair, now carried in a brown paper bag, rather than the childish and highly visible Hopalong Cassidy lunch box that I had been so proud of when it was new in grade two. Lunch was usually a flattened peanut butter sandwich, or worse again, flattened potted meat. There might be a Wagon Wheel or a cookie, a drink of milk or chocolate milk, and an apple was possible, rarely. It was dull and no great sacrifice, but it was lunch, so for several weeks I went without it. I would simply leave it on the desk of the lunchroom. One day I watched as a boy picked up the abandoned sack, looked into it, poked at it, took out the Wagon Wheel, and flung the rest into the garbage. The gesture put my sacrifice in its place. If it had been a better lunch, it would have been a bigger sacrifice. Still, it felt good to go hungry and feel closer to Dominic and his world, and with his story again in my bookbag I headed for home.

By the time I left school it was close to five o'clock and pitch black. The school and the campus were empty. I was hungry now and the night was frigid, but I felt dull and ordinary. I longed to feel more, to come closer to my patron saint, to suffer with Dominic. I took off my warm wool stocking cap and my mittens and immediately the hard cold wind swept over my hands and head. Yes. This was better. Now I was awake. I stuffed my hat and mitts into my bookbag, undid the top button of my duffle coat and let the cold air rush in, crossed Bonaventure Avenue to the empty sidewalk of Merrymeeting Road, and walked up along the black wooden fence of St. Pat's, alone with Dominic.

The pole lights lit up the hard lumps of icy snow on the sidewalk. Overhead the wind howled through the power lines. In the distance I could hear the shouts of several St. Pat's boys who were leaving school late like me. As I drew alongside the gate I could see there were three of them coming out of the shadows. The biggest one shouted something when he saw me but I kept on walking. I could tell from his tone that no answer was expected. I began to walk faster and so did they. Running would have been a provocation and there were still no witnesses when they caught up to me just past Parade Street. Perhaps this was it.

"Hey, look it's a St. Bon's boy. Where you goin' so late, St. Bon's boy?" said the biggest boy.

"Yeah," chimed in the other two. "Where you goin', St. Bon's boy?"

I walked quietly on, looking down. They started to laugh. Then the big one turned nasty again.

"St. Bon's boy is too good to talk to us," he said and he gave me a smack across the side of my bare head, then jumped in front of me, stopping my progress.

The others laughed and poked me on either side. The big one was a little taller and bigger than me and the other two were smaller but made bold by their larger friend. I could not run. The story of St. Dominic weighed heavy in my bookbag. I could not, would not, fight.

"I'm going home," I said.

"Oh, St. Bon's boy is going home, is he," he roared and poked me again. "You're not going home, St. Bon's boy."

He pushed me back. I held my ground.

"This is our territory. Anyone who comes this way got to get permission. Did you get permission?"

By now he was in my face and his two companions had worked their way around behind me, poking and laughing.

"You're not going home, St. Bon's boy," he said and pushed me with both hands.

I fell back over the others, who had stuck out their legs, and hit the icy concrete hard on my tailbone. A stab of pain shot out into my legs and lower back, and I rolled over onto my side, trying to appear calm.

"Look at him. Look, St. Bon's boy is gonna cry."

I could barely feel their kicks. They paused for a moment, uncertain.

"Fuck him. Come on."

"Don't let me see you here again, St. Bon's boy. You won't be so lucky next time."

They faded down Feild Street. I tried to get up. I couldn't. I took off my bookbag and got on my knees and crawled a little, and then slowly got up. Blood rushed into my head. There was a deep, sharp pain right at the bottom of my spine. It hurt to bend over or walk. I couldn't put my bookbag on my back because it would bounce against my throbbing spine, so I slung it over one shoulder and tried to get my legs working. I had to walk. I hunched on with a crippled rhythm until I reached the end of Merrymeeting Road, where I stopped to rest. Before me, the top of Walsh's Field lay covered with a thick glaze of snow, shining under the sharp moonlight. Far above, the deep black sky was flooded with icy cold diamonds stretching far away.

I no longer felt the cold. Hot tears rolled down my cheeks as I looked up at the firmament. The rush of feelings, the pain, the humiliation, the cold were now creating another sensation. I had wanted to suffer. Surely this was it. Yes, I had been blessed, was being blessed. These were tears of joy in a vast and ruthless world. Dominic must have felt something of this. Yes, I was suffering but I was not unhappy. I stood like a statue until I thought I would become one. The cold dug in deeper. I felt light-headed and suddenly very tired. Unsure how many more blessings I could survive, I pushed on, struggling to keep Dominic beside me, and when I finally arrived at 18 Mount Royal Avenue I felt as though I had travelled a great distance.

Everyone else was home before me. Even Dad was home from work, and all were sitting down to supper at the kitchen table. The steamy warmth and the thick aroma of mashed potatoes with sausages and onions overwhelmed me. I walked, frozen, into their midst.

"Where's your hat?" said Dad.

"My God, look at his ears," said Mom. "What's that?"

"They're frostbitten," said Dad. "Where's your hat?" he asked again.

"I forgot to put it on," I lied, coming back to earth with a thud.

"You what? And you got your ears frostbitten!"

"Why didn't you wear your hat?" asked Mom.

"We give you a hat and mitts, look, and you don't put them on. How stupid are you at all?" said Dad. "How stupid is that?" and threatened to give me a smack in the side of the head.

"What are we going to do about the frostbite now?" said Mom.

"There's nothing you can do for that now," said Dad, thoroughly poisoned with me. "He's just gonna have to suffer. Now, go get out of your good clothes and come down here to supper, for the love of God."

In the small mirror over my dresser I could see a section of the outer edge of each ear was now white, frostbitten. The section was very clearly defined, like the core of a thermometer, and as the temperature rose they began to turn from white to the palest puffy pink and began to sting like tongues of flame on the sides of my head. More tears sprung uncontrolled to my eyes. More suffering, more joy? No, not joy. Confusion and exhaustion.

Dad was right. He had gone to the trouble of providing me with a warm hat and mitts and a coat, and I had discarded them to create suffering. Dominic would have worn the hat unless, of course, someone else had needed it. His suffering was authentic. He didn't invent it. But I hadn't invented the boys from St. Pat's, nor could I now complain about them to soften Dad's anger, or think of gaining sympathy on that account, and I certainly could not ever tell him the real reason I had not worn my hat. So, I must hold it all in. There, at least, was some dignity, and so, swollen with secrets and pain, I went downstairs and humbly ate my supper.

Bristol's Hope

We did not go to Topsail Pond to spend Dad's summer holidays at the Murphys' cabin anymore. They had a large family and there were great demands on the little place, and now, with our own car, Mom and Dad wanted adventure and a spot of their own. Dad found just such a place on the other side of Conception Bay, between the old towns of Harbour Grace and Carbonear, in a beautiful little cove called Bristol's Hope. On both sides of the cove the hills were mostly bare, the trees having been felled generations ago by the sturdy fishermen from Dorset and Bristol, who named it with such expectations. Where pine and spruce forests once stood, overgrown gardens and meadows now rolled down to the steep, rocky cliffs. There were few houses left on the south side, fewer on the north, and half of those were abandoned ghost houses.

Coming down into the cove through the woods from the highway above, you first encountered the old Thomey house, an ancient, weather-beaten, Georgian structure, which once served as an inn. It stood opposite the beach road, which ran across to the south side with a small freshwater pond, bound by grassy banks on the right, a favourite spot for swimming and picnics. The beach itself stretched from the north arm of the cove to the south arm, and on misty June evenings the caplin would roll in on it in such numbers, children could easily scoop them up in buckets. Dad would roast the small silver fish on top of the little wood stove and eat them with bread and butter, a great delicacy.

We had come to Bristol's Hope several times for picnics and to explore, and we all loved it, so Dad arranged to rent a small house on the north side of the cove from Mr. Taylor. It was a simple, one-storey place, with white shingles and red trim and a path of beach stones leading to the back door. A small verandah ran along the front, looking out over the meadow and the cove.

When the time came to move there for the holidays, we could hardly contain ourselves. As soon as Dad got off work on Friday evening, Nellybelle was packed up to the gunwales. It was impossible to say who was more excited, us or Dad, who had us whipped up to a state of near-hysteria, as was his habit. When he finally jumped in behind the wheel of the Chevy, he put the heels of his hands together like a hinge, and clapped them at furious speed, faster than a butterfly's wings, to the accompaniment of his own little jingle.

"Ding diddle ling diddle ling diddle ling!"

And with one final clap of his hands, he pointed, like a shot, out the windshield and announced, "This is it! We're going to the Gullies!" and, to a chorus of cheers from within, Nellybelle pulled away from the curb on the great adventure.

We were not actually going to "the Gullies," Dad's Gullies, those shimmering chains of clear pools far back in the woods, on the quiet barrens and fens, away from the common commotion, where fruit was thick on the bush and trout were the size of small children, those secret sacred spots and sunny moments where the sweetest memories are born. We knew it was not exactly that, but

we knew it was "as if", and even "as good as" and we longed
for its graces with our very souls.

The four of us played constantly in the back seat. We called
out and claimed every horse we saw along the way, the one who
claimed the most horses was the winner. The last stretch of
road from the Conception Bay highway just past Harbour
Grace to Bristol's Hope was gravel, but we were delayed by only
one flat tire. Nevertheless, it was almost dark by the time we
reached Bristol's Hope. Uncle Bob and Aunt Mil and the girls
were due to join the party the next day, but they had never been
to Bristol's Hope before and, as there was no sign to tell them
where to turn off, we stopped and Mom printed the name BRIS-
TOL'S HOPE with her lipstick on a piece of cardboard. Dad
attached the sign to a tree and we were all very pleased with the
result, which we supposed was the first road sign the village
had ever borne.

We drove past Thomey's old inn and over the very rough road
along the north arm until it divided, with one little-used path
going on out to the point and the main road turning sharply up
the hill to our place. Halfway up we came to the railway tracks,
which were rather high up on the bed and, as Nellybelle's front
wheels rolled over them and down the other side, the rear wheels
left the ground and the car came to a gentle stop atop the rails,
not two hundred yards from the house, and would not budge.

"When does the train come through?" we asked.

"What time is it now?"

"Ten o'clock."

"It's already been through then and there isn't another one,
not till tomorrow."

"Are you sure?"

"Pretty sure. Okay, everyone out and we'll see if she'll go
over."

But she would not, and we were forced to unpack the car
almost completely before it rose up enough to clear the rails.

Another tired cheer arose, and we repacked the car and drove the final stretch to the dark little house.

Dad and Mom worked all the next day, cleaning and ordering the place. Wayne and I were sent down the road to bring back water from the well. It was a long walk, almost back to the tracks past the two deserted TB houses that had not seen inhabitants for some time. Their clapboard was bare and grey, the most recently stricken still held glass in its windows. Inside we could glimpse broken furniture and even a model of an old steamer. All of this we spied from the road. Nothing could tempt us to cross the threshold of a TB house, not even the mysterious ship. We had been well warned of the deadly dangers of tuberculosis and it was assumed that any deserted house must be so because its occupants had fallen dead and, further, that the house itself was still infected. We stared in awe at the dilapidated shape and colour of disease, debated whether or not the root cellar and sheds were contaminated also, but chose, ultimately, not to cross the fence line. Instead we continued on up the dusty road with our pails of clean water, two buckets each, but only one wooden frame to hold the buckets steady and out from your legs.

There were few chores: fetching water, cleaning up, collecting wood for the fire and picking our own cup of blueberries for dessert in the sprawling meadow out front. We were not often in the house, but lest we falter in our enthusiasm for the great outdoors, Mom initiated the suntan contest.

"I have what they call 'sallow skin.' Imagine! What a word, sallow. But like everything else, it looks better with a bit of sun, don't you think?"

We did indeed, and could find no fault with her appearance. Mom was already well tanned, needing only to look at the sun to go dark.

"Now, I want to see which one of you boys can get the best suntan. So I don't want to see any more shirts on you today, and shorts only."

"How long is the contest?"

"Two weeks."

"What's the prize if you win?"

"Oh, don't worry. It'll be a good one."

Let the games begin. For weeks we roamed around virtually naked. Mom plucked our shirts off as fast as we put them on, unless it was raining, and all long pants disappeared. I burned as best I could, but I was no match for Kerry, who turned brown as a berry within days. He too had "sallow" skin. Wayne was a very close second. Eventually I showed some colour and promise, but Beni pulled up the rear, glowing red, and had to be covered up again.

At the end of the second week, Kerry cavorted around, cockily displaying his wiry native body in front of us, sensing his edge. The kerosene lamps were turned up to eliminate any shadows that might give a false positive. Wayne gave a fine runway performance, which made us laugh, and Beni was generally oblivious. Mom gave us all a careful inspection, comparing all arms and legs.

"My, Greg, you're a lot darker than two weeks ago. And Wayne, you really have a nice, even tan," before she concluded with what we already knew, that Kerry was the winner then, and for every summer after in the annual, and eagerly contested, suntan contest.

Kerry and Beni were too little to wander far from the garden, but up on the ridge behind our house the road narrowed and wound its way up through the remaining woods, inviting me and Wayne to explore. The road finally emerged on the south side of Carbonear, with the town settled prettily across the water on the north side. I was astonished to find it just behind us and so close to our remote little cottage.

When we drove through Carbonear, Dad would point out the landmarks.

"The Malones had a store there and, across the street, there's Kennedy's corner, Mommy Lone's people, but she lived in Crocker's Cove. And we're related to the McCarthys in Crocker's Cove and the Hogans too and God knows who else. You don't want to dig too deep."

On special occasions we went into famous Fong's Restaurant, a cool, pale blue establishment in the heart of busy Water Street, for chips or milkshakes.

"Take your pick. We can't afford both."

But there was rarely spare cash for such extravagances.

The Murphys and others came out for the weekends.

"Ada, we saw your sign on the tree with the lipstick."

"That's the only thing I had to make it with."

"And I knew it was you too because it was your colour."

"Coral."

"But you know, Ada, you need to get a brighter shade because we almost missed it."

"I'll put it on with nail polish the next time."

"No. That's too permanent. Everyone will be down here next."

Tents were pitched in the meadow to sleep the overflow. The largest of billies was produced to boil the biggest of dinners, and there were games of horseshoes and cards long into the night. Wayne and I showed Karen and Robin all the trails and secrets of the ridge. We warned them about the TB houses, which they were not inclined to investigate, but to which temptation Wayne and I eventually succumbed. Ignoring our own cautions, we went in, holding our breath and stood next to the kitchen table . . . on which were still dishes! How quickly had the poor inhabitants been overtaken! We rushed out gasping into the sunlight.

Our stay extended long past Dad's summer holidays. He worked in town all week and came out for long weekends. One

Sunday evening Wayne and I went with him to explore the point, which Dad had called Malone's Point. Uncle Bob laughed openly at that, and was truly astonished when it was confirmed by no less an authority than old Mr. Taylor himself.

"I didn't know the Malones. They were gone before I can remember. But my father remembers Malones out on the point."

The road out to the point had turned grassy from little use and ran down into a low wood, which extended to the cliffs on both sides. Inside was shady but the air was still warm from the day. We walked on for some time through deep woods, which opened up into small fields and clearings, until we came into a large meadow surrounded by tall trees. To the left were the ruins of the old plantation, several smaller structures and two large ones with little left but the shape of gabled roofs and the remnants of shingles on the bare ribs. There was a sense of grace and charm in the secluded old refuge. Still the wind sighed with melancholy in the dark trees, gloomy sentinels of some distant sorrow that could not settle and did not wish to be disturbed. Abandoned and forlorn, it was still too full of ghosts.

We walked quietly on through the field and once more briefly into the woods. The narrow trail suddenly emerged onto a ragged strip of rocky ground stretching out into the ocean. To reach the very tip we had to walk single file along a narrow, winding gravel path that dropped away precipitously on both sides to rocky beaches below. At the end was a small, wild, rocky headland with a grassy patch on top. There we sat, at the tip of Malone's Point, in the middle of the sea, surveying all around us. We were almost out as far as Carbonear Island, where the English held out against the French, while Carbonear burned behind them. Beothuk may have watched from here as the famous pirate Peter Easton brought his hostage, Sheila NaGeira, the Irish Princess, to Bristol's Hope. Did she stay here on the point?

Walking back, we discovered a path that ran through the woods along the south side, very near the edge of the cliff, where the trees were smaller and sparse and the forest floor, a mat of mosses, ferns and roots, projected right out over the cliff.

"Be careful. Don't go too close to the edge," warned Dad, as I slipped right through the ground and almost disappeared.

One of my hands shot out and grabbed the turf. Dad grabbed the other and pulled me back up to safety. Hearts pounding, we gazed back down through the neat hole at the waves rushing onto the rocks of the beach far below. Dad was very quick and strong, and I was saved again.

"This is a dangerous place. We'd better get out of here," he said.

We emerged from the woods and climbed the hill back to our little place in the last rays of the evening sun.

During the week, the days were endless. Very early on Monday morning Dad left for Town while everyone else was still in bed. I sat out in the sunshine, which was already intense at 6:30. Sometimes Mom and I would sit there together, reading our books, or simply sitting. Today she was behind me in the house, content with her chores.

Far below, the sound of a trap skiff on the platinum water broke the quiet and trailed on out into the silent sea. No wind interrupted the eons-old work of the bumblebees among the buttercups and Indian paintbrushes in the meadow. The shiny leaves and grasses seemed to shimmer and disappear in the sun's glare.

The little white houses on the far side of the cove sat like toy models in the grass, and over the crest of the pale ridge behind lay headland after headland of bays and coves on up the coast, receding into hues of green and azure, and over them all, the misty blue hills sat in cool solitude. Beyond them was where the gullies lay, far in the deep distance, as far back as the past. But I could not imagine any greater joys than the ones that filled me as I sat on the sunny little verandah in the grassy meadow.

Dad Is Promoted

D ad was promoted to sales rep with Imperial Oil after winning an award for signing up the most contracts for Esso in all of Canada. He now went to the office every day in the modern Imperial Oil Building on Elizabeth Avenue in the new part of Town. We were so excited, Kerry and I hid on the floor in the back of our new car after lunch to drive back to the office with him. When we got to the corner of Anderson and Elizabeth, Dad pretended to discover us with great surprise, and took us along for a tour of the modern new building. Our new car was an impressive, black, four-door '57 Dodge Regent, with immense fins on the back, and we were all ecstatic. Even Monsignor Fyme asked Dad to drive him to a special dinner in his honour because he thought it looked like a limousine.

The family was pretty well established by now and everyone had settled into their roles. We were the four boys. Beni was past the three-year mark, the usual time for the appearance of the next boy child, and it was concluded there would be no more. There were three years between each of us. Wayne was oldest, tallest and left-handed. I was second oldest, second tallest and right-handed. Kerry was third oldest, third tallest, and left-handed, and Beni was the fourth, the youngest, the shortest and right-handed like me. Mom arranged and photographed us in order, like steps, in various locations around the house and in the yard, while she and Dad, still glamorous, beamed alongside us. Auntie Vera said we were the perfect family and always said how lucky Ada was to have a husband who thought so much of her. Dad was very proud of Mom. He admired her beauty, athleticism and ambition. He knew how smart they looked together and strove to live up to the image. He kept the little front garden full of dahlias and gladiolas for her and let her sleep in on school mornings while he got us off to school. Dad called her "Lovey" for everyday endearment, but when he was poking fun at the arrangement between them, he called her "Queenie," often enough for it to be a standing joke with everyone. Mom accepted "Lovey" without undue irony, but she would brush off "Queenie" with a sidelong glance. "Excuse me, the Queen has to go out now and wash the supper dishes and pack the lunches for tomorrow."

We ventured further on our weekend trips. Bellevue Beach had salt and fresh water for swimming and was a popular destination for dusty Townies in need of diversion. There were always people out there, but we got a good spot, and Dad, always impatient, did a quick change into his swim trunks behind the imperfect screen of the opened back door of the car.

"For Heaven's sakes, Bill, that woman over there can see you!" said Mom.

Dad looked over at the woman craning her neck.

"Well, if she's ignorant enough to look, then I'm ignorant enough to show her," he retorted.

"Bill!"

This was in the days before designers thought to put little pockets in bathing trunks for valuables, and so what to do with the car keys while we were all in the water was a continuing problem.

"I'll put them under a rock," said Dad finally.

"How will we know which rock it's under when you come back?" asked Wayne.

"I'll spit on it," said Dad, running off to the beach.

"Where did you leave the keys?" asked Mom, after a long day of swim and play.

"Under a rock," answered Dad.

"Under a rock!" exclaimed Mom, gazing across the beach. "Which one? There's millions. Did you mark it?"

"Well, I spit on it," he confessed sheepishly.

"You spit on it! Cripes Kate, Bill, that dried off hours ago. What were you thinking?"

"Not much, I guess," said Dad, and we all laughed. "All right, come on, let's find them."

We were the last to leave that day and had to rearrange the beach before our little holiday was over.

Dad was on his wooden seat in the car a lot now, cruising the city, especially the new subdivisions, for new homeowners to sign up with Imperial Oil, and we often went along, waiting in the back seat for Dad to return with the contract signed. More often than not he was victorious, and kept going until he had filled the daily quota he had set for himself. Dad was very handsome, with a broad chest and an athletic build. His coal-black, wavy hair curled over thick black brows and smoky green eyes, and he was always smiling or beaming. He loved women, young and old, and courted them constantly. He loved to chat them up, and with the greatest of interest in their concerns and the lightest of touches, he got them laughing, and kept them laughing with shameless doses of flattery for good measure. Mom generally smiled at all this. And, in fact, Dad had much the same relationship with men.

On our Sunday drives he would mark down the houses to

come back for.

"There's a nice house," said Mom, looking at a new split-level in the northeast subdivision during one of our Sunday drives.

"Yes, I know him. He's already signed up," said Dad.

"I'd like to have a house like that."

"It's a beautiful house but they pay for it."

"How's that?"

"They don't eat," Dad told us. "Every cent they make goes to pay for that house."

"Don't eat!" we cried in alarm.

"What do you mean 'don't eat,' Bill? Who are they?"

"What's his name, Parsons, married Ethel Morgan, you know her."

"Oh yes, I can believe it then," said Mom.

"They have the same small bowl of porridge every single day."

"Now how do you know that?"

"She told me. They don't believe in food. The big new house takes his whole cheque."

"Right," agreed Mom.

"They never have a real dinner."

"Or people in," lamented Mom.

"They can't afford it," concluded Dad.

"I wouldn't want to live like that. Would you, boys?" asked Mom.

"No! No!"

We went as far as the old RAF airport and turned back, passing two houses on Torbay Road that stood side by side, identical in every aspect, down to the trim. Both Dad and Mom told a good story, and Dad was easily spurred on to heroic dimensions by the enthusiasm of his audience.

"Look, those two houses are exactly the same," said Wayne.

"They're a twin," said Mom.

Dad weighed in with the goods.

"Those two houses there were built by two brothers."

"Two brothers?" Mom was already skeptical.

"Yes, two brothers. Twins."

"Twins?"

"Really?" we said.

"Yes, and they married two sisters."

"Bill! Okay, you don't have to believe that, fellas."

"Dad, that's not really true!"

"Yes, every word."

"Bill!"

Later that night with Uncle Bob, Aunt Mil and Uncle Bob's sister, Aunt Sheila, at the card table in the living room over canasta or gin rummy, with drinks and cigarettes going, the conversation continued.

"No, Bill, no one's going to believe that, so you can forget it," challenged Mom.

"Bob knows I'm right."

"Don't drag me into this, Scully," said Uncle Bob.

"You know those identical houses on Torbay Road? Two brothers built them, right, Bob?"

"Two brothers?"

"Yes, two brothers. And they married two sisters."

"Oh God, here we go," said Mom.

"Scully, you're thinking about your own crowd now," said Uncle Bob, "your Aunt Mary . . ."

"No, no," said Dad. "Two brothers married two sisters. It happens a lot in Newfoundland."

"If you say so, Professor," conceded Bob, and everyone laughed.

"You're making this up, Bill," said Mil.

"No, no, it's all true. Two brothers married two sisters, and I don't know but the sisters were twins too" (more laughs) "and they built two identical houses. You can go out and look at them now, everything the same, matching fence and car."

"And I suppose they had twin cats too," said Mom.

"No, dogs," said Dad. "They had twin dogs."

"Oh for God's sake, Bill!"

More laughs and the clink of drinks.

"Even the kids won't believe that, Bill," laughed Mom. "Speaking of the boys, I better go up and check on them. I know they're not in bed."

We were listening in the upstairs hall, of course, to the story of our day and darted back to bed on cue. We listened to the laughs and whoops from the card games and finally fell asleep to the strains of a heartfelt, if uneven, rendition of "Oh Danny Boy." During the week they had sandwiches and cookies, but on the weekends they had a big dinner on the stove, and went on laughing long after we were fast asleep.

The crowd got together every Friday night for a snort of rum for the boys and light drinks for the girls. Whatever topics were up for discussion, Dad could be counted on to furnish outlandish, ready-made answers and solutions to the most complex of the world's problems, and Bob could just as surely be counted on to shoot him down on cue, to the delight of all. It was a great game to guess when Scully was lying and when he was actually telling the truth. They liked nothing more than to get together, have a drink and poke fun at each other over a game of cards and a boiled dinner, often getting quite giddy. But they were never drunk or out of the way. The other ongoing game was to catch Scully scoffing off with tastes of the dinner, usually the best bits, before it was ready.

"I caught Scully at it again, Bob!"

"Okay, Scully, that's it, no dinner for you."

"No, no, that was just a little piece," Dad protested.

"It's called the filet, Scully."

Sometimes Auntie Vera would be one of their company, especially now that she and Uncle Ron and their children, Buddy and Joan, had moved in to 7 Mount Royal Avenue, a drab house just below the Churchills'. Auntie Vera came up to our house often, but we rarely went there and never for long. Uncle Ron was a policeman, heavy-set, surly and never smiling. He liked to drink, after which he smiled less. We knew their lives were unhappy and that they rarely "had people in." Mom and Dad did their best to include Ron but there was no fun to Ron. He rarely laughed at a joke or rose to the occasion. Ron was a heavy and he had reason to be.

A constable with the Force, as they called the Newfoundland Constabulary, Ron McGrath came from St. Mary's Bay. His father was dead and he had two sisters, Jean and Blanche, who was considered simple or retarded by their mother, who dressed Blanche poorly and kept her indoors by the stove in the kitchen where she could not be seen. Jean looked out for Blanche as best she could, and when their mother died, she scraped everything in the house that related to their mother into the garbage. She bought new furniture and a television set. Then she bought Blanche new clothes and shoes and took her for a full medical examination, which revealed that she was smart enough, only deaf. Blanche's life was happier after that. But Jean sacrificed her life to stay with her sister, and lived with the conflicting sweet satisfaction and bitter regret. They moved into Town next to the West End fire station on Lemarchant Road, where the firemen became their great friends. When Blanche died, they all attended her funeral, carrying her coffin in their full dress uniforms.

Jean thought Vera too grand.

"She only thought of herself, spending money on expensive clothes for herself, while Ron had nothing. There was this beautiful, black velvet dress with jewelled clasps on the shoulders that Vera wanted, and it looked fabulous on her, but it cost a lot of money. Well, they were going to a big dance for the Force and Vera had to have it. So she spent all their money on it and Ron didn't even have a pair of pants to wear out the door, only his uniform. But she didn't mind that. It only made her look better,

I suppose. Anyway, I couldn't let Ron go with an old pair of patched pants. So I put some money down on a suit of clothes. I worked for a major down on the Base at Fort Pepperrell, and I could get it for a good price, but I still had to pay it off. Ron went to the dance and he looked really good, and Vera couldn't figure out where he got the suit."

Vera, meanwhile, thought Jean was a saint and would not hear a word against her. But she was not about to watch Ron drinking and pissing away their bit of money without at least getting a good dress out of it for herself.

Auntie Vera and Uncle Ron's children, Joan and Ron Jr., or Buddy, were older than us and in high school. Buddy was the oldest and very handsome, with brooding dark eyes and dark, thick, wavy hair, which he wore in a ducktail, like Elvis. When he saw Wayne playing in the street, he would throw a quarter on the ground for him with a grunt, and that was as close as we ever got to our cousin. We knew that he and his dad argued constantly and had terrible fights and we were on Buddy's side.

When they moved up to Mount Royal Avenue Auntie Vera decided they needed more money than they got from Ron's police cheque, and so she determined to get a job. Uncle Ron was dead against this. No wife of his was going out working and showing him up.

"One night we were fighting about it again, and I was drying the dishes," said Auntie Vera, "and I was so frustrated, I just took a plate and dropped it on the floor and smashed it. Well, he noticed that because I saw him kind of jump back a bit, so I thought, all right, and I threw another one and another one, and it worked. He let me go and do it, as long as Joan got him his supper on time and I made sure the household routine didn't change. Then I got a job at Bowring's."

Joan used to babysit for us. When we saw her, we would send up a chant.

"Joan, Joan the ice cream cone!"

She bore it with practised patience and put Fats Domino and Elvis Presley on the hi-fi and taught us to jive and jitterbug. Joan was fun, so we took full advantage and drove her nearly crazy. Vera and Joan liked it more at our house than their own. Vera would come after work from Bowring's and sit down with Mom in the living room for a cup of coffee and a cigarette. Dad would put a cup towel over his arm and wait on them.

"And what can I get you beautiful ladies today?"

"Oh, just a coffee please," Vera would laugh. "Gee, the service here is good, Ada. I'll have to come back more often."

She'd bring little presents and lots of gossip about Bowring's Department Store. I could never get enough of her stories, and long after the others had left, I would still be there, begging for more.

"Greg, you really like my stories. But I'm going to have to take a break soon before I go hoarse. So anyway, you could see the ring around the collar of the shirt and there she was trying to return it and get the money back, as cool as a cucumber," reported Vera, wide-eyed in disbelief. "She said it was too small," Vera laughed.

"People will take anything that can be moved, you know. But I don't confront anyone. If I see something suspicious, I tell one of the floor walkers and they take care of it. You'd be surprised at the kind of people we catch. But I'll be off the floor soon, I hope, and away from all the action. I won't have any more stories," she declared.

Ron stopped coming up to our house. He got too drunk, and he thought Dad and his friends were foolish, laughing at nothing, and so Vera came by herself, which was better.

✳

Mom and Auntie Vera were very excited about Len's upcoming wedding, and Dad was nervous because he was to be the master of ceremonies. He practiced his speech all afternoon in the same American accent he used on the phone with customers.

Uncle Len's second marriage was a very special event. He was marrying Jeanette Warren, the sister of his first wife, Yvonne, who had died in the car crash. We liked Len and Jeanette a lot. Len, with his easygoing, smiling, pleasant ways, was a favourite with everyone, and Jeanette was very smart in her airline stewardess uniform and was very polite and kind to us boys. They were fond of Mom and Dad, and when they came to tell them of their engagement they sat on the big green sofa chatting with me and Wayne. Jeanette gave Wayne a St. Christopher's medal on a ribbon and also a pretty cross, which she did not want anymore. Wayne was pleased enough to get it, but not nearly as pleased as I was devastated to receive no such proof of preferment or affection from the lovely couple. I excused myself and unaccountably burst into tears in the back bedroom. But the truth and I were soon discovered and I received a great deal of awkward but not entirely unwanted consolation for my dismay at the unintended slight.

At last, on a very pleasant June evening, Mom and Dad set off for George Street United Church. Dad had received a special dispensation from Monsignor Murphy to take part in the non-Catholic ceremony, but he swore he would have gone anyway, and what were they afraid of at all? We said goodbye to them on the front steps, and Wayne took a picture of them with Mom's camera, looking their radiant best as they set off.

When they returned they were not smiling. Mom threw down her purse in disgust and shook her head at Dad.

"My God, Bill, how could you!"

"I didn't do it on purpose, Lovey."

"For God's sake, Bill, of all things," Mom was beside herself. "To propose a toast to Jeanette, and call her Yvonne, the name of her dead sister, Len's last wife!"

"I didn't even realize I'd said it."

"I know because then you called her Yvonne again!"

"But I didn't realize—"

"Well, everyone groaned. I was out of my mind. I don't think I have ever been so mortified, and then, you actually said it again. Three times!"

"I don't think I said it three times."

"Bill, yes, I counted. Well, the wedding was over then."

"What can I say, Lovey? It was on everyone's minds and I guess—"

"Well, it's on their minds now for sure. I don't think I have the face to see Len and Jeanette again."

"Jeanette understood, Lovey, she said—"

"What's she going to say, Bill! No, the wedding was ruined, Bill, my God."

Poor Dad was uncharacteristically speechless. When Uncle Bob heard about it over a glass of Old Sam, he shook his head.

"Oh my, Scully," he said. "You should have called them all Andy."

"Yes, but it wasn't funny, Bob," Mom reminded them.

Even then it might have faded from memory if Dad had not repeated the mistake again and again . . . and again.

★

Our last tenants were too much for Mom and Dad. Glen was a skinny GI, and his unfriendly wife, Tracy, could only cook hamburgers and hot dogs, which they had every day with bottles of Coke. They had a small, skinny boy who cried a lot. When he cried, they smacked him, and when they smacked him, he cried. It was hard for us to listen to. Mom talked to her, but the beatings continued, so the decision was made, and Mr. Layman was brought back to cut an archway in the wall that he had put up along the stairs five years earlier, and we at last took over the whole house. Renovations always improved my parents' spirits.

They installed a new fireplace and before it was fully bricked in I deposited a holy picture of the Shroud of Turin inside with vital information for future archaeologists.

Here lives David Gregory Dominic Malone, born October 19, 1948, 18 Mount Royal Avenue, St. John's, Newfoundland, Canada, North America, Earth, The Universe.

Dad had a little office now in one of the old bedrooms on the main floor. Mom helped him improve his reading and math and went over all the Imperial Oil contracts with him. It was she who handled the household accounts and paid the bills. Dad handed over his cheque and weighed in on general policy.

Wayne and I now shared a large bedroom upstairs, which was a great disappointment to me, and to Wayne. We each thought we would get our own room when we took over the whole house. His alliance with Don Piercey and his beagle had cooled our brotherly friendship to a low point. And Wayne was poisoned with me for not playing softball with them when they were trying to make up a team. But I did play sometimes. Once, at a critical moment in a big game up in Walsh's Field, I even caught the batter out and got a big cheer.

"Yeah, that's good," Wayne said, "but if you weren't so busy celebrating, you could have thrown it to third base and we'd have two out."

He was never satisfied, nor was I, so I mostly played with Brace and Lioney, and the girls. If I played house with Barbara Lynn or Sharon or Gwenny, he mocked me, but I managed to ignore it for the most part. Further to my ignoring it, I now wanted to put a partition down the middle of our new bedroom. We lay in bed, both excused from Sunday Mass, Wayne because he had a cold, and me because I was getting it. I could tell he felt hurt that I was so unhappy to be stuck with him. But he managed to cover it up very well, making fun of my ears, which stuck out, especially the left one. The mood was getting ragged.

"Hey, Dumbo," he teased.

"Shut up," I said miserably.

He laughed.

"Ha ha, don't get upset, Dumbo. You could always fly away with those ears."

I had to match him.

"Well," I said, "at least I don't have a head like a building."

"I don't have a head like a building!" he cried suddenly.

Now, Wayne was very handsome, dark and tall, with thick eyebrows like Dad, a pleasant smile, and perfect small ears. He had, after all, won the Beautiful Baby Contest. But his head was rather square, and, viewed at a certain angle, it did sort of resemble a building. This had not been noticed before, and certainly it had never been stated, but he got it right away. I might vainly make fun of his thick eyebrows or his height, but his whole head? His handsome head? He was devastated and started to cry. This shocked me. I'd never been in this position before. Clearly I had gone too far.

"I do not have a head like a building, Dumbo, shut up."

"Building Head, Building Head," I persisted. "There's the door and there's the windows."

He was inconsolable and Mom was as shocked at the bitterness of our fight as we were.

"He said I had a head like a building."

"What! No, Wayne, you don't. Greg, what a thing to say. A building?"

"He does."

"Now, Greg, what did you say that to your brother for?"

"He called me Dumbo."

"Wayne, that's not nice. Now you boys see what happens when you try to hurt each other, you both end up crying. I want you fellas to be friends now."

We came to a truce and divided the room with invisible barriers.

He was entirely correct about the Dumbo ears, of course.

I openly lamented this fact to Mom, who sympathized entirely with my distress and strove to console me.

"I had a big mole the size of a quarter on my neck when I was younger, and I was so embarrassed and ashamed of it. You can see me in the pictures, I have the collar of the dress pulled up and pinned over the mole because I didn't want anyone to see it. When I got older, a doctor cut it off for me, but he did a bad job and left a scar. You can still see it."

I looked. It was true.

"Can these ears be fixed?"

"Well, maybe we could tape them back when you go to bed so you don't buckle them back over and sleep on them during the night."

"Yes," I agreed.

And so we taped my ears back at night—Band-Aids worked the best—and watched every day for progress, which was slow, even imperceptible, to the fast-moving eyes of a ten-year-old, and the practice eventually died out. My ears, however, unlike Prince Charles's, whose mother may have been too busy to tape his ears back, are not stuck out today, not even the left one.

Our bedroom used to be the tenants' kitchen, and there was a sink in the little closet. The door had been removed, but I soon curtained it off, claimed it as my laboratory, and filled it with vials of coloured liquid for my experiments. Kerry and Beni were fascinated by this, and I would let them in if they agreed to play school, so I could dress up as a woman and play the teacher. St. Bon's had a few lay teachers for the early grades by then—Mrs. Hann, Mrs. Sexton, Mrs. Murray—and I liked them. My kindergarten teacher, Miss Snow, had not inspired me to emulation, and I could not imagine dressing up as Brother Brennan or Brother French, and certainly not Brother Clancy. Being a woman was more fun.

I did a lot with scarves and shawls, and scavenged as much from Mom's room as I dared. I would have had her good shoes and stockings and more, but she protected them and gave me some jewellery with reluctance. Kerry had some notion of school by now, but Beni was hopeless, and it took all of my ingenuity to educate him. It had been a hectic afternoon, and I had given up and let them both go by the time Dad got home from work. I heard him and Mom talking in their bedroom.

"Greg got all my stuff dragged out everywhere today, playing school."

"Playing school on a nice day like this? You'd think he'd have had enough of that."

"Yes, and a woman teacher, no less. You should have seen him."

"A woman?"

"Yes, and he was good at it too. He had the boys going all afternoon. I suppose it's all right, I don't know."

"I don't know, Ada. I don't think we should be encouraging that."

"I'm not encouraging it, Bill. He doesn't need any encouragement from me. I just don't know what to do about it."

"Well, I don't think he should be at your stuff. It's not right."

"I told him he can't have my good things."

"I don't think he should be dressing up like a woman at all. It's the wrong influence on the others."

"Well, they're only little."

"He's growing up now. It's time to be doing other things. He shouldn't be indoors at all. He should be outdoors, kicking a ball around like the other kids."

"Well, I'll have a talk with him."

When the time came, I argued my case against Mom, who was left to enforce this new policy, which seemed completely unnecessary to me.

"Why can't I dress up anymore?"

"Because you're a boy, and you're getting bigger, and it's time to play boys' games."

"I play boys' games too."

"And I don't want you taking my things, Greg. They're my good things and I don't want you at them. Now that's final, Greg. There's lots of other things you can do."

With great reluctance I abandoned my promising teaching career and consoled myself with games of kings and queens. On the back lawn I'd set up pavilions made of appliance box "tents" arranged in a circle with a pole in the middle to hold up the big sheets of brown water silk, made from old drapes found in the back of the closet. It made a wonderful cover for our tents with the sun bleeding through the silk. I filled them with pillows and blankets. I was mollified enough by cloaks and crowns, and Mom even donated a medallion that was as fit for a king as a queen. The entire royal compound made a very comfortable retreat from bouts of sword fighting and jousting.

And I went back into the cart business. I had already pushed Dad to the limit by using up every metal bar and long nail that might do for an axle, and every spare wheel from old prams and wagons from the basement for carts, but when it came to it he didn't explode. Instead he brought me some good, thick rubber wheels from Esso, and a decent axle (always hard to find), then he actually lent me his hacksaw, and I set to work. The body of my cart was a long, narrow piece of plywood, with the front corners cut off and repositioned upright to create a flared, more aerodynamic appearance. I attached the long axle to a two-by-four in the front, and bolted it onto the body with a single bolt, which allowed you to steer the cart by pulling the ropes attached to either end. In the back of the long cart, I attached a sawed-off high chair, which tilted back, and over that I hung a white canvas canopy. I nailed a hand brake next to one of the back wheels, which were positioned close to the seat. The entire appearance was very impressive, like a coach or an old-fashioned roadster, and definitely the limousine I wanted.

It was not difficult to convince Kerry and Beni to play this game with me. I hauled them around the neighbourhood for weeks, and took them for fast rides down the street, always pulling into Churchills' driveway at the last second to avoid going over the steep hill and out onto St. Clare Avenue. The turn into Churchills' was tricky, and more than once I cornered too fast and buckled the back axle, or turned over altogether, causing a great roar of laughter from Wayne's crowd, who seemed always near at hand to laugh and jeer. The rear end required as many long nails as I could scavenge and straighten, and eventually the frame holding the canopy broke, the axles wore out completely, and the glory days of the long, long cart were over, but not forgotten, even though its place was filled with a more practical mode of transportation.

The summer of grade four, I finally got the bicycle I had been pleading for. The only occasion it marked was the end of a drawn-out period of intercessions. I had been driving Wayne crazy riding his big Raleigh with one leg through the crossbar, up and down the driveway, whenever he wasn't on it. When I fell down and dropped the bike, he exploded and complained to Mom and Dad. I followed up with a lot of begging for my own. Finally one afternoon Dad brought home a bike for me. It wasn't a Raleigh like Wayne's, or a Hercules like Andy's. It was a Royal Enfield, which we had never heard of before, but it looked great, and I was thrilled, although less so that the brakes were always breaking and could never be adjusted to satisfaction. But it was fast, and it took me all the way to Rostellan Street, a new neighbourhood in the fashionable East End, to visit Andy.

I was welcomed at the Joneses' in their new, one-and-a-half storey home just off Elizabeth Avenue, overlooking Rennie's

River. There were girls there, Andy's two younger sisters, Marywin and Cathy, who were very friendly and polite, and Mrs. Jones was warm and welcoming and very funny. His big brother, Mike, was older than Wayne, but I didn't see much of him. Their father was dry and sardonic, and reminded me a little of Pop, with his riddles and word games and tweed jackets on at home. Mr. Jones had the franchise for General Films and a store on Water Street, and he brought a projector and movies home to watch. In the den there was a big Philips tape deck, which we recorded ourselves on, imitating teachers and making up our own radio plays. There was no mention of hockey or basketball, and I never heard the score on the radio at their house. In fact, I never heard the radio. Andy and I would play records, and he had tapes of English comedies like Stanley Holloway's reading of "Albert and the Lion".

Except for Scouts, these were my first long forays away from home, and Andy and I went on many long bike rides. I did not entirely neglect Brace and Lioney for my school friends. Both Brace and Lioney had bikes too now and we roved the paths of Walsh's Field at the top of Mount Royal Avenue, and the Knights of Columbus field at the bottom, playing cowboys, and we could now ride to Bowring Park instead of getting the Cowan Avenue bus or walking. But Lioney now often went off on hunting trips with his father and Spencer in the Ford hard-top. The Braces had a car now too, a blue '54 Pontiac, in which they all went for excursions, and when Don Piercey went off with his brother to their cabin on Salmonier Line, fishing and fighting mosquitoes, Wayne and I were sometimes left to amuse ourselves on our bikes.

One day we rode to the end of Pennywell Road and around the long Ropewalk Factory by Mundy Pond. It was a wonderful ride over grassy roads and then down Pearce Avenue. We knew this was a tough area, we just didn't know exactly how tough. The smaller kids on Pearce just threw rocks at us and tried to

poke sticks through the spokes of our wheels, but they were very
determined and managed to slow us down. Then the older guys
spotted us and dug their eyes into us like hawks.

"Where the fuck do you think you're going, boys?"

"Look at the boys on their new fuckin' bikes," they snarled,
coming at us, shirts open.

"You don't come on our fuckin' street."

"Let's get out of here now, Greg, go," said Wayne in deadly
earnest.

"Give us those bikes, *Greg*," the leader mocked. "They're
ours now."

I had just got my bike and I didn't need any more motivation
to pick up speed.

"Get 'em, boys! Get 'em!" they shouted, grabbing their
wrecks of bikes and tearing after us. We looked back. There was
no doubt they were in full chase. We sped down over Blackmarsh Road, with them gaining, and made a wild, fast turn
onto Bennett Avenue, barely holding onto the turn, and belted it
towards the intersection at Lemarchant Road at full speed and
pushing it. We checked behind, they had taken the corner at
Bennett too. One guy lost it and slid into the gutter but two
made the turn and were still coming on. We had no choice: we
completely ignored the Stop sign at Lemarchant Road and kept
going. We might be killed, but we would not be caught now at
any cost, and so, choking on our own hearts, we streaked across
the busy intersection, as the traffic closed in behind us. It was a
miracle we were not hit. The Pearce boys finally stopped at this
omen and flung a few weighty curses after us. We were free. We
were almost downtown, but we were free. We hadn't gotten
pounded and we still had our beloved bikes, so, after the shock
subsided, we gave each other hearty congratulations, and
declared Pearce Avenue off-limits to ourselves from then on.

In September, when I got back to school, our grade five classroom was in the new building. The elegant old tennis courts,
where we had once looked up in such awe at the senior boys,
swinging in their whites, had been swept away for classrooms
for the baby boomers.

Having been thoroughly terrorized in grade four, we were
prepared for the worst, but hoped for better from grade five. All
the survivors were excited to see each other in the new building.
Andy said big hellos to Michael Harrington and Richard Simms
and Eddie Taylor, but only a very casual one to me.

"Gee, you don't seem very excited to see me," I complained.

"I saw you only two weeks ago."

"Well, you could be a bit more excited."

"I am excited. But I haven't seen the other guys all summer."

"I thought we were best friends."

"We are best friends."

"Are you sure?"

"Yes, I'm sure."

"Okay then, get excited."

"I am excited. See? I'm extremely excited. If I were any more
excited, I'd get the strap."

"Okay, okay, that's better. It's great to see you too. Come on,
who's our new teacher?"

"That's him. Brother Pigott."

"Oh. He looks strict."

But he was not.

The new class was bright and sunny, and Brother Pigott, an
easygoing New Yorker with a wry sense of humour, was firm
but fair, and a great relief from the previous four years. He even
had us write poetry, which I loved, and he singled out my very
sentimental poem about Mom as an example. He asked if I had
any more, which I did, and I happily furnished him with a whole
scribbler full of sentimental ramblings.

"Come with me," he said to me one day. "Someone wants to

meet you," and we went down the hall and knocked on the door of his friend, tall, handsome Brother Mitchell.

"So this is the great poet," enthused Brother Mitchell, when he opened the door.

He took me up in his hands and spun me playfully over his head. As he brought me down, my front tooth hit his head, and he winced but kept smiling.

I was in shock. To be free of the random terrors of the early grades was one thing, but this boisterous affection from big, handsome Brother Mitchell! I was utterly speechless but wrote many more poems so I was not completely surprised when Brother Pigott selected me and Andy to enter the school oratorical contest. I was given a very corny poem about sheep, which I rendered with every cliché in my arsenal, and won. Andy came second. This came as quite a shock. I had no idea there were such things as oratorical contests, much less that I could win one. It wasn't the Boyle trophy, the coveted cup of senior intramural hockey, but I was pleased, and so were Mom and Dad, which was helpful.

The Truck

We combed through the pages of the Christmas catalogue, feverishly pouring over pages of glossy, red-, green- and gold-striped Christmas candies and explosions of fruitcakes. I knew Wayne was looking at bras, of course, but then so was I, but all of that was the most fleeting of side shows to the main attraction. The once-crisp pages of the toy section were worn to soft tissue. Pages of cars and trucks, complete garage sets, the complete Fort Apache set, the best double gun and holster sets with pearl handles, the Lone Ranger set with silver bullets, derringers, rifles, shotguns, everything a boy could want, and more.

We knew that our only chance was to narrow our choices down to one or two main items that the parents could easily grasp, and so for Christmas I wanted a truck, but not just any truck. There were several in the catalogue of the type I wanted: what is now called an eighteen-wheeler, or a tractor-trailer as we called them in 1958.

In the long evenings before Christmas, as I repeatedly pointed out my choice to Mom, I added extra enthusiasm to my voice as I expressed how much I preferred tractor-trailer trucks over tow trucks or dump trucks and so on. Mom acknowledged mechanically my preference. But I knew it had not yet registered, that she did not know that I wanted that truck or no truck at all. So I said so.

"What, Greg? Yes, that's a good truck all right."

I offered a choice of three possible models. I carried on, praising the thin, silvery metal of the cargo box and the friction engine. I repeated myself until I risked insulting her formidable intelligence. But this was a blind spot whose logical and practical cause I could not comprehend. Mom nodded and smiled and pretended to look at the catalogue, but her eyes did not seem to see it and she turned back to her business. I turned back to Wayne for consolation and confirmation in my delicate and desperate quest.

Christmas came after hard work from Mom and Dad. The big tree, hung with fat, silver balls and exquisitely draped in hundreds of strands of silver tinsel, stood motionless in the living room corner. Darkly festive in the blank winter light of early morning, it stared back at us. Wayne and I glimpsed it breathlessly, but postponed the warm pleasure of adoring this pagan god. Making an invisible, heretical genuflection, we sped to the bulging, navy blue wool Scout stockings that, by special dispensation from Santa Claus, hung on the kitchen wall, instead of the perfectly functional fireplace mantle in the living room. But Santa, like Mom, understood that you could not fill the good mantle with tack holes, Christmas after Christmas. This aroused considerable anxiety in Kerry and Beni. Would not Santa, after coming down the chimney and seeing no stockings, merely go back up and leave? Why would he go into the kitchen? But my mother was convinced of Santa's intuition, and this Christmas morning proved her right as on all others.

The stockings bulged with fruit in the toe, a mysterious shape in the heel and the rustle of small, tissue-paper packages of chocolates and grapes in the middle. Strange feels in the early morning. The linoleum was ice-cold on our bare feet. We freed the wild treasures from the kitchen wall and, checking each other's booty, went back to show Mom and Dad. They roused themselves sleepily with tired smiles to be "surprised" at the familiar goodies and prizes that poured out of the stockings.

The smell of the turkey filled the house. Dad plugged in the coloured lights. The tree glowed and the presents lay proudly beneath it. But they must wait a little longer, till after Christmas Mass, to reveal their secrets. The damp cold, the empty stomachs and the dull routine of Mass sharpened the expectation of the rare treats awaiting us.

After Mass, everyone gathered in front of the tree. There was a large box for me from Santa, which Mom and Dad seemed especially impressed with and anxious that I should open. The box was exciting but felt a little heavy to me, considering the picture in the catalogue and the thin, silvery metal of the transport box.

Wayne knelt next to me, looking down at the box, preparing his excitement. I could sense Mom's anxious, keen eyes and Dad's pleased smiles behind me as the paper vanished, the cardboard packaging fell away, and the fender of an oversized metal pickup hit the floor. It was a lovely metallic blue and had a bright-yellow cargo trailer. Excellent for farm work. There was the barest moment of quiet. My stomach turned over. My face, which I kept down, fell. Struggling to master my shock, I raised it now in strange surprise. I am not sure if I risked a look at Wayne before I mouthed, "Wow."

Wayne quickly added his own pretend enthusiasm for the crucial present.

"Yes, Mom. I'd say this is a great truck."

He knew as well as I, pretense was the only course that could save the rest of Christmas Day.

"Hey, Greg, let's take it and play with it down the hall."

Yes, I thought, let's throw it down a hole.

"Yes, let's play with it."

Mom and Dad seemed satisfied and pleased with Santa's work, and they returned to the preparation of the much-longed-for and much-needed Christmas dinner. We slid along the hall, pushing the ungainly pickup on its sturdy, fixed rubber wheels, struggling to steer it over the grille of the floor furnace, its yellow cargo trailer rattling out of control. I looked through its empty windshield to the hardwood floor below and swallowed down a low, sick feeling. My empty stomach folded in half and turned over.

At the end of the hall, we played quickly through the bright, steamy kitchen, passing under our parents' busy bodies as they prepared the always delicious Christmas dinner. Everything was on schedule. It didn't matter that the truck was obviously meant for someone younger, not to mention for summer dirt, and not at all suitable for the couches, hardwood floors and rugs of midwinter. That was past now and there was just the large metal truck to bury. The low, sick feeling of the upper respiratory resentment hardened into a small ball in my throat. As soon as we were alone in the storeroom behind the kitchen, I spit it out. We seriously put the truck in its place verbally, abandoned it under the bed and returned to the tree in the living room in search of some overlooked surprise.

But the imposter truck was large and strong and would not die so easily. In fact, it had to be resurrected and shown again, often in play mode, several times throughout the day, always at my mother's request. In fact, Mom's interest in trucks was now keen.

"Greg. You're not playing with your truck. Where's your new truck?"

I had to be careful that my enthusiasm was undiminished. But my heart was not in the role and I failed.

"Don't you like your truck?"

YOU BETTER WATCH OUT   223

"Oh yes . . . Yeah."

I fell asleep at my post.

"I just parked it."

My uneven enthusiasm eventually proved to Mom the correctness of her views: Children really don't value toys. One is as good as another and they will drop the expensive offering and go on to something else in a few minutes. So why waste money?

Wayne knew the truth. You never got what you wanted in that house. But the cost of saying so was great. You risked hurting Lovey and rousing Bill's protective wrath. So I'll pretend and thank Santa, whom I now knew could not exist, but must pretend to still believe in, for a present I did not want, but had to be grateful for, as if my wishes, which could no longer be specified, had been fulfilled.

My brothers and I, after long years of less-than-perfect pretense, came to be seen by Mom and Dad as ungrateful, a description we had to agree with and accept with guilt and shame, for Christmas moments not lived up to, and for Christmas moments we had not really had.

Standards Were Falling

The new car and the promotion notwithstanding, standards were falling. Wayne and I were quick to notice. It started with the milk, and it was understandable that, with one hungry man and four hungry boys, one quart of Kelsey's milk would no longer do. We now needed two or more, and so Mom bought one quart of fresh and one quart of Starlac, the new powdered milk. This was mixed half and half until, finally, the clean, sparkling bottles of creamy milk were entirely gone, replaced by cloudy, opaque plastic jugs of sour white liquid, which tasted like the box it came in. We didn't care to drink glasses of this, even when masked by toast and jam or cookies, and Mom was forced to harass us into finishing it off. Inevitably as much found its way down the sink as down our throats. With a shudder, we ran from the table, complaining bitterly.

"It tastes awful."

"It's just not cold enough, that's all."

"It's cold enough. It's just bad."

"Well, it's not mixed right. I'll put more powder in."

"No, no," we cried in unison. "That's the problem, the powder."

But Mom was adamant.

"I can't afford to feed you boys fresh milk and cookies every day. You'll just have to drink this if you want milk. And if you don't want that you'll have to drink water or tea."

Next came tinned spaghetti, not that we had ever had real spaghetti, but even so the canned version was a keen disappointment and one of the few foods I could not swallow without suppressing the gag reflex. Now this noxious novelty was presented with a slice of bread and margarine and called supper! The butter was gone too, of course, replaced by the local margarine, Good Luck, and the eggs were no longer Mrs. Nash's. Mrs. Nash had traded in the old Nash for another car and lost all mystery before she too disappeared like her lovely farm in the rush of new subdivisions.

The new order extended far beyond the kitchen. Turning out four boys in starched white shirts for school, five days a week, was an oppression that, to Mom, bordered on injustice. She was not about to become a laundry slave to St. Bon's pretensions, and so one weekend, she unilaterally dyed all our school shirts from various hues of white, to various hues of blue. In this great dyeing process many other articles, hats, shorts, stuffed toys, anything that needed a pick-me-up, were thrown into the vat, and we lived in a blue world for many months.

The Brothers were not slow to notice the colour shift, but a little nonplussed by what to do about it. We looked respectable. The blue shirts looked good with the navy blazers and blue and gold ties. It all tied in very neatly but it was not technically the school uniform. White shirts were the regulation, even though there was always someone with another colour shirt, or the wrong tie, or a sports jacket instead of the blazer. But these breaks with conventionality were usually just temporary, or an exception, like Johnny Violette and his uniform of corduroys and red plaid shirt. His older brother wore a green plaid shirt and corduroys. It was a wonder to me they wore these casual clothes for as long as they did, but before any explanation was given, the Violettes vanished.

This left the case of the blue shirts, which was of a more delicate nature than the plaid. With only two sons at St. Bon's, and Mrs. Coady to help with the laundry, Mrs. Jones found no difficulty in turning out Andy and his older brother, Mike, in clean, white shirts every day. However, sons of the larger, poorer families, and even those of the larger, middling or well-to-do families, could frequently be seen in collars that could no longer be called white. Even to the eyes of a child, they were grimy, and so there was a problem and there were rumblings, and other coloured shirts did appear, and now Mom had thrown down the gauntlet.

But it was Wayne and me, and even Kerry, who were pushed into the front lines, where we concocted explanations from Mom's exclamations as best we could, until Mom herself could argue her case at the next PTA meeting. Like the Queen, Mom could rouse herself with great energy and fervour when her own interests were at stake. She would put me in a panic, grilling sales staff at the Royal Stores or Ayre & Sons over some irregularity or flaw in an item. She would ask to see the manager and always got something off the price. Her hauteur, her utter shock and amused disdain for the less-than-perfect or overpriced was usually enough to melt most managers and leave me sweating.

Mom took special care in her preparations for the meeting and looked very sharp, we thought. At the school she appealed to the Brothers. She was very personable and persuasive, even humourous. The younger Brothers certainly had no wish to see her beauty or her spirits diminished by the excessive use of hot water and harsh detergents. She appealed to other mothers. Was not the aim of the school uniform to make the boys look smart and well-groomed? The blue shirts did that. They were just as neat as the white shirts and much easier to keep clean, which was code for "did not show the dirt as much." And, finally, there was only need for one or two blue shirts a week, as compared to the three or four white shirts needed to look fresh, and everyone looked just as good in the blue.

"Perhaps white or blue shirts for everyday, and white shirts only for Sports Day and special events," suggested the Brothers.

Of course, that is exactly what Mom thought, and so a happy compromise was reached, and before long there were as many blue shirts as white to be seen on campus.

Mom's new economy was felt at school in other ways. The lunches had been getting leaner and the bags lighter for some time, and what sandwich did appear was more often the dreaded potted meat, or the dreaded dry peanut butter, and sometimes not even that. If Dad hadn't thought to throw in a Wagon Wheel or a Snowball, the bag would have been totally empty, which Wayne swore actually happened to him one lunchtime—nothing but a bag of waxed paper. All of these economies were introduced so gradually that the trend was not immediately recognized, but now we questioned the policy directly. Mom was ready.

"If we want to move up at all and get the things you boys want, then we have to economize. We can't afford everything."

We could not disagree entirely but on the question of lunches we dug in.

"We don't want to be like those people with the nice house who don't eat."

"We're not like the Parsonses," she countered defensively. "You boys get lots to eat."

"Not the lunches."

"Mine was empty the other day, nothing."

"Now, Wayne, you didn't get nothing."

"I did. I swear."

"There wasn't much there, Mom, and I had potted meat, so it was like I had nothing."

"All right, all right," Mom surrendered, and the protest did bring the standard of lunches back up for awhile.

If Mom wanted to encourage economy, she also wanted to avoid jeopardy. That, at any rate, was part of the reason she gave for her unwillingness to take in the orphan saxophone I brought home from school.

Brother Michael was recruiting for the band of which he was the leader and chief reason *not* to join. But Brother Michael was supposed to be "all right" with the band, which must have been the only place he was "all right", and offered proof of the possibility of hope, even for the darkest of characters. I found it hard to refuse Brother Michael, but Mom had no difficulty.

"No, Greg, you don't want that," she said when she beheld the shiny instrument. "If it breaks or gets scratched, it will be your responsibility. And the noise in the house. You'd have to practise for hours. You won't want to do that. And where are you going to practise?"

She left little room for argument, and as I had no particular interest in the lovely saxophone, the matter was quickly settled.

"My mother won't allow it," I told Brother Michael the next day, and he seemed to understand that readily enough, as did Wayne.

"I know," he said. "Mom said exactly the same thing to me last year when I brought home a clarinet."

Apparently the roots of this opposition were deep, as I discovered when I later made noises about getting a piano. Mom would not hear of that at all. There would be no piano, and if we were mini-Mozarts, we would have to amuse ourselves with something else, because the lid was not coming off the music box in that house. This was a little perplexing, as Mom had grown up in a house with a piano and music, and she liked music on the radio, or so I argued. But on the question of an instrument in the house, whether piano or piccolo, she was not to be moved, and so our lives remained simple and uncluttered by either music or milk.

✸

It was a naive age, when merit earned reward, and Vera too got her promotion. She was now a buyer for Bowring's and often away on buying trips. She also modelled the clothes she brought back on *News Cavalcade* with Don Jamieson. Don had a large, round, shiny face and sat at a small desk in front of a picture of Bowring's Department Store. He looked straight at the camera and delivered all the news and weather for Newfoundland and Labrador, Canada and the world, and never once referred to the paper on his little desk in front of him. Everyone knew that Don Jamieson had a photographic memory and could talk all night, or all year, if need be, without once looking at that page, and everyone was quite proud of the fact. Then, during the commercial break, Auntie Vera would appear, sometimes under a flowered arch or next to a plant, in a neatly tailored coat and hat, or in the newest cocktail dress from New York or Chicago. We could barely believe our eyes as we watched her carefully posing and turning, looking at the camera, then sashaying off.

She was regaled with praise for her new stardom, with me leading the chorus. Regardless of the sparse competition, Auntie Vera was far and away our favourite aunt, which I never tired of telling her. As her chief fan, I was always in attendance and at her and Mom's beck and call during their many tête-à-têtes, and only banished out to play for the grown-up section of their chats. It was easy to be with Mom and Auntie Vera. I was entranced by their stories and their gossip, and they were sympathetic to my woes and amused at my adventures, and I was as much their favourite as they both were mine. Mom's partiality grew gradually, and naturally it was Wayne who first announced it. Mom immediately declared that there were no favourites, everyone was different and needed different attention, but she loved us all equally. Wayne was unconvinced and Kerry and Beni joined in on his side to gain whatever advantage might be had from the situation. I was secretly pleased but instinctively chose official denial as my best protection for the long haul.

It was not as if Mom exerted herself especially on my behalf or neglected the others. It was just that I was more concerned with cooking, fashion and movies than hockey, basketball and wrestling and so spent more time in her world, where I did get to lick the bowl of icing after we had baked a cake together. I was happy to join in her chores, though Dad complained that he couldn't get me to lift a rock in the backyard unless I wanted it moved to make a road for one of my games.

Being Mom's favourite, if it could be called that, did not mean that I was Dad's favourite; in fact, it meant quite the opposite, and whether I started it or he did, I felt that we were somehow in competition for Queenie's favours. I felt in competition for her with all the others too. We all did, and perhaps she enjoyed that. We competed to get her the most thoughtful and sophisticated present for Mother's Day. Kerry even asked me what he should get her, since I knew what she liked. Fortunately, I failed to deflect him with my suggestion of a flock of ceramic geese from the catalogue, and he got a more honest suggestion from Mom herself. I was forced to add this unkindness to my chain of regrets, along with the memory of pulling Sean Power back on Sports Day, but the stakes were high, very high.

I knew she had become fond of brass. A couple of decorative items had appeared in the living room and I resolved to get her a good pair of solid, brass candlesticks from my scarce earnings delivering the *Sunday Herald*, the local weekly TV guide and magazine. This industriousness, which Wayne and I shared, only lasted a few seasons, as it was finally judged too much trouble for the few cents. I did buy the candlesticks, at the enormous cost of $6.95, every cent I could gather, and the results were as hoped for. Mom was very pleased and surprised.

"Oh my, Greg, they are beautiful, and they're good ones too. Where did you find these?"

Dad admired them but without her enthusiasm, and I sensed, in his polite response, the beginnings of a standoff.

The standoff further down Mount Royal Avenue, at Auntie Vera's, was over. Buddy, having fought Uncle Ron and the Brothers at St. Bon's to a standstill, and accidentally broken the legs of his classmate, the future Brother Batstone, was finally expelled. With nowhere else to go, he left Newfoundland to join the United States Army. In Montana, he met and married the stunning Irene, a Ukrainian-American, and brought her home the following year to show her off. She was very pretty and very tough, with frosted blond hair, lots of make-up, a skin-tight skirt that came somewhere above her knees and the highest spike heels I had yet seen. She offered to babysit us one evening and challenged us to a race. We had fallen into bragging and boasting, at which Irene was tops.

"I can run faster than you guys, I betcha."

"I bet you can't. I'm a really fast runner," I said.

"You won't beat me." Wayne was confident.

"I can beat you guys in my skirt and high heels."

"No way, you can't beat us in those."

"Just watch me."

She carefully butted out her long filtered cigarette, pulled her tight skirt straight, and we took our places at the top of Mount Royal Avenue.

"The first one to get to our house wins."

Kerry counted us down and we took off. Irene pushed us to our limit. Her shapely legs were a blur and the click of her heels became a steady roar, as she flew over the finish line first. Irene was quite the dame. She promised to send us every new kind of cowboy gun, ones that fired like real guns, and real cowboy boots and hats from the West, but nothing ever showed up after they went back. They were busy with their new baby girl, Levida, and Mom said, "I wish they wouldn't promise those boys things they have no intention of sending. They've got me worn out waiting for it."

And so we finally left off expecting guns from the States.

Marilyn and the Monster

It was the end of summer. But Dad and Mom wanted to get in one more weekend out of town, camping and a boil-up.

They took us out to a motel, which had cabins on the side of the road, at the junction of the Lewisporte turn-off and the Trans-Canada Highway. We had been out there earlier in the summer and run into a slightly tipsy Mr. Benson from Town, who greeted Dad.

"My God, Bill, you run into Newfoundlanders wherever you go."

We'd all had a laugh at that.

Now it was cool and getting dark. Dad and Mom were unpacking and cooking supper in the main room, but the stove wouldn't work and Dad had to get the Coleman stove going, which irritated him. Wayne was off by himself and I was playing with Kerry and Beni in the bedroom, fairly giddy and exhausted by that point.

Kerry and I were still looking for some sort of game to play but Beni was too restless to stay at anything and left us.

"Let's play movies," I said. "You can be Marilyn Monroe, and we'll play a movie love scene."

I wanted to do this and Kerry didn't care what we did. He was game for anything.

"Okay," he said.

So we smooched and hugged and argued and kissed with appropriate "Oh, darlings" until Kerry became bored and wandered out into the main room.

Dad had become aware of us and when Kerry and I came out, he asked suspiciously, almost angrily, what we had been doing in there. Kerry spoke up brightly and said we had been playing Marilyn Monroe and movies.

"What do you mean you were playing Marilyn Monroe and movies? What were you doing in there?"

"We were kissing and hugging," Kerry said.

"Just pretending to kiss," I stammered.

Dad was growing blacker. Now he erupted.

"What were you doing to him in there!" he roared at me.

"Nothing. We were just . . ."

I thought he was going to hit me and backed up a step.

"Come back here!"

I did.

"You little . . ."

He sneered and went to strike me but didn't.

"Don't you ever do that to him again," he yelled down at me. "Do you hear?"

"Yes. Yes," I said quickly, hoping he would stop.

But he did not stop.

He kept yelling and yelling down at me. Everyone was watching: Mom, Wayne, Kerry and Beni. I was unmasked, shamed, hot and cold. The roar of his voice finally stopped and Dad turned back to the Coleman stove, grumbling in disgust. He was disgusted with me, by me. I was shocked, cleaved in two by the force of his attack, but not surprised. As soon as I could, without drawing further attention to myself, I went out the door and stood on the small wooden step and held onto the rail in the dark.

My chest seemed stuck. I tried to suck in air. The trees in the woods at the edge of the gravel parking lot were black. I wanted to run into them. Where was there to go? I looked at the dark sky and the stars. "How can I escape? What can I do?" I thought desperately. It was cold. My legs were shaking. My hands were shaking on the rail. How could I return? How could I face them all? They were all decent people. I was not. But they would tolerate me. He would tolerate me. Me? Who was I? I was ashamed. Stripped of my status in front of my brothers, an outsider, safe, for the moment, outside. It was all so impossible. How could I see any of them again? I just needed to catch my breath, to calm down. This will pass. I took in a breath. There is no escape, nowhere to go, and soon I must find a way, a way back in, as if nothing had happened.

But something had happened. I heard Dad's voice, still angry, calling us to come and eat. I dared not delay. But so deeply did I not wish to return that something of me must be left behind. My obedient shell returned with enough of me left inside to animate it, and my father was satisfied. What was left outside was not needed or wanted here, and I would only feel its loss much later.

I moved carefully over the brittle ground. The atmosphere was sour, unpredictable, as though my behaviour had awoken some sleeping monster in the family, and it was me. The bare overhead light in the cabin, the steam on the black windows—summer was gone. The others regained their good mood quickly, or had never lost it. I did not regain my mood, nor my father his, and when the storm had passed my father's position and mine had settled into something hard at the centre.

Watchfulness settled over me. There would be more camping trips, in better weather, and pleasanter picnics, and we would play cowboys and Indians and other games, and push the edge, but I would be careful now to remember not to awaken Marilyn, or the Monster.

A Fountain Pen Hero

Brother McGoohan had the reputation, like all the Brothers who taught the other classes, of being tough and quick to deal out physical punishment. But he came to us in grade six with a changed philosophy.

"You boys are grown up now. You're not little children anymore and I expect a certain maturity from you. So I will not be using the strap to punish you. But that does not mean there will not be consequences. I expect you to do your best. I hope I can trust you."

The class crackled to attention. There were some smirks and raised eyebrows as boys checked out each other's reaction to this revolutionary concept.

Brother McGoohan was slightly built and he moved with a casual, athletic lope. His light brown eyebrows met over his serious blue eyes, as they focused on us with conditional trust. He flexed his wide jaw bones and rippled the surface of his cheeks, which were always dark even when freshly shaved, and his full lips pursed slightly in deliberation, as though questioning his own decisions.

I certainly appreciated his philosophical change of heart and the thought he gave to making it. I admired him for it, but then maybe the choice had already been made by those above him, that our class would be spared physical punishment as a sort of sociological experiment. Whatever the reasons for Brother McGoohan's choice, and in spite of my own sincere wishes to justify his new faith, the freedom from fear it gave me sent me to giddy new heights, and I became, with the already well-established Bobby Tilley, the class clown.

We sat in rows, two to a desk, the bench seat of which was attached to the front of the desk behind. The double desk, with its ink well in the middle, was bolted to the floor, likewise the seat. From this fixed position I was driven to amuse whomever in my immediate neighbourhood I could reach.

I developed elaborate dramas with the available props and derived the greatest pleasure from making my friends laugh at nothing. The sillier and more ordinary the object, the more energy I invested in it. My new fountain pen was the hero of my most famous "tragedy," which improved with every perform- ance. After a thrilling and brave but doomed battle with a lead- headed dullard of a pencil, the proud pen was mortally wounded, bled his last drop of ink, and died, his cartridge spent. The fountain pen was very beautiful, a great and beloved hero who must have a hero's burial. With much pathos I lay the slain hero in his sleek, black pen-box coffin, checking that those nearby had a chance to pay their last respects. With a show of restrained grief I reluctantly closed the lid for the last time, and then began the painful journey to its final resting place.

This sad tale was engaging indeed. The more studious and law-abiding tried vainly to ignore the unfolding drama. Andy gave me a tolerant scowl and straightened himself in his chair to signal his non-involvement. The un-studious were puzzled and the athletic types, like John Byrne and Pat Royal, looked on sideways, half scornful, half curious.

But when the lonely pen-box coffin turned away from the desk top and wobbled onto the narrow ruler bridge spanning the gaping chasm to the cemetery on the far desk shore, there was an involuntary groan, and the air around sparked with new attention. Would the ruler bridge hold?

Slowly the pen-box coffin inched onto the bridge, and slowly the ruler bridge took its full weight, shifted slightly, and held. There was a moan of relief from the crowd. John Byrne hissed with disgust and looked away and then looked back. It was too late to retreat and no room to do so. The coffin must continue to the other side.

The bridge began to twist and lean to one side with the uneven weight. But the procession was now almost halfway across and hopes were high that this time it would make it to the other side. Again the bridge slipped. Again it held. But the coffin had shifted. The tension was unbearable.

No one dared to look down to the curved oak seat of the canyon floor far below. Slowly, carefully, the coffin was righted and bravely the procession pushed on to our silent urging, over the weakening supports past the sagging middle, the weakest point, and even seemed to pick up speed as it climbed the last quarter to the safety of the far desk.

Everyone's hopes were now pinned on that bright spot and so they failed to notice the moorings on the shore behind suddenly give way. The bridge tilted to one side, then dropped down, hanging for a moment by one end. The cortège strove to mount the sudden incline. Desperately, bravely, the coffin tried to scramble up the final inch to safety. But it could not. The bridge let go completely from behind. The pen-box coffin, now in slow motion, twisted backwards and down in a freakish fall. The lid suddenly swung open, and in one ghoulish moment the corpse pen, laid to rest with such care only moments before, came tumbling recklessly out and crashed to the bottom like a broken doll, with the coffin and lid on top of it. It was over.

A stifled wave of grief and laughter followed the desperate finale.

"What's so interesting down there?" Brother McGoohan turned around suspiciously from the blackboard, the chalk still held in his dusty fingers.

He walked slowly down the aisle, his soutane swishing, his lips pursed, half angry, half hurt.

"What's that?" he asked, gazing down sadly at the ruler, pen box and pen lying on the seat between me and Eddie Taylor.

"It's my pen and ruler, Br."

"And what are they doing there?"

I liked Brother McGoohan. I wanted to please him, to validate his trust, but I knew he would not understand the Drama of the Fountain Pen Hero. I could hardly understand it myself.

"What were you doing with that ruler?" he asked quietly.

"Well, I was using it for a bridge."

"A bridge?"

"Yes, sort of."

"And what was the bridge for?"

"The pen, Br."

"The pen?"

"The pen box needed to go across and . . ."

"Put it away and pay attention," he said quietly.

I would have another occasion to disappoint Brother McGoohan later.

＊

Brother Darcy, the principal, also thought we were growing up. He took over Brother McGoohan's class one afternoon for a special talk.

"You boys are growing up and you will notice changes in your bodies. Not just getting taller. Some of you are already taller than me, but don't get any smart ideas—I can still handle

you fellas. I'm talking about other kinds of changes, more sub-
tle changes as you grow into men. For one thing, you'll get more
hair in different places. You might lose it in other places like me
on top, but that happens later. It's all perfectly normal and it's
nothing to worry about. Now, as you become young men, it is
important that you respect your body and keep it clean and
healthy. Your bodies, after all, are temples of the Holy Spirit.

"You will notice other changes in your body too. If you have
begun to feel those changes and have any questions, you can ask
me, not here, not now, I don't want you to ask them here now,
but later, in private. If any of you have felt any discomfort or
want to know more, you can see me later. Don't tell me who you
are. I want you all to take a small piece of paper and write your
name down, and then if you want to see me privately write
"yes," or if you don't want to see me, write nothing. No one will
know if you have come to see me or not. This is private and
between you and me."

Although I felt no particular complaint except ignorance, I
wrote down my name and then "Yes."

Brother Darcy's office was in the new building, which had
once been the lovely tennis courts. I waited in the cool, jade-
green gloom of the borrowed light in the waiting area with the
secretary, who managed to communicate with every glance and
gesture both her knowledge and disapproval of these "appoint-
ments." Above me, a new picture of the Crucifixion hung in
framed meditation. Sunlight bathed the muscular shoulders and
back of the Saviour as he hung out and away from the cross. His
head was bent forward away from our view, and he stared down
on the dusty troubled earth beneath him.

"Brother Darcy will see you now," said the secretary with
neutral censure.

Brother Darcy had studied psychology and he studied me as
I entered. He was short and solidly built. His balding head was
rescued from total exposure by a small battalion of black and

grey hairs that still marched in some formation across the shiny dome between two perfectly paired ears. He cocked his head to one side as I entered, regarding me with a half-amused, half-curious expression, as though surprised by my choice to visit.

"So, Mr. Malone, you answered 'yes' on your paper."

"Yes, Br."

"So what would you like to know? Are you having any problems?"

"I don't know, sometimes it feels . . . ah . . ."

"Are you uncomfortable?"

"Well, it feels uncomfortable sometimes."

"Um hum."

"I don't know if that's okay?"

"Well, why don't we just check it out, all right?"

"All right."

"First I want you to go in the storage room there and close the door and take down your pants and check yourself just to see if everything looks all right to you, and then you can come out and I'll have a look. How about that? Is that all right?"

I went into the storage room, unzipped my pants and took my wrinkled, sleepy penis out of my snowy white underwear amid the boxes of papers and pens. It blinked up at me, confused. What did I want? I did not know. What was I looking for that I had not seen before? Nothing. It was what it was. I could make no more of it. I did not feel I had anything to show Brother Darcy. He seemed to agree. He sat with his legs apart. I stood in close, almost touching his soutane. He took a good look, like a doctor, from behind his rimless spectacles, breathing regularly.

"Well, everything looks fine. You're not having any problems? That wasn't giving you any problems, was it?"

"No, Br."

"No, there's nothing to worry about. So, young man, what else did you have on your mind?"

"Nothing," I replied.

"Well, you're still young. How old are you now, Mr. Malone?"

"Eleven."

"Come back and see me when you are a bit older."

Through the window behind him, I could see the Aula Maxima door in the main building open. Someone was going in late, I thought.

You Better Watch Out

Christmas Eve was busy. In the afternoon I was singing Christmas carols in the parade on the Boy Scout float with Wayne and a few of his Scout buddies from the brand new First St. Bon's Troop. We had some songbooks but we had never sung together before, and it wasn't really a float so much as an open Land Rover donated by Uncle Bob and Adelaide Motors. We crowded on and sang into a microphone. I was the youngest and not quite sure why I was included. Dad had arranged the "float" but he wasn't there. Even though it was all last minute, I was happy for the adventure. Wayne and the older boys were a bit cynical about the whole "carolling Boy Scout" thing, but I was guileless and eventually we all got into it. I was laughed at for being too loud and flat, and laughed at again when I did a solo verse.

"Too loud! No more solos for you!"

It was cold standing in the back of the Land Rover in the snow. "Jingle Bells," "Santa Claus is Coming to Town."

You better watch out, you better not cry.

Even my enthusiasm was flagging. We stopped on New Gower Street at Adelaide Motors and got hot coffees with milk, which I had a mouthful of, but it was too strong for me. I wasn't used to coffee. After the parade we delivered boxes of groceries and frozen turkeys to needy families around Mundy Pond, and were finally dropped off at Mount Royal Avenue after dark, leaden with exhaustion, but satisfied with our full day of worthwhile activities.

Wayne and I went in. The vestibule was dark. We kicked off our gaiters, hung up our coats and went down the hall. There was a noise in the kitchen.

"Hi. We're back from the parade," we said, as we turned into the kitchen.

A plate flew across the doorway and smashed against the wall.

"Go on," sneered Dad. "Throw another one."

Mom threw another dish hard at him. Dad didn't hesitate. He threw one back at her.

"Shit on you."

Mom's voice was twisted in anger and bitterness. Dishes were flying and smashing. Mom screamed and then lashed out. "You bastard. I'm not staying here for Christmas."

"You can go to the Newfoundland Hotel for Christmas if you want, but I'm not paying for it," Dad flung back.

"Stop it," we cried. "This is Christmas."

They ignored us as though we did not exist, or had not been born, like we were someone else's children. It shocked me. Mom screamed "you bastard" again, and smacked at Dad. He raised his hand to strike back but checked himself.

"Don't you hit *her*," I yelled.

Dad lunged at us but pulled himself back.

"Get out of here," he sneered in contempt. "You little . . ."

We ran out. Really, you couldn't choose between them. Mom and Dad went back at it, and Wayne and I walked up the stairs, lost and overcome.

"Now see what you've done," Mom cried

"I don't give a damn," Dad said.

Halfway up the stairs, feeling quite righteous, I joined in, loudly enough to be heard over the fight, which was starting up again.

"This is not a house. It's is a hellhole."

Dad shot out of the kitchen and up the stairs after us.

"What did you say? Who the hell do you think you are? I'll show you a goddamn hellhole!"

He was fast but so were we. Into the bedroom we ran, shutting the door only halfway, not fully shut, so as not to incite or inflame him, but Dad only came to the top of the stairs.

"Now shut up and stay out of it." The door of Kerry and Beni's room was already shut. They were lying low.

Dad went back down. The voices continued downstairs, lower then louder, then lower. It was Christmas Eve. The carolling was long over. The whole reason for carolling was gone. Christmas was gone, swept away. Maybe the family was gone. We waited in the dark. The night passed on and things slowly came around. We hung up our stockings humbly and went to bed, hopeful that the small things that kept our world together would hold.

The next morning the Christmas tree appeared, fully dressed in the dark morning light, with presents underneath, and the long Scout socks were full of fruit and candy and toys. Christmas had come again, as if by magic.

That Christmas was not, and could not be, the fun-loving affair we used to think it was. We stepped around the holiday highlights carefully and were on our best behaviour. Everyone was strangely polite. Wayne and I could not think what to do about it. Dad and Mom had had fights before this one, but this was the worst one we had seen, and never before had we been so close to the storm. They often made up over renovations or vacations, and the growing tension in the house would suddenly break with peals of laughter from Mom in the bedroom—but not that night. We thought Mom might leave and the family might split up. I had long discussions about the situation with Andy. But there was nothing to be done, except wait and see, and pray of course. We prayed.

High Mass

It was about this time that Wayne took an unexpected turn and became pious. He began getting up at six o'clock on weekdays and walking all the way down to St. Patrick's for early morning Mass and Communion, and then back home for breakfast before going to school. I watched him getting out of bed in the faint blue gloom of winter mornings, onto the cold floor, and dressing, day after day with growing apprehension. This devotion was very disturbing.

"You should come with me," he invited kindly, but not as a challenge.

If I were truly holy, I would get up and go with him, but I could not convince myself to follow him down over the snow to Mass.

At the same time as he began to grow in my esteem, I began worry about the poor light his devotion might cast me in, for while Wayne was actually devout, I was the one who had developed the reputation for devotion. But while Wayne struggled through snowstorms down to St. Patrick's, I preferred to

celebrate Mass in the comfort of my own home, where I conducted many elaborate religious ceremonies. I was generally the
archbishop. Only rarely did I allow myself to be the Pope. I
pressed Kerry and Beni into service to assist at my Masses. I had
to promote them from altar boys to sub-deacons, to deacons,
and even elevated Kerry to monsignor to keep his attention one
Saturday night.

I made all my own vestments: the alb, the stole, the chasuble
and the cope, out of old bed sheets and drapes, trimmed with
bits of ribbon and cord. At the Arcade store on Water Street, I
acquired spectacular scraps of silk, satin and brocade, perfect
for all my ecclesiastical needs. I even had my own archbishop's
mitre, made of two triangular pieces of cardboard stapled
together, painted gold and encrusted with the finest costume
jewellery Woolworths and Mom's jewellery box could offer.
The staples dug into my scalp, which discomfort I deemed
appropriate for a pious prelate of my rank, and I offered it all
up for the souls in Purgatory.

The problem of a proper silver chalice was also solved.
Actually it was silver plate, and this memory forms another
link in my chain of regrets because I broke the remaining handle off Mom's canasta trophy to make it. Well, one handle was
already missing, and I thought it would look better with the
other one gone too, more balanced. So one day, snap. Mom was
crushed.

"Who broke my canasta trophy? That's the only trophy I ever
won. I was quite proud of that."

"I did, Mom, sorry, but one handle was already gone so . . ."

"Yes, but you didn't have to break off the other one."

"Sorry, Mom."

"Well, you might as well use it now."

"Thanks a lot, Mom."

"But ask me next time, Greg."

Using a flat iron, I pressed circles of bread from Mammy's

Bakery into sacred wafers, and with grape juice for wine, I was finally ready.

In the finest bed linen and satin robes, my jewelled mitre stapled to my head, the sacred canasta chalice in my hands, my upturned face held in an otherworldly gaze, I walked, flanked by my two awestricken younger brothers, sombrely out of the upstairs bathroom, which served as our vestry, and continued in procession down the hall to the candlelit bedroom and up to the chest of drawers, where I intoned High Mass.

"*Introibo ad altare dei.*"

And waited for the response. Oh, those slack brothers.

This elaborate dress-up attracted Dad's notice, but fortunately he got a good kick out of this production and so it was allowed. After a few snorts, he even dragged Uncle Bob and Aunt Mil up to take a look. They gazed in amused disbelief at the altar, the candles, flowers and tabernacle, and the vestments. Uncle Bob knelt and asked me for my blessing. But their mirth was not mean-spirited, and they returned incredulous to their game of 120s, laughing and shaking their heads.

I was vastly relieved when, some months later, Wayne abandoned the practice of actually going to daily Mass. The allure of St. Patrick's and Monsignor Murphy were not strong enough to satisfy his practical nature.

"That's enough of that," he said. "I'd rather go to basketball practice."

And he did.

In the meantime, I was surprised to find an ecclesiastical colleague in the grade junior to me. James Kelsey was tall with pale red hair and carried himself with all the ironic disdain of a dispossessed duke. He was a natural snob and so we quickly became allies.

We told each other elaborate lies about our respective families. James was tremendously well connected by his own account, and having once doubted some of his more extravagant claims of lineage, I felt free to invent a pedigree all my own. My mother was transformed into the daughter of a Russian prince, her real name was Adalacoskya. I even produced a glorious emerald ring from Woolworths to back up my claims. Kevin Whittle was amazed but James was doubtful, especially as the ring was adjustable.

James was very well read and mixed enough genuine information in with the wildest assertions that it was not always possible to tell the difference. He was a real master, as deeply steeped in Catholic ceremony as I was and very impressed at my collection of ecclesiastical paraphernalia. We lacked only a suitably sacred and secure location to co-celebrate. We were both familiars at the Basilica, and James, the "snob", had struck up a great friendship with the janitor, who shall remain nameless for his own safety. He let us use the altar boys' dressing room one Saturday afternoon. It was not within his power to give us the Marian chapel next door, or the archbishop's sacristy just behind. Monsignor O'Keefe or Monsignor McGettigan might come in unexpectedly, but in the spacious altar boys' room he could guarantee our safety, to which end he locked us in for a leisurely afternoon, and a near-perfect High Mass in the Basilica.

That spring brought terrible news from Labrador to our street: Lioney Churchill's sister Wow had died. She was the brightest, sweetest and most affectionate of the Churchills and had gone to Labrador to teach after receiving her certificate. She was riding across a frozen lake in a snowmobile when the ice broke, and Wow, who could not swim and was terrified of the water, drowned. One of her fellow teachers, an American, tried to save her but lost his own life in the attempt. The whole street grieved the loss of Wow. Lioney cried and cried and all the candy in Hodder's little store could not console him.

Mommy Lone had died too and was waked in the old house on New Gower Street. Before the year was out, Skipper was removed to the newly constructed St. Patrick's Mercy Home on Elizabeth Avenue, across Rennie's River from Andy's new house, where he continued to decline and where Wayne and I amused ourselves on the new elevator until Dad snapped at us.

"What's wrong with you two, for God's sake? Your grandfather is in there dying. Try and show some respect and stop playing in the damn elevator."

We hadn't realized that Daddy Lone was at his end and exuded as much respect as we could in the time remaining, but neither of us could understand what Skipper's death meant to Dad, and he could not tell us.

It was not long after Daddy Lone's death that Uncle Tom sold the house and went off to New York on his holiday. In spite of the big blow-up over the furniture and the hard feelings between Dad and Uncle Tom, when Tom returned from New York, Dad managed to be gracious as his brother passed us all impractical gifts Dad could not afford. With the remainder of his inheritance from Daddy Lone, Tom bought a ghastly, pale yellow and white, two-door '58 Chevy sedan. He was a strange sight with his wide, brown homburg and his pale coupe, which before long was deposited in our driveway, where it sat interrupting all driveway games. Ordinarily an abandoned vehicle would have provided a wonderful toy, but this sad car, with its grey, faux-brick fabric upholstery, was so repulsive that it was rarely disturbed. It also had a scurrilous history that kept us at bay.

While driving the sickly car one evening, under the considerable influence of alcohol, Tom struck a woman and killed her. There was a trial, a sobering experience, and Tom was found guilty of manslaughter, but he received only a minimal sentence, to be served at the Salmonier Correctional Farm. Uncle Ken was thunderstruck.

"I've only got one question, Bill, and that is, what did Tom have on the judge, I wonder?"

Dad had no answer, but he saw Tom through his legal difficulties and kept the car in the driveway until his release.

✦

We abandoned our yard and took to the trees. The bungalow next to Churchills' was rented out to Americans, who didn't mind us up in their trees, which were some of the best on the street. Jimmy "Hot Dog" Wadden was there with his brother "Hamburger," and Wayne and Don and Bruce. While the Americans didn't mind me up in the trees, Jimmy for some reason did, and every time I got off the ground and onto a branch, he pulled me back down. This went on for some time.

"You don't have to take that, Greg."

"Don't let him get away with that."

"You're as big as he is," came the advice from Don and Wayne and Bruce in the treetops.

I swung up into the branches again, and when Jimmy grabbed onto me I suddenly wheeled around and, taking him by the shoulders, pushed him back down on the ground and sat on him.

"Now, stop pulling me down out of the tree! Do you hear? Stop it," I yelled at him.

Jimmy was as surprised to be on the ground as I was to be on top of him, but he couldn't move.

"You should have done that a long time ago," said Wayne.

Wayne was right. I suppose I should have, and I was pleased to have prevailed, but this little triumph came in a miserable wrapping. Jimmy was humiliated, which made me very uncomfortable. But he got up, surprisingly philosophical about it, and thankfully did not press for a rematch then or later, and although we did not become best friends, we decided that we were not enemies, and there was no more trouble between us after that.

✦

Kerry was sick again. He was a very loveable and lively child, but he had always been frail and excitable. If little Kerry got giddy and started laughing, he might just keep on laughing and laughing uncontrollably, until his neck swelled up the size of his head and his face turned blue. Or if we had a fight over something and Kerry got mad, he might get madder and madder until, again, his neck swelled up and his face turned blue. Mom and Dad had taken him to the hospital once before. Now they explained the situation to me and Wayne.

"You know Kerry is very excitable. Well, the doctor thinks he may be having some kind of seizure and that we have to keep him from getting upset and keep him calm."

Mom was in tears.

"So I want you boys to play gently with him, and if there's a disagreement about something, don't make a big deal out of it. Just let it go and come to us if you have to and we'll sort it out. He might grow out of this, but for now we have to be careful about the way we treat him. Okay, fellas? Can you do that?"

"Yes, yes, we will," we promised, and we tried.

We watched Kerry like he was a madman on a day pass for at least two weeks or until we felt he was using it and getting away with too much, fair is fair. Now here he was quite unexpectedly in hospital again. Uncle Bob and Aunt Mil, who were very fond of Kerry, visited him there. He was in the Grace Hospital and we all hoped and prayed he would be home for Easter, which he was, smiling and looking the same as when he left.

The family went to High Mass at the Basilica to give thanks, which was unusual, and Mom came with us too, which was even more unusual. When we returned home we discovered a beautiful, big, yellow and purple basket filled with chocolate and marshmallow eggs and candies, wrapped in cellophane with little chicks on the top. Wayne and I were flabbergasted and in little doubt as to whom it belonged. Next to the basket were two clear plastic bags stuffed with bars and candy, looking very practical but tempting enough. There were no names or tags on these items. Unable to tell exactly who got what, we ran to Mom and Dad for clarification.

"Who owns the basket?"

"How come there's only one?"

"Who owns the bags? Who owns which one?"

"Goddamn it," erupted Dad. "You don't even say thank you. You just start in arguing over who owns what, you ungrateful bunch."

"We just didn't know who gets the basket."

"Aunt Mil and Uncle Bob bought that for Kerry because they thought he would be in the hospital for Easter, but now he's home," Mom started to explain.

"It doesn't matter who gave it to him, you should be grateful for what you got."

And we were grateful, but all that was lost in the explosion and could not be recovered, and so Wayne and I retired to swallow down these misunderstandings with boxes of colourful Smarties.

May Altars

The new Confederation Building, the pride and joy of Premier Joey Smallwood and a monument to his successful campaign to bring Newfoundland into Confederation with Canada, had not yet officially opened, but a delegation from our class was invited to tour the city's first skyscraper and report back to the class. I was very pleased to be chosen by Brother McGoohan, which reassured me that I had not completely alienated him with my antics. He was less than pleased to see me in my old sneakers and scowled at me, which made me grieve, but he thought it over and let me go nevertheless. Brother Stoyles was to be our chaperone. Mr. Quinlan, the high school math teacher, had loaned him his brand new Dodge hardtop with push-button drive, power steering and power brakes.

Brother Stoyles spent some time looking for the clutch, cursing the foolish new car and pushing buttons, until he finally hit "D" and we lurched away from the curb with excessive speed. He then hit the power brakes and sent us all flying into the windshield. And in this fashion we made it up the hill, pretty

shaken up and fairly hysterical by the time we arrived. The tour
was enjoyable and I was particularly impressed by the blue velvet curtains in the assembly chamber and the spectacular view
of the city from up on the observatory.

We were assigned to write an essay about our tour and report
back to Brother McGoohan and the class. I worked hard on it
all weekend, struggling to convey the richness and colour of the
official furnishings, the size and scale of this glamorous new
seat of power. Having let Brother McGoohan down over the
sneakers, I was looking forward to delivering an excellent essay
to him on Monday. I felt sure he would appreciate the trouble I
had taken. Unfortunately I didn't finish my regular weekly essay,
but I convinced myself that he would let me hand it in on Tues-
day. I could not have been more mistaken. That essay was the
first thing he asked the class for and my excuse was the last one
acceptable to him.

"You should have done your homework like everyone else.
That's the most important thing, not this other essay."

"Yes, Br. I intended to do both, but I started the other essay
first and took so long with it that I couldn't finish the homework essay on time."

"Well, that was a mistake. You should have done your homework first. I don't care about the other one. Put it away now. You
won't read it out to the class after all."

I sank, stupid and humiliated, in my crummy sneakers,
clutching my pages of adjectives while the rest of the delegation
read out their essays. His dismissal was awful. There was nothing more I could do other than turn in the required work and
keep quiet in the faintest hope I might regain some small footing. But there was one more thing I could do, and that was to
break one of the glass vigil lights on the May altar.

Every classroom had a May altar. To begin with, every
classroom had a statue of the Virgin Mother Mary, often featuring the Virgin standing calmly on a serpent's head, garbed

in white and pale blue, May blue. The Virgin's eyes too were almost always blue. These statues sat on a special shelf or pedestal, and during the month of May, the month of the Blessed Virgin, they were decorated with far more white and blue crepe paper, bunting, vigil lights and tissue-paper flowers than present-day fire regulations would allow. May altars were competitive and it was common to tour the May altars in the other classrooms to determine the best.

Brother Stoyles had a particularly elaborate shrine in Wayne's classroom. There was no crepe paper here. Brother Stoyles used real white and blue silk, pleated and tied back. Tissue-paper flowers were an innovation he did not approve of and the many steps of the altar in his class were lined not only with vigil lights of blue and white glass, but vases of the finest artificial flowers the Arcade store had to offer. It is fair to say the Arcade was virtually denuded of its stock of blue fabric and artificial flowers every May. Brother Stoyles's May altar was the ultimate, followed by Brother McCarthy's. He taught high school but occasionally he would come into the younger classes with an orange stuck in his hand and pretend his hand was permanently frozen into that shape from squeezing oranges so long. The smallest students were invited to try to straighten out his hand but we always failed, and in the end he fitted his orange back in and went on smiling. We laughed nervously at this playful interlude. We knew very well Brother McCarthy was strict and quick to strike like Brother Stoyles, still their May altars were the most elaborate and I was very impressed with them. It seemed to me that the toughest and most violent Brothers had the most elaborate May altars, while the milder-tempered Brothers, like Brother Pigott and Brother McGoohan, were content with more modest displays.

Wayne was in Brother Stoyles's religion class the day the great work there was completed and several sly students initiated a discussion about the theological dangers of statues themselves.

"Some Protestants think Catholics are idolaters, Br, and that we actually worship statues."

They had no idea they had struck the bull's eye with the word "Protestant." Brother Stoyles was an older Brother, a former boxer from Bell Island, and as tough as a bulldozer. His misshapen nose bore testament to the many rounds he had gone in the ring, and in some ways Brother Stoyles was still in the ring, waiting for the bell. He heard it that morning, ringing loud and clear, and came out swinging.

"Protestants! Idolaters? What do they know about Catholics? The one True Faith! What do you think?" he challenged the class as he rushed up to the glittering May altar he had just finished. "Do you think this is the Virgin Mary?"

He whisked the large pastel statue off its base and held it up in one hand.

"This is not the Virgin Mary," he announced. "We don't worship this. This is only a piece of plaster," and he twisted the head right off the Virgin in front of the horrified students. "This isn't the Virgin. We don't worship this!" he shouted, and with that, he threw the Virgin, body and head, out the window.

There was pin-drop silence in the class, enough to hear the quiet crash of plaster on the pavement below. The Virgin's body was recovered, but her head was never found, its blue eyes scattered in all directions. This had been a shock to the class, even though they were used to seeing Brother Stoyles throw things out the window. There were no lockers, only cloakrooms or hooks in the hallways, so on hockey days many students were forced to keep their duffle bags of equipment and hockey sticks in the classroom. If Brother Stoyles tripped, or was obstructed in any way by these, he would fling open the windows and throw the equipment out. It was an arresting sight to see shin pads and skates and hockey sticks flying through the air, and it was a miracle that none of the grade ones below were decapitated by a pair of flying skates. The luck of the madman.

I, of course, had my own altar at home. I had constructed it myself using the ornate top of an old chair for the arch. It had pillars and I lined it with pleated white silk, all carefully pressed and stapled into place. I was forced to use my old St. John's Cub Scout neckerchief for drapes, but the overall effect was splendid. Wayne's wild story from Brother Stoyles's class, however, forced me to reconsider my devotion to decoration. Was I praying to the beautiful shrine of my own creation, or to the Virgin beyond? Yes, yes, I was praying to the Virgin beyond, whom I imagined inhabiting a white silk heaven much like the shrine of my own creation.

Brother McGoohan was inclined to a more modest display, but I believed his devotion to be very sincere. We were permitted to augment the basic altar. I added flowers left over from my own devotions, and one lunchtime, as I and another appointee blew out the few vigil lights, I accidentally dropped one and it smashed.

I was very discouraged and simply did not have the face to tell Brother McGoohan. I could not bear to be the cause of any more disappointment to this handsome, trusting, quiet and pious man. I left school immediately and started walking home. If I walked fast and did not dally, I could reach home and get my own vigil light off my own altar and be back with it before lunch break was over. It was a pleasant May day, but my mind was filled with Brother McGoohan's many possible reactions. I arrived back in time and went straight up and presented the vigil light to him.

"What's that for?" he inquired.

"I accidentally dropped one of the vigil lights from the May altar when I was blowing out the candle and it broke."

"What's this then?"

"It's mine. I went home and brought this back to replace it."

"You went all the way home and got this?"

"Yes."

He looked at me with some surprise.

"You didn't have to do that. It was an accident."

"I know, but I wanted to."

He looked at me again in mild disbelief.

"Well, that's all right then, thank you. You can go and sit down, and don't forget to take it back after."

"Yes, Br."

He clearly thought I had gone too far and overreacted, but I was glad I had replaced the light. I wanted to leave him in no doubt of my devotion, not just to the Virgin Mary, and I could see that I had succeeded in climbing back up a rung on the endless ladder to his respect. I also saw that he did not care especially about vigil lights and May altars, in fact, but about a deeper devotion, which I hoped he might think me capable of, and I sat back immensely relieved, pleased, and even relaxed for a moment.

Brother McGoohan was ill and we prayed for his return to health and to us, not least because his replacement was none other than Brother Stoyles. Brother Stoyles would have been a bit of a laugh to us now if he wasn't still so dangerous. We had encountered him in grade four when Brother Clancy taught chemistry to Wayne and his class, and he would come in and take our grade four class. He insisted on nice neat pencil and no messy ink. And as he called out the words for Spelling, and spelled them out, he would casually bang on the nearest boy's head with his speller for emphasis.

"Band. B-A-N-D."

"Brain. B."

Bang.

"R."

Bang.

"A."

Bang"

"I."

Bang.

"N."

Bang.

"Brain."

Bang. He was still doing it to us in grade six. But Brother McGoohan was gone too long and it was inevitable that Brother Stoyles would one day again hear the bell of the boxing ring calling him to action. When that day came, it was hapless Larry Connors who, unbeknownst to him, was seated in the opposite corner.

Brother Stoyles held a grudge against Larry's older brothers, which he sought to nurse here with the younger Connors. This came to a head one spring day when Larry came to class with his head shaved. Although everyone wore his hair short, clipped at the sides, and crew cuts were commonplace, the shaved head was unique. Perhaps Larry had gone up the side of his head with hair clippers like I had, and his mother had to buzz it all off, but the real reason was never heard.

Brother Stoyles took Larry's new haircut as a personal insult. Larry was light-hearted in his response to Brother Stoyles's question about the haircut and Brother Stoyles thought he was being smart.

"Don't think you can make a fool out of me, Connors," he snarled and drew a long black strap out of his sleeve.

"No, Br," stammered Larry in confusion.

"I know your brothers. I know what you're trying to do. You won't get away with it," he yelled and raising his arm swiftly, he struck Larry across the face with the strap.

We were stunned. There was an audible gasp from the class. No one had been hit that year, and to be struck in the face. A red mark appeared immediately on Larry's face. The entire class was in shock at this throwback to the days of terror, but there was something more. There was real anger. The class could not settle, as if our visible indignation might mitigate some of the humiliation and pain that Larry endured, and perhaps restrain Brother Stoyles. But he turned on us as if cornered.

"Don't think you can put one over on me just because I'm a substitute. I'm not Brother McGoohan, and I don't care what he does. You'll listen to me now, or else," and he brought the strap down hard on the desk.

Unlike so many other incidents past, this one shocked more than us students. Larry's family had words with the principal, as did others. Brother McGoohan had words with him too. Someone had failed to call the fight in time. A student had gotten hurt and Brother Stoyles was forced to hang up his gloves for a time out. The sight of meek, self-effacing Brother McGoohan returning a little paler to class was an occasion of great relief and rejoicing, which we directed at him with such energy that he could not, and did not, fail to feel it.

Second Home

There was no one on the street. I couldn't find Brace or Lioney and there was no sign of the big boys when Sharon and Gwenny appeared and asked me to play house. It had been a long time since I had dared to play house with the girls. If caught the penalty was heavy, the mocking of the boys was relentless: "Greg with the girls," "Sissy with the girls." I just couldn't listen to it again.

"No, I can't," I decided.

"Oh come on, Greg."

"No, I can't, if the boys catch me they'll never leave me alone."

"They won't see us. We're allowed in Sharon's back porch," said Gwenny.

"And I've got dishes and food and everything," said Sharon. "It'll be a good game."

"I can't."

"Come on, Greg, you're the best at it. You can be whatever you want."

"I don't know."

"Yes, yes, just one game."

"Okay, just one game, but you can't ever tell any of them."

"No, no, we wouldn't do that."

They really did have a good set-up that day, with a little table and chairs in the McGraths' roomy porch. We settled into our roles. Sharon was the mother, it was her porch, Gwenny the daughter, and me, the husband. With everything set up at home, it was time to go to work and I swung open the porch door to a chorus of laughing and hooting faces. They had been waiting, watching through the door, and now they erupted, all of them, Bruce and Don, even Lioney and Brace, and Wayne was the loudest.

"Oh ho, Dad is going to work, fellas!"

"Where are you going to work, Greg?"

"Ha ha ha."

"What have you got to eat, Mom?"

"Hey, we'll be your children. Ha ha ha. Come on, boys."

I was horrified. Sharon and Gwenny attempted to shoo them off and restore order. I went cold and, with eyes straight ahead, ignoring their taunts, walked stonily out the little lane between McGraths' and Martins' to the empty street, through the laughing, jumping gauntlet delighted at their perfect ambush. It really was rather perfect, I reflected, and what joy it gave them! I don't know if I was angrier with them or Sharon and Gwenny, but it was, needless to say, my last attempt to play house, and it seemed that I was now on the outs with the boys and the girls on the street, but I had other options.

I continued my visits to the Joneses' on weekends and holidays. At first Mom telephoned Mrs. Jones to see that my visits were welcome, but eventually she stopped calling unless I was invited to stay over for the weekend, which was becoming more frequent. When I arrived at the front door and came into the little vestibule, Cathy would run out in a pretty dress, her shiny black hair bouncing, and stand by my legs, looking straight up at me with her bright black eyes. Marywin hung back, looking and half laughing at Cathy, followed by Mrs. Jones.

"Let poor Greg come in now, Kitty. I think someone likes you, Greg. He's very handsome isn't he, Kitty?"

Cathy nodded.

"But just remember, 'Handsome is as handsome does,' right, my darling? But we love you, Greg, because you have a kind heart. I can tell, right, Kitty? And that's everything, Gregory, my love."

All of these observations were made before we were in the hallway where she turned to Cathy and Marywin.

"Come with me now, Kitty and Boo, I have something for you girls, and we'll leave the boys alone for a while."

I would do anything for Mrs. Jones and Andy was devoted to her. He was the good son and if Mike were rebellious, or Kitty went wild, or if Mr. Jones got mad, Andy and Marywin would circle the wagons of good behaviour, and with exceptional maturity deflect the danger and keep a bad situation from getting worse. I was not so mature though I understood the tactics well enough. As my visits became common Cathy would still run out for a look, followed by Marywin's practical observation: "It's only Greg, Cathy. He'll be here all weekend. There'll be lots of time to look at him."

Occasionally Andy paid a return visit to Mount Royal for the sake of form. Andy was extremely uncomfortable at our house full of boys. The shoulder to shoulder contact at my house with the boisterous energy of the basketball stars, Dad and Wayne, was a nerve-racking challenge. I was practiced from years of ignoring and deflecting these challenges, but there was no reason for Andy to develop such skills. We both knew we were far more comfortable on Rostellan Street with Kitty and Boo, and Mrs. Jones and Mrs. Coady catering to us, and where there was no danger of the man of the house harassing us to go out and kick a ball around.

At first Andy's big brother was still at home. Mike knocked about with Barry Lynch, John Scott and Jim Hanley. Handsome and smart and in all the clubs at St. Bon's, they were the picture of privilege, hanging out of Barry's Austin Healey sports car, roaring up Rostellan Street, shouting and laughing. It was a wholesome Catholic shock when all four went into the religious life: Jim to the priesthood, Barry giving up his sports car and the mansion on the hill and his troubled family inside, and going with John and Mike into the Irish Christian Brothers at the tender age of sixteen.

The shock over, and Mike gone, I quietly moved into his bed on the weekends. It was a large, bright room with two beds and a functioning sink in the corner, and was practically a self-contained apartment for me and Andy where we laughed late into the night. There was always an excellent breakfast and the Joneses still had real milk and real butter. I could not have been more comfortable.

Our bike trips now took us as far as Logy Bay over rough gravel roads. Sometimes the extended gang would come along, Andy's friends from the neighbourhood: Greg Campbell, Brendan Walsh and Mike Harrington. Just before the road down into Logy Bay, we stopped at a small store for bars and drinks, which proved awkward for me. All these boys from the East End had allowances and money in their pockets. I did not, and I had not anticipated this stop. By the time we got into the store, Brendan Walsh had bought and consumed his entire ten-cent bar, which still hung out of his mouth, preventing him from speaking or offering some to anyone else. We understood perfectly.

"What are you getting?" Andy asked me.

"Nothing."

"You should get something; this is the last store."

"That's okay, I don't want anything."

"Here, have half of this."

Andy shared all and made light of it all, for which I was very grateful.

The next weekend I was reluctant to go back to Rostellan Street. I couldn't return without money. It was just too awkward and so I was forced to confront Mom.

"Why can't you go back to Andy's?"

"I can't. It's too embarrassing, They all have allowances and I have nothing. Andy had to buy me something last week and I just can't go back."

I was just about in tears at the thought.

"Now, now," soothed Mom, "that's terrible. I know how awkward something like that can be. But you should have told us, Greg. We would have given you some money."

"I didn't know I'd need it. They all have it."

"You and Wayne need an allowance now too. You're both big boys now. I'll talk to Dad and see what we can do."

At her kind response, the tears held back all week flowed freely. A weekly allowance of fifty cents was therefore instituted, which was just enough, if I saved it all week, to get me through the weekends with my more affluent friends. There was always money available to Mom and Vera and Ray and Len on Charlton Street for the children to participate fully in the social life of their peers, so despite her frugality and schemes for "moving up," Mom was not about to see us embarrassed or lose our social footing for lack of necessary funds. As weeks went by the allowance would sometimes dwindle to forty cents or even thirty-five cents. Wayne and I, having grown to expect it, complained, which caused Dad to grumble and bark that we were damn ungrateful, the two of us, and should be thankful for what we got because he damn well didn't have fifty cents in his pocket, case closed.

*

That year Mom announced with great and guarded pleasure that she was thinking of converting to Roman Catholicism and that she was taking instructions from Monsignor Murphy at St. Patrick's. We could see she thought this would please us all enormously, and it did. We were astounded and congratulated her and asked her all kinds of questions, and offered all kinds of help. Dad was certainly pleased, as this completed the picture for him on Sunday morning, which was now totally changed with the whole family heading off to Mass together. It was a great novelty and we all played it up.

Mom didn't want to go down to St. Patrick's, so we went at first to the Basilica of St. John the Baptist, which was grand, but distant and boring, and then out to Mary Queen of the World Church on Topsail Road, which was quite plain, and there was a school above, but it was bright and airy and the priest gave very short sermons, which, combined with a good drive there and back, suited our new Catholic family exactly. In these heady days we even attempted to say the rosary together as a family and almost succeeded. Many Catholic families I knew said it faithfully every night but there was no danger of that happening at our house. Mom was not a religious person. She spoke of God with reverence and affection, but as you would an unpredictable grandfather, and the thought of an afterlife held no great comfort or interest for her. But it was she who taught us our first nightly prayers, simple, short and, of course, Protestant.

"Now I lay me down to sleep . . ."

And now she was converting to Catholicism. But Mom would never be a dyed-in-the-wool Catholic like Mrs. Jones. She could never understand that kind of devotion, and her nature and upbringing were too practical to accommodate the preoccupation of Catholic guilt, occupied as she was with a growing discontent with her own earthly lot and fortunes. Confession was, therefore, baffling to her. But Wayne and I eagerly furnished her with sample Confessions and lists of all the familiar sins that might be safely confessed to without undue alarm or embarrassment. And in the end she managed her conversion with all the grace and decorum of the Queen at a fertility dance in Africa.

In the wake of all the pleasure and satisfaction in this event was the faintest shadow of a loss. If Mom was not religious, she was even less a Catholic, and was closer in temperament to her own United Church, whose polite, common-sense theology basically boiled down to nothing more demanding than "have a nice day." It was, in that sense, a loss of one fragile identity for another that was even less her own. The reason for her conversion was perhaps best expressed by Mom herself: "I thought it would be nice for us all to go to church together."

Makinsons

There was no escaping Scouts. Even though the First St. John's had officially folded and provided a short but glorious reprieve, it was not long before Dad, Tom Furlong, John O'Dea and Dr. Bill Higgins had organized the First St. Bon's Scout Troop and eventually the Cub Pack, and persuaded Brother Darcy to have the school sponsor the troop as an official College activity.

It was also in Mom's interests to have the venture succeed, as the weekly meetings gave her a regular break on Friday evenings, and the annual camp took us off her hands for a full two weeks every summer, her own Scouting holiday. The Scouts were such a good deal that Mom didn't even complain about the uniforms, which were less trouble than the school uniforms, except for the constant sewing-on of badges and stripes. Every year I asked to get out, and every year the request was denied. Insufficient reason. No ironclad, urgent, alternate activity to take me away from the long and ever-winding Scouting trail.

The First St. Bon's camp had gotten off to a shaky start with a hastily organized camp at Beachy Cove. There was no Cub pack yet, but even though I was not old enough to be a Scout, Dad took me along with him on his many visits to set up the troop and run the camp. Being an unofficial Scout was more fun than being a real one. I hung out with Mr. O'Dea's son Brian, who was, like me, a Scout in waiting. Brian was a wild ball of energy and required no convincing to embark on the most treacherous adventures over the surrounding cliffs and woods. We quickly became a gang of two and set up our own patrol called the Loon Patrol.

I was at the time a regular visitor at the Ewing Fur Factory on the bottom of Pleasant Street and I walked down every Saturday to pester them for fur and leather scraps, until I was finally barred, but not before I had amassed enough raw materials to furnish us with leather pouches, fur headbands, and, of course, fur and leather woggles galore. I was responsible for the Indian theme of our improvised uniforms while Brian, born to barter, always made sure we had access to the stores. We set up our headquarters in the beach house the committee had rented for the summer from where we bothered Wayne and Brian's brother John and the other real Scouts as much as we could get away with.

But now I was the real thing, my native amulets were gone, and I had amassed a line of badges and the single stripe of patrol second. Being a Scout was at least more comfortable than being a Cub, the itchy wool jersey having been replaced by a cool, green cotton shirt which left only the knee socks to suffer. With membership booming, the energetic Scout committee had rented a large campsite in Makinsons. Accordingly we all boarded the train on Water Street for a grand trip around the other side of Conception Bay to Brigus Station, where we disembarked in the hot sun for the final bus ride in to the campgrounds.

Thankfully, I was now the owner of an ordinary plaid sleeping bag and could see no evidence of bed rolls. Later I discovered that Dad had gotten sleeping bags for the boys who had none so they could go to camp, and the hard-working and visionary committee saw to it that camp fees were waived for any boys who could not afford them. All this was known, and not known. Dad was very popular and friendly with the boys. I watched him laughing and joking with them during the communal dinner held for the troop and visitors under a big khaki marquee one of the committee members had gotten from the Army. The other boys loved him and he seemed easier with them and to have much more to say to them than he did to me. He made the rounds with good-natured comments to all, radiating happiness. He was the very spirit of Scouting. Clearly I was the "odd man out", as Dad would have it.

After that came a spectacular bonfire with the usual songs. *Val-deri, Val-dera, my knapsack on my back.*

Opening ceremonies over, Dad and the other parents returned home and left their charges to Mr. Colford and Mr. Linegar and the eternal woods. My disinclination for Scouting extended to camp, with its rules and regulations without reward. Mediocrities from school, now wearing badges and stripes, barked frivolous commands amid stacks of damp sleeping bags and smelly duffle bags filled with rumpled clothes and the crumbs from many bars and biscuits. The committee had purchased highly controversial new tents, not the old traditional bell tents of the First St. John's. The new tents were pink, albeit a dark pink, shaped like cabins, with a separate front section and large screened windows, which were pleasant and bright. Unfortunately the window covers were on the inside with a seam along the bottom and zippers on each side. This formed a perfect pocket and when it rained they filled up with water like goatskins. We had to carefully push and squeeze the water back through the exterior screens. Needless to say this design flaw caused constant flooding in the wet weather, but everything was fine when it was fine.

The troop was divided into patrols with troop leaders and patrol leaders. I was not in a position to command and terrorize yet. My day would come but now the patrol leaders were all

Wayne's crowd. I was second-in-command of our patrol, which was led by Gary Mooney. Ours was not an elite patrol as Mooney did not command the full respect of the elect. In the *Adelphian* yearbook his wide, round face, like a jack-o'-lantern, out-grinned all the others in the Scout picture. Mooney was simply too enthusiastic, too respectful of rules, too good a student and too friendly with authority to orbit in the super-cool clique of top Scouts, consisting of Wayne "Mugs" Malone, tall, handsome Joe Murphy and Jack Cochrane, followed hard by Mike Furlong, John O'Dea, Mouse French and Tony Murphy. Scouting suited those favoured sons. They were comfortable in the wild and made their own treetop lookout deep in the woods where they smoked their illicit cigarettes and conducted their business, looking down on all around them.

They cut a fine form as they sauntered back to camp from one of their jaunts in to Makinsons one evening: Joe, Mugs and Jack Cochrane in the middle, with several local girls running after them. Jack was not tall but he was indeed impressive, built, as they say, like a brick shithouse, and he moved with the easy assurance of a mountain lion. You had to be impressed by Jack; at least, I was impressed by him. His thick blond curls were cut short over his watchful, smoky blue eyes, and his full chiselled lips curled slightly, almost cruelly, under a proud aquiline nose. Not given to expressions of enthusiasm, he walked on steadily, even sullenly, as the girls swirled around, galeing after them.

One, a Chinese girl, with white bobby socks, saddle oxfords, lots of crinolines under her flared skirt, and lots of bright red lipstick, was the noisiest of all, squealing and dancing around. It wasn't clear if the girls were chasing the boys or chasing each other around the boys.

"Here, catch this," screamed the Chinese girl in her perfect local accent, as she flung her friend's sweater at Jack.

The angora arrow caught on his chest for a moment then fell unacknowledged to the ground.

"Who owns the Chink?" he deadpanned without breaking stride and passing by me on the sidelines.

I went cold, but the Chinese girl only laughed louder as she picked up the sweater and threw it at him again. This time he brushed it aside with a curse under his breath.

"Okay, calm down now, girls," interposed Mugs. "We'll be back later to sign autographs."

"No, we're going with you," said the Chinese girl, to gales of laughter.

"Yes, yes," her friends agreed.

"No, that would not be a good idea," objected Wayne.

"No girls allowed in camp," confirmed Joe Murphy, the boys cleaning up after Jack.

Such incidents as these cut into the glamour of the golden boy. But cruelty was common, even among the less magnificent. The victims were invariably the weak: the deservingly snotty, like myself, and the undeserving, awkward boys, fresh from their mothers' care, nervous of the wilds, with little or no natural athletic ability, and delusions of fair play. These were the ones who caught the handsome predator's eye, and the occasional ritual kill, with the spilling of tears and feasting on humiliation and embarrassment, was the sad but necessary sacrifice they made on all our behalf, to placate and plump up those in positions of power and privilege.

I numbered friends among these martyrs and spent considerable effort negotiating for their release from petty tyrannies. I myself was not often one of their prey for several reasons. I was not a greenhorn, and had an extensive, if unwanted, knowledge of Scouting and I knew my way around the woods. My most powerful weapon was desperation. I had nothing to lose. I didn't want to be in Scouts or at camp. I would rather be riding my bike and philosophizing with Andy. As much as I was attracted to the Rat Pack and wanted their approval, I knew that if they knew of that attraction there would be no power on earth that could, or would want to, protect me. I knew the dire importance of hiding any such need, and of showing the opposite in fact, and camouflaged my feelings with a sharp, sarcastic tongue, so that although an attack might succeed, the counterattack would be so unpleasant, it was generally judged not worth the effort. I could also outrun them if necessary, which I did on Sports Day, and beat them at their own games.

"A big fish in a small pond," said Wayne, after I won all my events and was declared champion in my division.

There were even decent prizes this time, and I walked away with a flashlight, a hunting knife and a compass. These prizes meant a lot to me—too much, in fact. These were trophies taken from the enemy and treasured like the shrunken heads of my would-be tormentors. Wayne came that afternoon to inspect the proofs of my standing.

"You did all right for yourself," he said with some surprise. "Hey, this is a good knife. I'm going to take this."

"No, you're not," I countered.

"Sure, you won't use it. I'll bring it back later."

"No. Don't take it!" I yelled after him as he walked through the pink flaps.

I followed after him in my bare feet and underwear.

"Come back!"

"You can come and get it," he taunted, and he headed into the woods, sure I would not follow. But I did. I was not going to let him get away with this, and I struggled through the thicket, calling after him to stop, stepping over the broken branches and rocks until I stepped on a sharp stick and yelled out.

"Go back, boy," Wayne said. "I'll bring the knife back later."

"No," I screamed, totally beyond myself now. "Give me back my prize! Give it back."

Wayne stopped, and looked at me.

"All right, boy, don't have a fit. I was gonna give it back. Here then, take the stupid knife," and he pitched it into the loamy forest floor.

I grabbed the knife and stumbled back out of the woods, ignoring as best I could the feelings of futility and stupidity that accompanied me back to the tent, where I wiped off the stupid knife and put it back with the stupid flashlight. My foot was not cut. I lay back and contemplated my advanced state of nerves. Oh well, tomorrow would be Sunday and a day of relative rest.

After the ritual excursion to Mass in the strangely modern new church in North River, we were bused back to camp and set free. Uniforms were stripped off with glee and replaced with T-shirts and shorts. It was hot and beautiful and it was a superlative luxury to lie on the stack of hot duffle bags outside the tent and do nothing in the sun. Gordon Bailey sat himself down next to me and leaned over.

"Just feel this," he said.

"What?" I asked, raising my head and squinting at my old enemy.

"This won't hurt," assured Gordon. "Just stay there and leave your arm with the palm up. Now close your eyes."

Could I trust him? I relaxed into the heat. Gordon barely touched the inside of my forearm with his fingertips, and then very lightly drew them down, all the way from the inside of my elbow to my wrist and over my palm to the tips of my fingers.

"Doesn't that feel good?" he enthused.

I had to agree.

"Do it to me," he went on.

I had no objections. Gordon had recently been friendly, even made a point of it, as though we had never been anything but friends, and so that's the way I played the scene too. His white forearm was tight and muscular, and could no doubt still throw a good punch. But I felt no danger of that now as Gordon's eyes fluttered back in his head and he half laughed as I drew my fingers down along his arm to his fingers, the savage beast soothed.

This was a much more interesting activity for strong forearms than punching, I thought, and Gordon, it seemed, couldn't get enough of it, so back and forth we went. I did my best to meet expectations and we were quite numb and reduced to the barest of touches, just grazing the fine hairs of the inner arm, when Mr. Colford abruptly interrupted us.

"What are you fellas at?"

"We're just playing around," answered Gordon brightly.

"Well, you shouldn't be at that, so if you can't find anything useful to do, I can find something for you."

As far as friends went, camp was a patchy affair. You knew all the boys there by sight from St. Bon's, but were not always lucky enough to have your regular friends there, and so you had camp buddies, sort of second stringers and guys from different classes you did not usually get an opportunity to be with, guys like tall, pale Earl Benson, or "Bean and Sons" Benson, as I called him, which did not please him, and vivacious Paul McCormack, adopted son of the local dry cleaning magnate, who looked like a satyr with his large, seductive almond eyes, and was to that point the most brazen sissy I had ever met. I had a strange admiration for this, although for Paul it was not altogether a matter of bravery. Very comfortable with himself, and indulged at home, he was determined to be indulged abroad. Paul could speak up for himself.

John Kendall could not so well. Tall, awkward and shy-seeming, he was actually very intelligent and articulate, but utterly unable to disguise his true feelings and opinions, or his ignorance of things Scouting, and so was bound to rouse the curiosity of the sporting set, out for game. For some reason, John in particular came in for it, and I saw him more than once heading off on his own into the woods to escape, and it made me seethe with anger.

The beauty of Makinsons was a great comfort. The camp was laid out in two sprawling fields in the valley, which was bordered by a high ridge covered in dark spruce woods. The Makinsons River flowed through the valley and a smooth dirt road wound along its banks through the woods to an abandoned cotton mill where the machines still stood in tangled disarray. The sun streamed through the large shattered windows onto the rough wooden floor now littered with millions of tiny metal pellets. This bright, ghostly haunt made an ideal destination for my walks and I sometimes brought a lunch and a book to spend the afternoon on the banks of the river by the mill, indulging in occasional swims. This practice I shared with other camp buddies in need of sanctuary, long walks and talks. Returning to camp the long way we stopped to visit Miss Annie Kelly in her antique saltbox cottage in a clearing of the forest. In the hayfield alongside, her hired man John stopped his work and leaned on his scythe, the top of his long johns soaked with perspiration, his sleeves pushed back up over his thick brown forearms. John was a big man with one eye slightly turned. He looked down at us with practised patience.

"Now that's my bread and butter there, boys," he said with the gentlest reproach, pointing to the fresh path we had just cut through the hay.

My literal mind struggled to get his meaning. Did they make bread out of hay, like wheat? Slowly I gathered that the hay was his cash crop and should not be beaten down.

"You have to go around," he said.

"Sorry, John."

"That's all right, boys. Miss Annie is inside."

"It's hot today. Would you boys like a glass of lemon crystals?" asked Miss Annie, as she always did, uncovering the top of the bottle and putting a spoonful of the yellow crystals and sugar in each glass.

She then filled the glasses with dippers of cool well water. The old, silver cast-iron step stove was not lit and the little kitchen was cool as we sat on the painted wooden chairs and chatted. She enlightened us on the challenges of farming and we told her of the dangers of Scouting. Miss Annie was no longer young, but not ancient. Her salt-and-pepper hair was pulled back in a loose bun, and she wore an apron over her summer print dress and a kind smile on her pleasantly weathered face, as always. We looked closely at Big John as he came in after us for his glass of lemon crystals. We spent much time trying to decide if John was hired help or Miss Annie's man. The occasional sudden familiarity in their routine of gentle respect convinced me of the latter, which both shocked and impressed me. Imagine Miss Annie! She had the manners and aura of a saint, but her humble cottage lacked the usual icons of nodding devotion. She was a woman of mystery.

John Kendall's mother knew Miss Annie and he took refuge there more than once, but he had to leave now because this evening he was on grub duty and responsible for, though largely incapable of, lighting the campfire, peeling and boiling vegetables, opening the tins, and keeping the fire going without burning the bully beef. I was certain he would get all the advice he needed to complete his tasks.

"I don't know what we'll do with those fields the Scouts are in next year," said Big John to Annie. "They won't be any good to grow hay."

"I think we're going to camp at Second Pond next year," I said.

"That's right," said John.

"I like it here better."

"Yes, this is a grand spot. We're going to miss you when you go."

"You won't have anyone cutting through your hayfields."

"Oh, did you walk through John's hayfield? He doesn't like that."

"I know."

"You're from Town. You didn't know the difference," said John. "But now you do. We all have to learn. Now if you cut through my hayfield again tomorrow, that would be another matter. If we're not going to use them fields, Annie, you should let one of them go."

"I'm not selling any land, John."

"Who's going to keep it up? I can just keep up with the hay we got here."

"Don't worry about that now."

As they talked, I was struck by a realization I should have had in the spring when I came out with Dad, Wayne, Kerry and Beni, and Brother French and Mr. Linegar to look over the new campsite, and Dad had talked to Miss Annie and John, but I did not understand then what I suddenly did now: that Miss Annie was the owner of all the land we were camping on and of all the land around. This was her empire, which she ruled from her little saltbox, and the First St. Bon's Troop were her tenants, mere serfs. As I processed this new information, a small plan formed itself in my mind for the liberation of at least John Kendall, if not others, from the dungeon. But how to enact my plot to greatest effect?

The next day brought the answer with a midsummer's camp drama that centered on Gary Mooney. I got the scoop from the horse's mouth.

"Yes, the boys tied him down to an anthill and put honey on him," confessed Wayne. "They were going to do the same thing to John Kendall but they couldn't find him."

"Why?" I asked unbelieving.

Sometimes, at odd moments, Wayne and I shed our Scout roles and talked "off the record."

"Well, you know Mooney. He was just being Mooney, getting on everyone's nerves, quoting camp rules at Jack and the boys when they were trying to have a butt."

"And so you tied him to an anthill!"

"I didn't, no, I didn't get involved. I tried to stop them, but you know the boys."

Yes, I did know them, and knew Wayne was probably telling the truth. The anthill wasn't his style, not that he was above deriving pleasure from hazing, teasing and even tormenting greenhorns, especially if they were at all snotty or spoiled or stuck up. But really Wayne prided himself on being an unofficial champion and protector of those in danger of being bowled over by bullies at school. These would include the intellectually superior but socially and physically inept, the rich and gullible but kind-hearted, and the less well endowed generally. In his role as defender he made several good but unlikely friends for a "big man on campus," friends like Edmund Mary McGrath, whose parents were so desperate for a child they promised the Virgin Mary to name their child after her should she answer their constant prayers. She did. The McGraths received their baby from heaven and the baby received the Virgin's name. But whether their prayers had been imperfect, or the Virgin wished to remind them of their promise, the baby was born with a cleft palate and grew up a shy and retiring boy, as you might expect of a boy child with a cleft palate named Mary. But no one made fun of Edmund Mary for long. His good friend Mugs Malone saw to that. But Mugs was either not able or not motivated to save his old friend Mooney. Mooney was more than capable of defending himself, and once freed from the stakes stomped off to the troop leaders and complained long and loud.

"The boys are out of control anyway, but they won't get off so easily with this one," continued Wayne.

Here was my cue.

"Well, they should be very careful about going after John Kendall," I drawled.

"Why," said Wayne, "they almost got him too."

"It's a good thing for them that they didn't."

"Why?" asked Wayne, genuinely curious now.

"Because Miss Annie is John Kendall's aunt," I lied, stretching John Kendall's family connection to the breaking point.

"His aunt?" cried Wayne.

"That's why John goes there," I continued.

"Oh is it?" said Wayne, following closely.

"Yes, and of course Miss Annie owns all the land we're camping on."

"I know that," shot back Wayne, of course he already knew that.

"Miss Annie has been noticing that her nephew isn't very happy at camp, so John told her why he wasn't so happy."

"Oh shit," said Wayne. "Who did he say?"

"No names yet, but Miss Annie said to tell her if it keeps up and she'd have a word with nice Mr. Malone."

Wayne jumped off the ground. I thought this was a nice touch and would bring the matter home to him, and I was not wrong.

"She didn't. You're making this up," he barked.

"Oh no, I'm not. She's John's aunt all right," I stated coolly, heady with the wonderful result of my deception.

"Oh shit. Okay, that's it. I'm not taking the shit for this. His bloody aunt. The boys are going to cool it. Okay, thanks for that and tell me anything else you find out and tell John Kendall to just shut up and everything will be fine. I'll personally guarantee his safety, tell him."

"I will," I said helpfully, astounded at my success.

I was back in Wayne's and the boys' good books, and got them to back off us. I felt very good about myself for at least a day, Visitors' Day to be exact.

It arrived with a cool, damp fog, which Mom was dressed for in a new beret and camel hair jacket. The boys crowded around. "I wouldn't mind having a mother like that," they chuckled, giving her the eye and me the wink as they tumbled back into the tent loaded with tins of chocolate cakes and biscuits, bags of oranges, bars and sodas, the usual offerings for homesick campers from worried parents.

"What did you bring me?" I asked Mom after opening greetings.

"Nothing," she said.

"Nothing!" I gasped.

"No, Greg," she was evasive. "I thought you were too old for that stuff now."

Too old for chocolate cake, I thought to myself. No, better not say it. Just let it go. Mom turned to continue her tour of the facility, leaving me to reflect on the advantages of being her favourite. Aunt Mil bounced in behind her, followed by Uncle Bob. The two couples were going on an outing after they visited the camp. Uncle Bob was still trying for a boy, so he often hung around with Dad and the Scouts, hoping the environment might somehow create conditions favourable to beget a son of his own.

Uncle Bob and Aunt Mil were very modern, and brought Wayne and me smart new instant popcorn kits, with the popcorn in its own small, aluminum-foil skillet with a cardboard top. I was very grateful not to return to the tent empty-handed. When they had gone on their way, I tried to cook the popcorn over the fire, but left the cardboard top on and burned the whole thing to a black coal, after which I removed the top, revealing a swirl of foil, which Wayne had correctly pulled up into a lovely dome, and consequently had the enjoyment of the fresh popcorn with his buddies. I knew it was the thought that counted, and for that I was truly grateful. But it was a bad omen.

The next day brought more cool grey weather. I was on grub duty and the fire was roaring with a big billy of soup on the grill, and as usual, I was arguing with Mooney over it.

"That soup is done, Gary. We should take it off."

"No, not yet, Malone. It needs to boil for another fifteen minutes."

"No, it's just going to stick on," I said, looking at the soup roiling up to the top of the pot.

"Just leave it. It will be fine."

The patrol leader had the last word, so I picked up the ladle to stir the soup, but as I leaned in, a spark flew up into my face and I jerked back involuntarily with the ladle full of boiling soup, which splashed over the inside of my thighs. I didn't realize this right away. I just felt the sudden, wildly stinging pain and ran screaming at the top of my lungs into the field with my eyes closed. Joe Murphy stopped me, putting his hands on my shoulders, and I started to laugh weakly.

"What's wrong?" he asked, looking straight at me.

I stopped and looked at him.

"I don't know," I said and started to laugh again.

He looked down at my pants. Gary Mooney came over and led me away to lie down in the pink tent. My screams were heard for miles around and a crowd had gathered. The troop leaders conferred. Would they take me into Town? Mr. Lahey knew first aid and they cut my pants off and found two large, wrinkled, red patches of scalded skin. The patches felt hot and cold to me, raw, impossible to touch, even to put cream on, so they just put clean bandages on, an agonizing process, by which time it was truly dark and I was glad to be able to fall asleep.

My next day was a very stiff one. There was no getting up and walking around. Nevertheless it was decided that there was no need to transport me to Town, or more precisely, there was no need to disturb Dad, and, therefore, Mom. This was the gist of Dad's instructions I deduced from the muttered considerations that came to me in bits and pieces from outside the flaps as I lay on my back in the pink glow of the tent.

I was given many comics and had visitors enough to read them. Chris Cumerford stayed cross-legged in the corner long enough to read two Batmans and the classic comic of *The Three Musketeers* before he tired and left. There were offerings of chocolate cake, biscuits and oranges from the recent booty of V Day. Mugs and Joe Murphy paid a duty call to inspect the damage and were surprised to find me still there.

Even the great J. C. himself came and shook his lion's mane over my pitiful state, and so I presumed my deception about John Kendall's "aunt" still held. But not even the regulars could stay for long, and by the third day on my back I knew every lump and depression in the small bit of ground that had become my home.

The boredom of day three was shattered by the changing of the bandages. The removal of the old bandages, and the skin that came off with them, was an experience that focussed my mind and the troop leaders', and rather than repeat that ordeal, Dad was finally notified. I was relieved to find my parents upset they had not been contacted before, and on day four I was removed to Town, where every day Mom took me down the street to St. Clare's Hospital to have the bandages and skin removed and fresh bandages put on. The new skin would take a while to grow back, but before the end of the summer I could walk properly and then finally ride my bike across town to visit Andy, where I was showered with sympathies from Cathy and Marywin, Mrs. Jones and Mrs. Coady too, who buttressed her concern with plates of cupcakes.

Teacher's Pet

I didn't understand why Brother Rogers liked me. It puzzled me. It almost troubled me. This was grade seven after all, not grade one or two. All the teachers' pets were well established by now and I had never been one of them. It was even possible to predict which of the small coterie of favourites the Brother would like this year if, in fact, he was the sort to like anyone at all. And if he was, it was usually little John Sullivan or little Danny Williams or even little Kerrin Martin, but never, ever me. I simply wasn't the type.

My brother had been the teacher's favourite, in fact, he had been my grade four teacher's favourite. Brother Clancy never lost an opportunity to praise him to me and questioned me carefully about his well-being.

"How is your brother Wayne today? He twisted his knee in practice yesterday. I hope he's back in school today."

"Yes, Br."

"Good for him. He's one of our basketball stars, you know. But Mr. Malone's brother keeps his marks up too. That's the sign of a real champion, right, Mr. Neville?"

"Yes, Br," answered Dennis Neville to he knew not what.

I was struck by his keen, steady interest in Wayne, his constant questions about him, which I could hardly answer. He seemed to know Wayne better than I did. What was I missing? How was it that Wayne shone in his eyes while I was merely a dull speck in the corner, whose only value lay in my relationship to the tall, dashing star forward? Yes, the basketball, of course that was it. Oh well, I was, and knew it, much safer out of the direct glare of Brother Clancy's fancy, where I might happily fail to meet his high expectations whatever they might be, leaving the hard work of maintaining Brother Clancy to Wayne, who through no apparent effort on his part managed to keep him in a radiant good mood at least during the brief minutes Brother Clancy was thinking about him. I was properly grateful to Wayne for these rare and radiant interludes, as indeed the whole class was, to the dullest boy, for any person, story, thought, notion or action that might please, soothe or subdue the volcanic perfectionist who guarded us. I was equally doubtful as to how long he could hold such power over the mercurial monk before the unpredictable, inevitable crash.

But that was years ago. Now we were in grade seven with Brother Rogers. Our classroom was not in the main school building but in the monastery, and was actually part of the library, which had been partitioned off. There was a short flight of stairs at the front of the room. At the back two tall windows looked out onto the back of St. Bonaventure's statue, whose vacant stone eyes stared out at the campus beyond.

Brother Rogers seemed very pleased with his new class and singled me out for comment, and not unpleasantly, right from the beginning. He didn't seem to care that I was neither basketball star nor scholar as he strode down the aisle towards me giving quick instructions and warnings to other boys in his path.

"Now take your time and write neatly. Some of you more observant ones may have noticed I'm wearing glasses. Have pity on me and do not make me go blind trying to read your chicken scratch. Oh my, Mr. Simms," he said, squinting and holding Richard Simms's scribbler at bay. "You weren't thinking of handing this in to me, were you?"

"No, I guess not, Br," blushed Simms, laughing nervously.

"Oh good," sighed Brother Rogers. "Thank you, Mr. Simms."

His tone, mock-serious and teasing, could become real enough if challenged.

Brother Rogers was not one of the most feared Brothers. He was playful, answered questions with questions, and he liked sports, which made me wonder why he liked me. But apparently he did. He had assigned us all our places, two to a seat, and he put me in the back by the wall. Passing the others, he came to rest behind me, leaned down over me, completely ignoring my desk-mate, John Sullivan, even pushing him slightly aside. What? What's happening?

Brother Rogers was a grown-up to me, but in fact he was only twenty-two, slight and quick on his feet. His wavy brown hair with its natural widow's peak was close-cropped in a perfect brush cut. His face was pale and narrow, his nose straight and fine, and his mouth, though small, was well shaped and turned up in the slightest curl, which suggested something unexpected. His front left tooth and the two next to it had been knocked out playing hockey, and the plate he wore didn't exactly match his own teeth and slipped sometimes when he spoke. The plastic frames of his glasses were dark on top and clear below and when he removed them his poor, grey-blue eyes looked dull and set back from being so long behind such strong lenses. It made me feel sorry for him. But he needed no pity. Athletic and cheerful, always with a hello or a quick boisterous tussle with the boys on his way through to the monastery for lunch, Brother Rogers was as close to "one of the boys" as a teacher can be, and although his looks could not be called strikingly handsome, his overall appearance was as pleasant as his manners were direct and engaging.

As he leaned in from behind, I could feel the warmth of his freshly shaven face close to mine. At least there was no stinky breath or dandruff. It was only Brother Rogers, after all. But I didn't know why he was there and I was completely tense. How long would he stay? I daresay John Sullivan and the others wondered too. But he was clearly in no hurry to depart. What did he want? What was he expecting?

"Relax, don't let me make you nervous," he said, squeezing my shoulder and making himself comfortable. "You just go on."

I nervously started the exercise while Brother Rogers looked on casually, correcting me occasionally. He answered Andy's questions from behind me.

"Turn around," he would say if anyone looked back. "There's nothing to see back here, Mr. Harrington."

"I'm not in your way, am I?" he asked me, half serious.

"No, Br."

"Good. Go on with your work then. Don't mind me."

And except for the occasional foray around the class, he stayed by me the entire morning.

I stumbled up the classroom steps to lunch, dazed and apprehensive. Yes, the others looked at me with widened eyes, all saying, what's going on with you? Yes, what is going on with me? What am I doing right? Or wrong? It can't be anything I'm doing. I'm just sitting there frozen. I'm not doing anything. It's him.

I had been an indifferent student to this point. Motivated primarily by fear and pride, I had some talent for writing and public speaking and had won the oratorical contest the year before with a stirring sentimental rendition of "The Highwayman" by Alfred Noyes. It had worked for Wayne and he was right in assuring me it would work for me. I had failed so far, however, to distinguish myself in anything athletic or popular except running away, of course, which I did well by necessity, anyone living in the West End having urgent need of frequent and speedy escape. My budding reputation in grade six as class clown had not endeared me to handsome Brother McGoohan. Now this favouritism. It was all very unfamiliar, even overwhelming, but not completely unpleasant.

This special arrangement did not happen once or even occasionally. No. This was it, our everyday routine. Brother Rogers would start class and then, moving down to my desk, lean in next to me. He smiled, chatted, explained my mistakes, encouraged me. He told me I was smart, prodded and nudged me till I lost patience and started to answer him back, which seemed to amuse him.

Every day it was much the same. I grew accustomed to his leaning in, joking, teasing, then bobbing up when another student wanted something, then back down to our little club. Sometimes after a long time with him bent over me I would be almost crushed down on top of my scribbler and I would have to push back up against him to get space to write, and he would poke me and laugh and lean in again till I complained again.

"Oh, you want me to leave, do you?" he challenged.

"No, Br."

More often now I would linger on after class talking with Brother Rogers, Andy and others, and sometimes on Saturdays he and I would go for a hike up on Signal Hill with Andy and Brother Pigott. The Brothers were not actually permitted to have particular friends, but Brother Pigott was Brother Rogers's friend and as close to sane as he could be, coming from Brooklyn and having been raised, as he himself professed, on a steady diet of B horror movies. In his favourite, which he described in great detail a year later, the pregnant mother is buried alive and gives birth to the child in the coffin and dies. The child eats the mother to stay alive and claws its way to the surface, a crazed infant horror hero. We were fascinated. Such movies hadn't come to St. John's yet, and I was amazed that Brother Pigott had not only seen so many, but had also survived them so cheerfully.

Brother Pigott was young and pale, a Yank with a slow, deliberate shuffle, he could not be hurried, even when he was running, at which he was very swift. His face was heavy and startling for one so young. He had a broad brow and a large lantern jaw, while his cheekbones and cheeks were sunken back. This all gave him an appearance not unlike a character in one of his favourite B movies. Brother Pigott had learned a great deal from these movies and was not above taking full advantage of his stern looks to frighten small, skylarking children. He would shuffle up to his victims and hang over them, looking down from under heavy brows with a well-practised deadpan, saying nothing. If that didn't produce the desired effect, he would flutter one eyelid and roll his eyes back in his head a little. That usually did the trick, unless you were very pathetic and made him crack, then his dark face would suddenly light up like a teenager's as he rocked with laughter.

He looked like a teenager one Saturday, leaning into the last of the winter gales on top of Signal Hill, the navy wool earflaps of his hat tied down under his big chin, his wild red face gasping for air and breaking up with laughter.

"Oh my gosh, I'm being blown away! We'll all be blown away."

Trying to climb the icy hill, we kept slipping back down, bumping into each other, laughing, grabbing at the rocks protruding through the ice to stop our backwards slide.

"Help. I'm sliding over," I said, laughing, and noticing there actually was a hundred-foot drop nearby.

"Jumpin' Judas," roared Brother Rogers. "What are you doing over there? I told you boys not to go that way. Malone, get back over here," he said, dancing along the dry rocks.

"I can't help it. I'm sliding," I laughed.

Out of breath and grabbing a sliver of rock, I slowed to a stop just as Andy, hysterical, slid into me and we lost the sliver and started sliding and pawing madly at the ice just to stay on the spot.

"Grab on here, look," said Brother Rogers, skipping over onto a piece of bare rock. But as we grabbed on, we slid into him and bowled him off his feet.

But he changed our direction, so at least we didn't fly off the edge, and we all came to a stop on a patch of ground, laughing helplessly at our hopelessly ineffectual efforts.

"Oh my, they're bad boys, Brother Pigott."

"V-Very, very b-bad, Brother Rogers," Brother Pigott stuttered, still laughing. "That's why we have to sp-spend extra time with them—to keep them on the path."

"That's right, but there's not much hope of that, Brother."

On another Saturday, the ice long gone, I sat with Brother Rogers on Signal Hill in the warm sun, finishing off one of the peanut butter and jelly sandwiches the maids in the monastery kitchen had packed up for him. I questioned him about his family.

"I have three sisters and three brothers."

"Are you the oldest or the youngest?"

"I'm the oldest."

"The oldest? What were your parents like?"

"My parents are wonderful people. I am very lucky. My father had a small business and worked hard all his life."

"And your mother?"

"My mother is a saint, and she put up with a lot for us."

"But not from you?"

"No, I was perfect."

"How old were you when you joined the Christian Brothers?"

"I was eighteen."

"Eighteen?"

"Yes, but I didn't know what I wanted to do with my life, and Brother Brennan, not the one you had in grade three, but his older brother, Brother Brennan Sr., suggested that I join the Brothers, and I liked Brother Brennan and I liked what the Brothers were doing, so I decided to give it a try."

"Right."

"So what are you going to do after school?"

"I don't know."

"Well, you better be careful, or you could end up like me."

"Are you ever sorry you joined the Brothers?"

"Only when you guys drive me crazy."

"So never, right?"

He laughed.

"What is your real name, Brother Rogers?"

"My real name is Brother Rogers to you."

"No, c'mon. Your real name?"

"You want to know my Christian name?"

"Yes."

"Why?"

"I just want to."

"Edward."

"Edward?"

"Yes, but you can't call me that."

"What did your friends call you, Ed or Eddie?"

"They called me Brother Rogers."

"No, they didn't. Come on, Ed," I said pointedly.

"Oh ho, Ed is it? Okay, that's it for you, mister."

"I think I'll call you Ed from now on."

"Oh you will, will you?" he said, grabbing the front of my jacket.

"Yeah."

"Oh no, you won't," he said, flushing and feigning serious, and pulling me towards him in a half headlock, my face close to his. "You'll call me Brother Rogers," he said.

✻

My voice was changing and I was thrown out of the Vesper choir.

"Someone is off back there," said Rainer Rees in his German accent, banging high C on the baby grand.

He turned on the stool, his wooden leg shooting out straight to the side, his good eye searching the unfamiliar faces of his choir. His glass eye stared out the window catching the light, the original and his other leg having been left behind on the battlefields of Europe. What was it like to lose your leg and your eye? How old was he? Was he fighting for the Nazis? No, he was fighting against the Nazis, he was trying to get out. He stepped on a landmine and lost his leg and one eye and took some shrapnel to his head. The Catholics took care of him . . . Wow! Now he was here.

"Okay, one at a time, *Pange lingua* . . . all right, now you. Okay, that's enough . . . yes you, *Pange,* good, yes you . . . no, it's him, that's the one. His voice is over."

I knew it was going to be me but I tried to fake it anyway. Brother Chaney bared his strong teeth at me and narrowed his icicle eyes.

"Goodbye, Mr. Malone. You can go back to class now. We won't be needing you anymore."

Brother Chaney had been brought in as Mr. Rees's enforcer after Brother McHugh's unfortunate collapse. Brother McHugh had been our earnest but ineffectual choirmaster until Vesper service one Sunday evening at the end of the last term when the whole choir, or at least those who had bothered to show up, had ground to a dead stop in the middle of a verse. He hurled several desperate threats at us before bursting into tears and fleeing the altar. Now it was my turn to go.

"Yes, and thank you for . . ." Rainer Rees trailed off as he swung back to the piano, the fringe of longish brown hair flipping over his ears. "All right, the rest of you, from the top, *Pange lingua.*" I left rejected and free, humiliated and elated, and took a slow walk down the cavernous staircase back to the classroom.

More than my voice had changed. I was a little taller, which I didn't mind, but my nose had gotten bigger and worst of all, right behind my own back, my bum had grown. My good brother Wayne was quick to point out these changing features for me in giddy, derisive tones.

"Hey, Greg, don't worry if you're getting a big arse. Your nose is getting so big it will balance it out." Gales of laughter from the other side of the bedroom.

Well, I guess Wayne was finally getting me back for saying he had a head like a building.

"Hey, Pinocchio. Ha ha ha."

"Very funny."

"Don't worry, Greg. The rest of you is bound to catch up with the nose and the butt, ha ha ha, eventually. Ha ha ha."

I closed my eyes and thought of Pat Royal's older brother Robert. I was sure he would never treat Pat the way Wayne treated me. He was the handsomest student in all St. Bon's and looked just like the guy in the Toro lawn mower ad. I'd torn the page out of the magazine. Pat looked up to Robert, and so did I. By this time I had long decided on the most attractive boys in the school and the most worthy, though they were not always the same, and I had no idea yet what to do about such feelings.

John Byrne was dark and good looking, but too surly to tamper with. His best friend, Pat Royal, well, Pat was perfect, beautiful, blond, blue-eyed, star of hockey and basketball, and most impressive of all, never mean to anyone, even when he had cause to be, which was the reason, and when you think about it, a very good one, for electing him class president year after year, a true golden boy. But for all I loved Pat, I could not imagine that he had anything but the most innocent and wholesome yearnings, and try as I might, I could not convince myself they were anything like mine.

I also really liked Denis Barry, with his shiny black hair and his merry, mischievous blue eyes. Denis was fun. He boasted he had webbed toes and I really wanted to see them. In a clumsy attempt to get more friendly with him, I playfully butted him out of the way with my hip as he was bent over his desk.

"You're blocking the aisle, Barry."

Unfortunately he shot forward and hit his head off the corner of the desk. He came up wincing in pain, holding his head.

"Oh my God, Denis, I'm sorry."

"It's okay," he said.

He wasn't mad.

"I didn't mean to hit your head. I mean . . ."

"I know."

"I mean, I was just . . ."

"Yeah, I know."

"Sorry."

"It's okay, boy, forget it."

Now I'd gone too far apologizing.

"Right."

My efforts ended in failure. I would have to try again.

But I was not thinking of anyone in particular when Wayne knocked on our class door for me one day. I had forgotten my lunch and he was dropping it off.

"Greg Malone is wanted at the door, Br," said Kevin Whittle.

"Go and get it," said Brother Rogers.

I sat rooted to my seat for I was, at that very moment, struggling to subdue an erection that was so hard it was painful, and though it wasn't an entirely new sensation, it had never come upon me so determined to have its way in public before. I stalled and looked up from my book. We had changed seats lately and I was nearer the front, but I would still have to walk across the front of the class and up the stairs to the door in plain view. Kevin Whittle was looking at me, still standing, sensing something. He was worse than Don Piercey's beagle.

I got up reluctantly and shuffled slowly into the aisle, allowing as much time as possible for the erection to subside. But the upstart member refused all attempts to get into lower gear. My attention and panic only increased its prominence and my crotch was so tight and tense, I was sure I'd get a cramp if I tried to straighten up. What was I going to do? How could I get across the room? As I slowly rose to a full hunch in the aisle, I saw that all my worst fears were realized. The front of my pants had all the appearance of a small bell tent stretched tightly over a large pole. I began to perspire.

Kevin Whittle spotted it right away and his face lit up like he had found a five-dollar bill. He sat back down and nudged Dennis Neville. I instinctively swung my hand in front of my crotch and kept it there as a screen, an awkward, vain gesture that only drew attention and guffaws from Dennis Neville and John Byrne in the front, which were quickly picked up by the seats behind. Brother Rogers looked up.

"What's going on there?"

I was in the middle of the steps, in full view. I felt his eyes on me. His face registered the scene but did not break.

"Hey, it's none of your business what Mr. Malone is doing, Mr. Neville.'

More sniggers.

"That's enough," barked Brother Rogers.

I arrived outside the door into the wide, cool hallway in a full sweat.

"Ho ho," said Wayne, taking in the situation in a glance. "What's going on down there?"

I could not have been more humiliated. I shot him a miserable look and took the brown bag containing my otherwise forgettable lunch. Nothing the sad sack contained could possibly be worth all the embarrassment.

"Better get a grip, Greg boy," said Wayne, and left.

I stood motionless and dejected yet still taut, waiting and praying for relaxation, which never came. I managed only to get it into second gear, which looked just as bad. There was nothing else to do but go back in. The door was open. Brother Rogers could see me from his desk. So, holding my lunch bag at a slightly unnatural angle in front of me, I descended the stairs into all the waiting smirks and sniggers, muffled titters and meaningful stares the boys could get away with.

"Quite the bone, Malone," whispered Danny Williams.

"Malone the Bone," echoed Kevin Whittle.

My dignity now gone, like the ephemeral pubescent display that now evaporated between my legs, I sat down, deflated, and looked coldly across the aisle at my tormentors.

More titters. God! Brother Rogers came to my rescue with only the trace of a smirk.

"Hey there. Mr. Whittle. Mr. Neville. Not one more sound out of you."

Of course Danny Williams escaped detection. And then to me: "You too. Back to work."

✦

"I'm going to open the window," I said to Andy, one warm afternoon after class. "Where's the window pole?"

"Wait for Br Rogers," said Andy.

"There it is."

I weaved into the tall casement window with the uplifted pole.

"Why don't you just open the bottom one?" pleaded Andy.

"It's all right. I've done this before," I said, thrusting the metal tip into what I thought to be the waiting hole, but in the glare of the setting sun I misjudged the distance, and drove the top of the pole straight through the large pane, sending slivers of frosted glass raining down into the classroom.

"Oh my God, Greg," whispered Andy in awe. "What did you do?"

"I missed. I . . ."

"Oh my God, this is it!" said Andy, twisted in fear and anguish.

"Oh no. I know. Oh no." I groaned.

"What will we do?"

"What can we do?"

"We can't do anything," hissed Andy. "This is it!"

I had gone too far this time. Our charmed existence was over and we waited miserably for the well-known boom to be lowered.

But that would not be today. Brother Rogers came down the stairs two at a time, relaxed and humming. He did a double take at the window.

"What happened here?"

I fumbled out the story. He was unfazed.

"Don't touch it. We don't want you cutting yourself. The janitor will get that. Now you two hoodlums better get out before you wreck the place and get me in trouble with Brother Darcy."

Outside Andy was incredulous.

"I don't believe what happened."

"I know. We are so lucky."

"Lucky! You can get away with anything."

"I don't know about that."

"I do. He's down by your desk the whole morning."

"I know."

"And in the afternoon too."

"I know."

"And you break the window out of the classroom and he . . . he must *really* like you."

"Yeah."

And indeed I flourished under Brother Rogers's patronage. I had risen to the top ten by Christmas, and was moving up. So I was smart enough if I cared to be. It was a revelation to me. Now I would have to keep it up.

Our famous friendship could not be denied. At first, of course, I had protested that I was not his favourite, but the guffaws this was met with put an end to any further attempt at denial. It was all "Brother Rogers and Greg," "Greg and Brother Rogers," and it wasn't just our class that noticed. The other grade seven classes, and even my brother and his friends—everyone knew. I was dismayed to see Wayne and his grade nine gang coming down the hall outside our class where Brother Rogers was giving me instructions. They caught sight of us and, with many silent guffaws and waves, pointed significantly at me behind Brother Rogers's back. The whole school knew. There was no escaping it.

At least Brother Rogers was popular with everyone, a fact which kept the situation from becoming nasty. And while I might be the favourite, I had to work for my marks. Brother Rogers was fair, which kept resentment at bay. But his fairness could not quiet the well-pleased chorus of "teacher's pet, teacher's pet, Malone is the teacher's pet" that greeted me outside the classroom and even at home, where Wayne made excellent sport out of the situation.

"Brother Rogers must really like you, Greg. Greg is the teacher's pet. Teacher's pet got it made."

"I can't help it if he likes me."

"Yeah, right. You love it, teacher's pet."

"You were teacher's pet with Brother Clancy. All I ever heard about was Wayne."

"Yes, Brother Clancy liked me, but he's Brother Clancy, not like you and Brother Rogers. I mean, you are the teacher's pet."

★

The seating arrangement was changed again and I was returned to the back, making another convenient spot for us. It was a slow, hot day and I was cramped with Brother Rogers breathing down over me, not saying anything, watching me work.

"Excuse me, Br," I said, getting a book out of my bag and pointedly making some elbow room for myself.

"Go on," he grunted, barely moving.

"Look," I said. "Denis Barry wants you. Talk to him for a while."

"Don't you worry about Mr. Barry, now."

He waved Denis's hand back down.

"I'm not disturbing you. Am I disturbing you, Mr. Simms?" he queried my desk mate.

"No, Br," chuckled Richard Simms, who was forever trying not to laugh and forever failing.

"See, I'm not disturbing Mr. Simms. Am I disturbing you, Greg?"

Sigh.

"No."

"No, what?" he teased.

"No, Ed."

"No, what?"

He drew back. Heads turned.

"No, Br."

"That's better there. You be careful now, my son."

"Yes, Br."

"That's right. Hey, Mr. Harrington, back to work. There's nothing for you to see back here."

That incident was just a little bump. I don't think it was that, but it was something. Something changed. Maybe he'd been hearing "teacher's pet" as much as I had. Maybe I had done something or maybe not. But things were different. Brother Rogers was all business for days now.

Our mid-term marks had not been great. But this was not just another serious, boring day, it had turned grim. I quietly closed the cover of my math scribbler, which I had not been able to resist opening to admire a fine drawing I had just completed on the back of a page full of equations. Brother Rogers was suddenly black, giving boys cracks with his thick wooden ruler for any excuse, he even snapped at Pat Royal. No one moved.

"What do you think you're doing there, Mr. Sullivan? You don't need to look at Mr. Kavanagh for anything."

He gave him a slap over the head.

"You can ask me. You got that, mister?"

Sullivan winced and bent his head over his desk. It's not that Brother Rogers hadn't given boys a smack, or even the strap before, but this was different. Usually cool, he was boiling now.

"No turning around. No talking. There's been far too much of that going on in here."

He didn't stop. He even gave John Byrne a crack for nothing. I knew suddenly that he was coming for me—that's what he was building to. There was no time to remove the scribbler from my desk. I made a weak attempt to cover it with my outstretched hand and felt the painful crack of his ruler. Oh! He hit me! He hadn't hit me before.

"What's so interesting in here, Mr. Malone?"

He snatched up the scribbler. I began to mouth a response.

"Let's see what has you so engrossed. Is it decimal division? I don't think so."

He flipped the page and revealed an elaborate blue and red ballpoint pen drawing of a British man-of-war, complete with masts, sails, flags and poop deck. He stopped, surprised for a moment, and then went cold with rage.

"Oh, this is what you're looking at is it, while I'm up there teaching?" he yelled. "This is what's got you so interested. You like this, do you?"

He tore the drawing out of the scribbler.

"I'll take this then and it won't distract you anymore."

He flipped the pages.

"Let's see what else is here."

There was more than one ship. He tore them all out, one after another, his rage increasing.

"I'll take this . . . and this . . . and this. You've been very busy, haven't you, Mr. Malone? Do you think you can do anything you want?"

His voice was ringing.

"Do you think you can take advantage of me because I've been good to you?'

Please don't, Br, I prayed. He hit me again, a sharp crack at the back of the head. Tears burst out of my eyes. I looked down, strangled, choking back any sound. I was mortified, paralyzed. I hated him.

"Is that what you think?" he screamed.

The class was deathly silent.

"Don't think that. Don't anyone think that."

He gave me another smack at the back of the head. I was crushed. "There are going to be some changes around here," he said, as he wheeled away, my drawings clutched in his hand.

I choked back another groan. I do not know if anyone looked at me. I didn't look at them. Outside, the others seemed to shrink away from me as I moved out of the building. What did I do? What did I do? Such contempt. But why does he hate me so much? I shouldn't have been drawing in my math scribbler. I shouldn't have.

The news had not reached Wayne yet. When we went to bed that night he started his usual chant. "How is teacher's pet tonight? Not saying anything, teacher's pet? Teacher's pet."

He didn't get far.

"Stop it," I said, but my words turned into a pitiful moan, as I started crying and crying.

Wayne bolted up.

"What's going on?"

I kept sobbing.

"Hey, Greg. Greg!"

"Stop. Just stop," I cried.

"I've stopped. I'm stopped. What is it, b'y? I was only teasing."

I could not answer him.

"There's nothing wrong with being teacher's pet. I was teacher's pet, Greg."

"Everyone is . . ." I sobbed, "everyone is always . . ."

"Who cares what anyone else thinks? Fuck them, Greg. Greg. Stop crying. It's not that bad. Well, it can be pretty bad, but stop now. I was only teasing. I didn't know how bad it was. What's wrong?"

"It's okay," I sobbed. "It's okay. Just don't keep saying . . ."

"I'll never say it again. I won't."

"Okay. Okay."

How could I ever go back? Did he hate me now? I hated him. Why did he have to humiliate me? They can't say I'm still the teacher's pet, at least. He hit me. I'll just act like one of the boys who gets hit by the Bro and I'll go back in, defiant, with my head up. Well, maybe not up. I did fill my math scribbler with ships and he had told me not to fill my scribblers with drawings. I was so stupid to put so many in my math book. Maybe I did go too far. I never thought he would hit me. He didn't have to do that, and say that! Now I'm not only teacher's pet, but I'm a spoiled teacher's pet who's taken advantage of his special and privileged position, and who went too far. I'm sure Pat Royal would never go too far. I'll just go in and I won't look at anyone and I won't look at him and I'll just do my work, and I won't say anything to him if this is how he wants it.

I coldly took my place and got out the books. Today he was moving about easily, being very reasonable about everything he had been so unreasonable about the day before.

"If you need to ask about something you don't understand in this exercise, don't go looking around at what everyone else is doing. Raise your hand and ask me. Mr. Sullivan, I'll get to you eventually . . . and if you don't finish on time, don't worry. The important thing is to understand what you're doing. Right, Mr. Malone?"

Was he going to pick on me now?

"Yes, Br," I murmured.

"All right. Get to work," he said cheerfully.

The class hummed to work. Brother Rogers strode the aisles, busily checking everyone's work, and he came to a stop behind me. I froze.

"Go on, do your work," he said and he leaned in over me, almost as usual.

"You're not drawing more ships, are you?"

I couldn't answer.

"They were good drawings. But you shouldn't be doing them in class. Oh, not talking today, are we? Mad at me, are you?"

"No, Br," I lied.

"Yes, you are, I can see . . . all right, go on."

He stood up.

"Just do your work."

And he went away. He came back, to pick on me, to tease me, and I relented in spite of myself. I even called him Eddie once as punishment, just to see. He faked anger weakly.

Then I asked if I could have my drawings back to see if the ground was really solid.

"You've got some nerve."

"Well?"

"No, they're mine now. You can do some more."

Gradually I got over the attack. It was full spring. Sports Day was coming and the end of the year. But that was not the end of Brother Rogers and me. He even joined the Boy Scouts. And as I had no plans to make an appearance for the annual Scout picture in the *Adelphian,* he endeavored to improve my attitude.

"Well, if I have to show up to get my picture taken, then you definitely have to show up, and if you don't, there will be consequences."

"What consequences?"

"Let's just say I will be very disappointed."

I showed up and we posed dutifully together.

In the last days, when exams were over, I sat with Brother Rogers and Andy, watching a group of older boys getting ready for long-distance runs.

"You should do that too, Greg," goaded Brother Rogers.

"Me?"

"Yes. You need to build up your long-distance legs."

"I'm not ready."

"They're not even racing, just clocking times."

"I don't have sneakers."

"Don't be so fussy. Go in your socks. There are guys in their socks, look."

And so there were.

"I don't know."

"Go on. Work on your stride."

I was talked into it. The first lap was respectable, but I was too fast, I'd never last. I tried to slow down and still keep a long stride but my socks were slipping. I ignored them and worked on my stride. Brother Rogers and Andy seemed to be enjoying the whole affair. Halfway back again my socks were definitely flapping but I finished the lap anyway to gales of laughter.

I had been the class clown and often played the fool to avoid being made a fool of. Now here I was taking the trouble to be serious about track and I turn out to look the fool again. Brother Rogers, having lured me into the run, was now leaning back, pointing at my flapping socks, laughing heartily.

"Oh my, you should have seen yourself. You look so funny, like you were running in clown shoes," and he flapped his feet and leaned back again, laughing with great satisfaction.

He's no better than Wayne, for God's sake! He only wants me for a laughing stock, a clown! Andy was laughing now too. I was furious. Okay, that's it. To hell with track. I'm going home. And the year bumped to an inglorious end.

Jordan Weedy

On the opposite corner from the Joneses', on the corner of Rostellan and Falkland, a picture-perfect bungalow floated on a flawless green carpet of such uniformity that it must be either magical or artificial. This illusion, which had cast a spell over the still-forming mind of young Andy Jones, was the work of amateur horticulturalist Jack Renouf, who was happy to mentor young Andy's budding interest in reproducing this magic on his own lawn. By the time I arrived on the first weekend of summer holidays and found Andy busy with the lawn mower and bags of fertilizer in the garage, I realized that I was almost too late, and his head was already too full of useful information on the subject of lawn care to be of any use to me.

"Ah, if it isn't my old friend Jordan Weedy," I exclaimed, taking liberties with his middle name.

He ignored my opening salvo and began by explaining to me that there was a very precise way to care for a lawn, which people did not appreciate. Mr. Renouf used only the hand mower on his lawn as anything else was barbaric. The action of the blades on the hand mower neatly cuts the grass, while the violent whirring blade of the power mower slashes and tears the grass, leaving ragged ends that can turn brown and spoil the health and fresh appearance of the lawn, which must be carefully maintained with regular applications of fertilizers and dustings with insecticides and herbicides, then mowed and cut around the paths with the edger and watered, or rather "sprayed," evenly every day before dawn and at dusk. I was aghast. Andy sincerely believed he could beat this lawn thing if he devoted his summer to its growing demands and I was very alarmed about the prospects for our holidays. "Well, Jordan Weedy, this has been very educational," I allowed.

"Jordan Weedy is it? This is actually very interesting stuff, you know."

"Yes, it is, but we're not going to do this all morning are we, Jordan?"

"No, Dominic Savio, we're not, but I have to finish my chores."

What were these chores, I wondered? Dad cut our little lawn with the clippers and didn't want us using them. As for the dahlias and gladiolas he grew for Lovey, he went at those with so much energy and single-mindedness, no outside efforts were required. We did make our beds and take turns washing the dishes. Mom had tried chores for "allowances," but her tone betrayed an uneasiness born of ignorance, and she failed to motivate us.

"If I don't mow the lawn today, Dad will be mad at me," Andy finally grumbled, almost under his breath, and so we set about it.

I am not sure I was of much assistance, but I hurried it along as best I could.

I could see Andy was as wary of his father as I was of mine though I did not fully comprehend his reasons. Mr. Jones was good to us and spoke to us as adults, seeing no reason to tailor his wit to suit smaller minds. He drove us out to St. Phillip's for picnics and always seemed to have a riddle or a word game of some sort to occupy us for the length of the drive. There he chatted with the local fishermen on the wharf, or sat on the beach in his shirt and tie and good brown brogues while we jumped off the wharf into the icy ocean.

He was very funny and kept us laughing with stories of all the ridiculous things that people coming into his store had said or done that day. All of this he delivered with a look of gravest concern and bafflement. He could be very scathing. Mrs. Jones would call for charity but laugh the loudest. Mr. Jones didn't put on funny hats or dance around to keep the party going like Dad, and, in fact, he wasn't really a party guy, but he was deadly funny and we had many laughs at the expense of neighbours, friends, and all radio and television personalities, great and small.

This lightly mocking attitude suited me immensely and I began to feel more at home at the Joneses' than at the Malones'. To be sure, my entertainments amused Mom and Dad well enough, but eventually Dad was apt to suggest that nothing or no one was good enough for me, and how did I get so cynical at all?

Dad was outgoing and optimistic, one of the boys. Mr. Jones was reserved, critical and had many acquaintances but no great friends like Dad. It was Mrs. Jones who filled the house with company, old school friends, nuns, Brothers, priests, and extended family. She was confidante to a long list of admirers whom she encouraged, cheered up and comforted. Like her husband, she was also very funny, but her humour was of the moment, explosive and warm, and she was very religious despite having been tortured by the nuns.

Jack Dobbin, her father, had died when she was a young girl. Her mother became the housekeeper at the Newfoundland Hotel and so little Agnes stayed at Littledale Convent during the school year, funded by a Knights of Columbus scholarship for which she was eligible because her father had been a Knight. Having lost her father, she was naturally regarded with suspicion by the nuns. Her high spirits were further confirmation of a wild, willful and fatherless nature for which she was regularly confined to a dark, cramped closet, where she might meditate on her behaviour to the rustling sound of the rats.

Due to the accumulated claustrophobic effect of these childhood chastisements, when Mrs. Jones left the house now and drove the big blue-and-white Ford wagon for the two-minute run to Churchill Square, it was a major production and required a great deal of encouragement from Andy, Marywin, Cathy and even me. She wore a large hat and sunglasses. Sometimes she was able to go into the new Ayres's Supermarket, but not always, and never for more than three or four minutes, before she returned to the car flustered and nervous, breathing quickly and close to tears. Gradually she became too nervous for even these excursions, and she ordered everything in, clothes and dresses from Gourley Gowns and the Model Shop, sending back what she did not want. Alec Cook delivered her groceries to her from his store in the Square, and so, with a network of devoted friends, shopkeepers and tradesmen coming to her door, she managed life at Rostellan from the telephone, where her husky voice was often mistaken for a man's.

"Greg, do I sound like a man?"

"No, Mrs. Jones."

"Greg is so sweet to lie to me. 'Yes, sir, Mr. Jones,' that little so-and-so said to me. I know my voice is a little husky, but you can't assume anything on the phone. I said, 'This is *Mrs.* Jones, young lady.' 'Oh my, Mrs. Jones, I'm so sorry,' she said. 'Yes, my dear, and I should really get a discount for that,' I said."

Mrs. Coady came in on Wednesdays and Saturdays. A big, friendly, down-to-earth woman with frizzy hair, she looked like a character in *Mad* magazine, which Andy got from Mr. Jones's sister in New York where Mike was now a novice at Iona College. Mrs. Coady cleaned and did laundry and cooked and baked, in a non-stop whirlwind under Mrs. Jones's direction.

"Mrs. Coady just sweeps up the middle of the kitchen, she doesn't get the corners, so I have to go around and do them after she's gone, you see, Greg. God love Jenny, she's the best, but she won't slow down. She tries to get too much done at once. I say to her, 'Jenny, let's just get the floor done first,' but she can't do that. She has to have the washer going, and something on to bake, and then start cleaning up, Holy Mary Mother of God, give me strength."

Thus it was that Mrs. Jones held court on Rostellan, playing at her piano in the dining room for Cathy, Marywin, Andy and me, with her silver bangles jangling on her smooth, plump, brown wrists, songs both serious and silly from her convent days, war songs and show tunes, all of which she sang with great wit and feeling in her warm, smoky, crackly voice. We were her connection to the outside and were pumped regularly for information about the Brothers and our friends, and if we were going to the Square, there was always something she wanted, and if it was also something she wasn't supposed to have, she would cup her hand against the side of your head, and whisper her order into your ear.

"A package of Bridge Mixture, but don't tell anyone, and a package of Matinée Extra Mild. I am trying to cut down."

Her warm fresh breath tickled your ear till you laughed.

"And keep the change."

It wasn't really a secret, of course, and everyone heard her dramatic stage whisper.

When Mr. Jones came home, the tone of the house altered. He was a man of some moods and masked it with a sarcasm that was sometimes brittle. He wanted the house to run on schedule and things to be where he wanted them. If they were not, he would only say, "Is that right?" or "Very good, my son," in a certain, long-suffering tone, or perhaps make only a grunt or a mumble, but it was enough to set the house on edge, and if supper was not on the table on time, he might just suddenly look up from his paper and exclaim, "Oh, it's too late now, the stomach is closing over."

"What! No, it can't be now, Michael, it's almost on the table, look."

"No, I can feel it. It's closing."

"Here have a cracker."

"No, a saltine won't stop it."

"What?"

"No, it's gone."

"It can't be, look, it's ready."

"No, sorry, my dear, it's closed. Well, enjoy your meal now, the rest of you."

"Now, Michael, don't be mean," said Mrs. Jones laughing nervously.

"No, Dad, you have to have your dinner," the girls insisted.

"I don't know if I can. Perhaps I'll try a small bit of roast beef, not too much. Is it rare, Agnes?"

"Yes, Michael darling."

"Not overcooked?"

"No, it's just the way you like it."

"I think the stomach's coming back."

It was all a big joke, of course, but it barely covered over a tension whose peaks and valleys I was not always there to witness, but sensed enough from my vantage point to respect Andy's caution around his father. But surely Mr. Jones had little to complain of in Andy's behaviour, I thought.

The Last Hurrah

The First St. Bon's Troop was encamped for the summer at the new Scout grounds at Second Pond, just outside Petty Harbour on the Petty Harbour Road. The camp occupied a pleasant peninsula of woods and fields that pushed out into the pond, and there were cabins from the former occupants of the camp. It had the advantage of being close to town but also secluded and rustic. But these advantages were nothing to me, who received no extra visits, and still no offerings of cake or cookies.

Mom toured the grounds on Visitors' Day again, looking very glamorous as usual, and received the usual oohs and aahs from the boys. I was hardened to Visitors' Day now but still disappointed that she did not think to bring anything but Beni and Kerry for me to supervise. I asked her to send me out a decent pair of swimming trunks so that I could go for a swim, but these too failed to materialize. I masked my disappointment with a cool exterior and a poker face. I gave Kerry and Beni the grand tour of the campgrounds and of my patrol. If I had to be a Scout, then I was going to be a leader. I had all the required badges and now had my own patrol under my command, and I ran a tight ship.

There is little else worth reporting from my last Scout camp unless it was that I had become a madman, a bitter, twisted, frothing madman. I kept all this under a tight rein, of course, very tight. No one would guess, after all our patrol won every single inspection at camp, every one. I would not tolerate so much as a gum wrapper on my campsite, and my patrol knew it. No inflated troop leader was going to find a flap down, a peg loose, a speck of paper, a sleeping bag unrolled, or a neckerchief askew on my campsite. However much they might try, and they did try, no quarter was left for correction. Gary O'Brien, my second, and the rest of the patrol were at their wits' end trying to appease me with offerings of chocolate cake and oranges, and so it turned out I had plenty of treats after Visitors' Day after all.

Nevertheless I was ready to explode, and in the afterhours I thought I might as well light up a cigarette in the woods. John O'Mara walked by as I inhaled my first sickening lungfull and docked me three points for smoking. I turned several shades of green. Real refreshment came from the fresh spruce beer at Donovan's Store up on the road, the perfect antidote to the hot and humid woods. The missing three points did not affect our winning the inspection for the year and we received an oversized lollipop for our efforts, which put our victory into proper perspective.

On the final night of camp, there was a big campfire with the Scouts and family members in the big new Scout hut, a long affair with a large fireplace at one end and a canteen and storerooms at the other, with a balcony along the top. After the usual songs, a boxing match had been arranged for the climax. I had much less than no interest in this event and loathed the very idea of throwing a punch even more than receiving one, but it was not possible to avoid a turn in the ring, fate would have its way. And my opponent, as it turned out, was none other than Gor-

don Bailey. I did not know whether to call him my old friend or
my old enemy. The match would tell the tale.

We were equipped with boxing gloves and told the rules of
engagement—no hitting below the belt, and no hitting in the
head—and so the match began. Gordon came out swinging. I
defended myself as best I could and even landed a few punches.
Mr. Colford pulled us apart. We came together again. I tried to
put on a good show, and without meaning to I landed a punch
to the side of Gordon's head. The referee separated us again.

"No hitting in the head."

Back we came again, and this time Gordon hit me in the side
of the head with a punch. The referee ignored this and waved us
on. Gordon succeeded in landing two more punches to my
head, which sent me reeling, before Mr. Colford intervened, but
even then he said nothing about hitting in the head, and the
match continued. The crowd was cheering madly. I looked up in
the dark to see them with their fists raised.

"Get him, Bailey. Get him."

No doubt my own patrol was among the crowd, well, I could
hardly blame them, but even the women were shouting. What
was Mrs. O'Dea doing cheering on this farce? I thought.

I failed, or was unwilling, to mount a comeback and Gordon
was declared the winner. He raised his arms and smiled at the
rabble as he turned about the ring, well-pleased with himself,
my old enemy. I left the building and stumbled into the field seeing nothing. I hated them, all of them. Let them have their
rigged matches and fake heroes, I thought. Let them thrill to my
humiliation and their own blood lust. I was out in the woods
and free of them all.

✦

The first bout of summer activities over, I now looked forward
to round two. Dad loved to make a party out of life and we all

happily agreed to that. But if Dad decided we were all going to have a good time, then you were going to have a good time, whether you felt like it or not.

"So get in the damn car, you're going, and you're going to like it."

But one cannot always be commanded to enjoy oneself, and too much forced gaiety can make a stone of the heart. Before that petrification process was complete however, Wayne and I found several legitimate reasons for missing the weekend drives. Wayne had basketball practice and dating. I had my weekend excursions to Andy's, although Dad was wary of my wanting to "live" at the Joneses' and occasionally pulled me back in. That was not always unwelcome, and both Wayne and I looked forward with genuine enthusiasm to our annual summer vacation.

For one thing, we now had our best car ever, a golden-beige 1960 Pontiac Laurentian with a cream top, wraparound rear window and white walls. It had a huge V8 engine and could that baby ever fly, which proved a key feature in Wayne's survival that summer vacation. We went to Bonne Bay Big Pond, on the west coast of our beautiful Island. We toured Gander, the Airport to the World, as well as Grand Falls-Windsor and Corner Brook, Newfoundland's paper towns, and we camped in the glorious provincial parks on the way.

Bonne Bay Big Pond proved to be a very big pond indeed, with a sandy bottom, and we had an excellent cabin on the beach, which belonged to a friend of Dad's at Imperial Oil. We had come out west before, though never this far. In previous years, we had choked on the dust of the Hodgewater Line, which was sometimes impassable and always caused at least one flat. It was stifling hot, but the windows were closed to keep out the dust, which eventually seeped into every crack and rose up through the floor until we had to stop and rush out coughing, or throwing up. Then we'd pile back in and continue on in search of adventure.

But now the roads were mostly paved and we were all very comfortable, cruising along in the Laurentian, the four boys and Mom and Dad, in spite of the addition of our large boxer dog, Bogey, as in the "Colonel Bogey March," from a favourite movie of Dad's, and the only time the car was really crowded was when the Colonel farted. Bogey was a gift from a grateful operator of a new Esso service station, whom Dad had helped to that position.

As in Bristol's Hope, a long line of friends followed Dad out west: Bob and Mil, and Charlie Derrin and his wife. Their little group had expanded. There was Frank "Nipper" Horwood and his wife, Pat. Dad had also helped him get the very desirable Esso station in Churchill Square. Dad was doing very well now at Imperial Oil and worked with all the distributors and operators. Nipper and Pat were great to party with and happy to live up to any funny hat Dad chose to put on them after a few snorts of Old Sam. And there we all sat on the sandy beach in the hot sun on an assortment of collapsible chairs and inflatable mattresses, with our Alpine hats on from the Regatta and the Kool-Aid and Old Sam flowing.

Everyone else but our family and Uncle Bob and Aunt Mil had gone back to Town by the time Wayne got sick. We had to hunt down the bananas and take them outside because they were making him gag. Everything was making him nauseous and he was starting to curl up with cramps. Mom thought it must be appendicitis. Hers had ruptured when she was a girl and she'd been in the hospital for weeks. Dad and Bob got Wayne into the back of the Pontiac and drove into Deer Lake, where the doctor confirmed Mom's diagnosis, and said further that it was about to rupture and they had better get him to the hospital in Corner Brook as soon as possible.

That was all the incentive Dad needed. Uncle Bob sat clutching the dashboard, white-knuckled and speechless as Dad flew to Corner Brook doing 120 miles per hour, everything the new

Pontiac could give. Wayne swore afterwards that the car actually left the ground, and Uncle Bob did not deny it.

"I'm glad you're still alive now, Wayne, don't get me wrong, but I thought we were all gonna die for a while there, Scully."

"No, no, Bob, I was in complete control the whole time."

Wayne was saved and a team of pretty nurses at Western Memorial Hospital brought him back from the brink. But he was thin as a rail and judged too frail for any further camping, and so it was decided to send him home on a plane with Mom. They posed for the camera on the steps of the little EPA plane on the gravel runway at the airport in Deer Lake, their very first flight.

Kerry, Beni, Dad and I were left to finish our annual adventure together. Enthusiastically I jumped into Mom's role and her seat in the front. Kerry and Beni, let loose, went to the dogs in the back with Bogey. I helped Dad set up camp and organized the boys into all the necessary diversions. It was not completely comfortable but it was entirely civilized, and we managed to finish off the remainder of the holiday with the remainder of the family in some remaining fashion.

Salve Sexte

We were all very satisfied in grade eight to fall mercifully into the waiting hands of our own patient Brother Pigott, and we soaked up as much about B horror movies and the mean streets of Brooklyn as he was willing to tell us. Grade eight was in our old grade three classroom, up over our grade seven class-room in the monastery. All the Brothers walked to and from the monastery and past our door every day, including all the new young handsome brothers, like Brother Barron, Brother Manning, and Brother Batstone, now fully recovered from his fight with my cousin Buddy. As Brother Pigott and Brother Rogers were friends, I saw him regularly as well.

In the middle of the year Brother Rogers took me out of Brother Pigott's class for a meeting with him in the principal's old office. There he informed me as tactfully as he could that the male sexual member, when excited, physically enters the female sexual member, where it ejaculates semen, which could fertilize the woman's eggs, and in due course, cause a child to form and grow. This, no doubt, was the information I had so unsuccessfully sought from Brother Darcy in his office two years before. It all seemed like a great deal of work. He followed up with a serious statement about the responsibility and sacred nature of the sacrament of marriage, and by the time he finished I had resolved to become a priest and perhaps that was the intention. It was naturally presumed that I would become a priest, or some vocation involving the wearing of robes, but soon even that long-term ambition became problematic.

Having been forbidden to dress as a woman teacher for playschool, the appeal of form-fitting feminine attire spread into the smallest creases of my confused mind. Skirts, slips, high heels and bandanas—I knew the location of every one in the house, and enjoyed their pleasures in private. As I lay on my narrow bed, employing a pair of nylons in ways never intended by the manufacturer, the thoughts that filled my mind were of no one I knew, none of my handsome heroes from St. Bon's and beyond. My mind was fully occupied with my Latin textbook, and more particularly with the ink drawing of a slave wearing only a slight tunic that barely came to the top of his strong legs. What wonderful attire! If only I had been a Roman. The thought of the slave, who must surely obey your every command, your every wish, was an intoxication which might have been liberation except for its foundation in bondage.

"Come, slave, let me touch thee."

And the slave, though startled and unwilling at first, must eventually succumb to the unyielding pleasure. My mind grew hot under the Roman sun. I took the slave into the shade of the villa to administer some light punishment for some imagined infraction. The strong surge between my legs was not unfamiliar, but now it burst over me like electricity, and I felt the full force of its pleasure. The fact of the final climax was a shocking and dizzying revelation and at the sight of the virgin white semen, tears sprang without warning to my eyes and I wept in defeat.

Such pleasure from such a source, I did not need to wonder if it was a sin. In fact, without checking, I knew it was a mortal sin and so realized that I might be going to Hell after all. I put away my Latin book and the nylons and resolved not to employ them again, but as I failed in this resolve like so many other impossible resolutions, even compounding my offence by adding a tunic-like T-shirt to the ritual, I was obliged to construct a Confession for Absolution. It was a sin of impurity, touching oneself. I would confess to being impure in thought and deed, to being impure with myself. That should cover it without putting too fine a point on it. No need to employ such heavy compounds as masturbation in self-condemnation. This expression of impurity, familiar and vague, was enough to distance me from the flesh without disavowing the sin, and it was thus I found myself confessing to Monsignor Fyme with alarming regularity. I alternated from a state of grace to a state of sin with such speed that my chances of landing in Heaven were completely a matter of timing, and there were now fewer and fewer hours of the week that I might, if found dead, also be found acceptable for eternal reward. In such a constant state of moral upheaval, passions must necessarily become morbid.

The Brothers were on the look-out for both passion and morbidity, the antidote for both being large doses of sports. I was tall, it could not be denied or minimized, and soon caught the eye of the basketball coach, our own Brother Pigott, who ganged up with Brother Rogers to press me into the team. It was a wonder they tried. I made no attempt at hockey. On our weekly afternoon in the Forum, the ice was divided into a hockey area and a general skating area. We were obliged to play a number of games, but Andy and I would much rather, and did, spend our time gliding around the other side shamelessly

playing the silliest of games, even using our hockey sticks for
witches' brooms, "folie à deux." Somehow few dared mock us.
Brother Pigott only gave us an ironical flutter of the lids. Ignoring all these warning signs, they now sought me out for the
court, and behind them stood Wayne, the basketball star, and
Dad, the great coach.

"My son, at least try it out. How do you know you don't like
it till you try it? You've got to get into something, hockey or soccer or basketball, or something. I can't have you just hanging
around the Joneses' all year."

There was no escape and in the end I was convinced to try
out.

There were basketball nets on the pavement at the side of
school where the team practiced when the St. Pat's gym was not
available. It was here I made my first foray. I managed to catch
the ball, even get it in the net a few times, but I would need a lot
of work on my dribbling. When the ball went flying off I ran to
get it, but there was a ladder lying flat alongside the school
behind the net. I tripped over it and plunged into the side of the
building with my hands extended for the ball. When I stood up
and looked at my aching right hand, the fingers in the middle
were missing, and there was just a large gap between the index
and little fingers. The middle finger was completely broken over
and the ring finger was sprained and fractured. Not even Dad
had a rejoinder for this outcome, and for a time I was harassed
no further to pick up a ball. The price was painful to be sure.
Dr. Harry Roberts dug a large needle into the bursting blood
pudding that was my felled middle digit. I felt the needle touch
the bone and then heard it scrape along the bone.

"This will kill the pain," he assured Mom and me, as the
colour drained from both our faces.

After several unsuccessful arrangements, a large wad of
cotton was placed in my ragged paw and the whole thing was
plastered over into the shape of a large ball at the end of my

arm with only my thumb protruding. We returned home thoroughly drained.

Brothers Rogers and Pigott were amused, and concerned too, of course, but mostly amused.

"Oh my, oh my, oh my, what have we done to him, Brother?" said Brother Rogers when he saw me.

Brother Pigott tried to restrain the smile that came to his lips with a wry twist. He put my cast in the palm of his hand and weighed it up and down.

"It's almost as b-big as a b-b-basketball. You can p-practice with this," he laughed.

"No, no, he won't be doing any more practicing, Brother."

There were advantages. The plaster wand waved away all danger of not only basketball but soccer and hockey as well, and was also the occasion of much conversation. I got all the boys, Denis and Pat and even John Byrne, to autograph it for me. It was on so long I had to learn to write with my left hand.

But the broken hand did not keep me from giving a helping hand, my other one, to the grade one teacher, Mrs. Hann, my very good friend, who coincidently had a broken leg. I helped to corral the grade ones into class as she hobbled along on her cane behind. I also did errands for some of the women teachers in the new building, down to Jim's Store for a package of Viceroy for Mrs. Murray, or a Kit Kat for Mrs. O'Keefe, but I was a regular in Mrs. Hann's class. I loved the little kids and she even let me teach them on occasion, a privilege I enjoyed so much that I was late getting back to my own class and Brother Pigott called a halt to my charitable works.

It was on my way back from the new school one day that I was approached by young Freddie Michael, whom I barely knew. Freddie was a couple of years under me and small, but very cute.

"My sister told me to tell you that she likes you," he announced.

Well, this was something, and a very flattering something.

I knew Freddie had a sister, Janet, who was my age. She was smart and involved in public speaking as well as class president, and I thought I would like to get to know her. Besides that, I found it hard to resist this charming declaration. Who was I to say no to such a daring offer of friendship?

"Tell your sister that I like her too," I replied in my most gentleman-like fashion.

Freddie rolled his eyes and suppressed a smile, well-pleased with the success of his mission.

Janet was as much fun as I had hoped. Not only was she down-to-earth and funny, but better still, she found me funny. She was also very exotic, especially when she snatched her butterfly glasses off her face, which she did regularly, squinting uncertainly around to see if it was still me standing next to her. We went ice-skating and roller skating at the Stadium on weekends with her cousin Pat Michael, and her friend Maisie Kelland, and hung out at her house playing Broadway musicals, a taste for which Janet had acquired visiting her Aunt Margie in New York. They were a very musical family. Her father was Lebanese and besides his regular job as an insurance salesman, he had a band which was famous locally. Mr. Michael was always very friendly and his wife, Anne, a Rockwood from Town, seemed just the reverse.

"Greg, it's great to see you. How are you? Come on in. Anne, here's Greg, look, isn't it good to see him?"

"Well, he got in this far, he might as well have a seat, I suppose," conceded Mrs. Michael.

Mr. Michael carried on as though his wife had just kissed and hugged me.

"Yes, make yourself at home. Janet, get something to drink for Greg."

I was fascinated by them, especially Mrs. Michael, for whom I was on my very best behaviour, and was rewarded with *mashi* and *kibbee* and other Lebanese delights.

After "dates" Janet and I would neck on the front verandah of their spacious home on Lemarchant Road, where again I tried my best to live up to expectations. I had seen enough movies to know my part, although I believe I gave a better performance dancing around in the living room to *West Side Story* with her and Maisie. Janet had two older sisters, Sandra, a famous beauty, and Lorraine, who was a nun with the Presentation Convent. This was a shock to me as Janet and Sandra were so va-va-voom. But there was Lorraine's picture occupying a position of prominence on the mantelpiece, from where she gazed down at us in full battle regalia. The quiet, dark walk from Janet's house to mine at the end of every date was a time to relax, and I did not hurry as I strolled along breathing in the cool night air and untangling my libido.

Wayne certainly was quite pleased, if not a touch relieved, that I was "dating" Janet. He, of course, was dating all the prettiest girls at Mercy Convent: beautiful Ann Kent with her coal-black hair and Irish ways, glamorous, vivacious Elaine Duff, and blonde, fun-loving Toni McGrath. I had no difficulty at all in sincerely appreciating the attractions of all three. After we'd listened to the Top Ten on VOCM Wayne would start in. Lying on his little bed across the room, he praised their beauties and virtues to the gathering gloom above.

"Ah Toni, Greg, Toni . . . I don't know. Ann Kent was good, I mean she is classy, and Elaine I really like, I mean, really, but Toni, Greg, I don't know. She's so . . . oh sexy. What am I going to do? I want to have them all, Greg, I do. Toni has a sister Robin, and another one, Carol. If you went out with Carol or Robin, that would be great, we could walk home together. That's a long walk boy from the East End, and I'm worn out before I start, ha ha."

Poor Wayne. He was so anxiously waiting for me to catch up and kick in with the girls so that we could talk about more than just the Top Ten or toys or Mom and Dad. We could talk about the real thing now. But that conversation had to be very one-sided. Luckily his own enthusiasm carried most of our talk along on this subject, and I was happy to listen to his exploits and offer a very sympathetic ear to his agonizing over which beauty queen to go skating with. I fashioned replies to questions about my own feelings with the greatest care, generating just enough enthusiasm to be credible, and changing the subject before being cornered into excessive fabrications.

In short, I agreed with him about Robin and Carol, but decided in the end to stay with Janet, all of which Wayne could understand perfectly.

"Yes, Janet is a dish, especially when she takes her glasses off. And her sister! Sandra is pretty too. I like her looks."

"Yes, yes," I agreed to it all and refrained from adding, "and what about that little Freddie?"

This reticence, this secrecy about my own true feelings, was certainly not comfortable. It was stultifying. But I could see no way out. I could not recognize the predicament; I was the predicament, and had not the language to tell Wayne, or the faintest desire to talk to him about what I, myself, did not comprehend.

I had certainly considered the problems of dating girls and decided without much struggle to risk it. I did not probe the contradictions too deeply. I had a handicap, to be sure, but dating girls was just a continuation of my childhood love and friendship with them. I would deal with the other complications on an improvisational, need-to-know basis. Not to date would deprive me of my share of society and I was not about to accept that.

I did not regard my behaviour as deceitful so much as a required tactic for survival. It had all started so long ago I could not remember, but I felt no guilt, only a sort of nervous defiance. I was the bold outlaw, unashamed of his ways. His crimes were for the good, after all. I was Zorro, posing as the gay blade, while the dark secrets of my true nature were hidden from the party-goers. Of course, like Zorro, exposure would mean ruin, even death. But I was as pleased as I was surprised by my new reputation as a wolf, which I said nothing to contradict. My disguise had worked. Skating with Janet on my arm at the Stadium I could safely watch all the boys at play. All the smooth, golden boys, who were so easy and confident at school and at Scouts, now suddenly turned self-conscious and even awkward as they attempted to win the favours of the ice beauties in their soft sweaters and white skates, leisurely circling the rink to the strains of Gene Pitney. The favoured were free to let their feelings show and their desires flow, even to excess. I was denied all this, of course, but in my disguise I was safe, and might steal visions of happiness to redistribute later to the starving heart at home.

The burden of this great silence was not fully felt until it was lifted. Andy was my very best friend and our partnership was well known by now. He was the funniest person I had ever known, plus he was considerate and we had a uniform curiosity. Our talks ranged from Church law to *Camelot*. We loved Jonathan Winters and Elaine May and Mike Nichols and Sid Caesar, *Mad* magazine and all the English comedians. It seemed that almost everybody I was interested in, Andy was interested in, and almost everything he liked, I liked too.

It had been one of our longer walks and we paused, as we often did, to look over the bridge on Elizabeth Avenue into the white water of Rennie's River, just before going up Rostellan Street. Andy had brought up the subject of girls, and the guarded, lacklustre nature of this conversation emboldened me. Somehow I did not think I was taking a great chance.

"Do you ever find guys attractive?" I asked tentatively, looking straight into the running water.

Andy paused. I waited, and waited some more. Had I gone too far again? Had I tripped the switch, awakened the monster and broken the bonds?

"I do find some guys attractive," he slowly drawled, and then quickly added, "Do you?"

"Yes, I do. I like Pat Royal."

"Pat is very handsome."

"And Denis Barry," I suggested.

"Yes, I like Denis, and I like John Whalen too. Do you?"

"Yes, yes, I do too."

We both paused. I was soaring inside.

"So what are we saying? That we like guys the way most guys like girls?" Andy asked for clarification.

"Yes, exactly," I replied.

"Okay, do you?"

"Yes, do you?"

"Yes. Yes, I think I do. I mean, I do find some girls attractive, but not like guys."

"No, not like guys."

We both paused.

"This is so unbelievable. I can't believe you do too," I enthused.

"Did you suspect?"

"Sort of."

"Why? What did I do?"

"Nothing. Nothing that anyone else would ever see. I just took a chance."

We skipped up Rostellan, our list of likes quickly expanding, and Andy swearing me to deadly secrecy before we went into his house. He soon realized there was no danger from me on that account.

This was an immense release. Now I could talk to someone, and not just anyone, but Andy, about "it," and the main topic of all internal desires and discourses could now be uttered in public for the first time. A new lightness had come over me. Andy was more cautious and reserved and kept both his feet, and mine, on the ground.

✦

The wear and tear on the Christmas catalogues was no longer confined to the toy section. My interest in toys had been whittled down to a small collection of Corgi cars and trucks that now sat arranged on a shelf. My interest in the underwear section, I must confess, was expanding. There were the brassieres and girdles, and the girdle-bra combinations, shapely armour for the modern woman in a man's world. And then there were the men, standing stalwart in their underwear, gazing into the distance, with friends, also in their underwear, pointing out invisible objects of interest and smoking pipes so casually it was hard to believe they were only in their underwear. But there they were, handsome men, the same ones in different underwear, in their jockeys, their big legs and feet bare. And the scene of them, standing around in their tight, white long johns, like Wyatt Earp in the memorable episode where he gets out of bed wearing just his long johns in the morning, was a special feature of the undercover excitement of the underwear section. I often allowed the book to fall open to those pages, careful not to finger it so much that the crisp pages turned to tissue and provoked questions I could not possibly answer.

But the need for clothes for dating, and especially sweaters for skating, now dominated all other considerations. Last Christmas, Wayne had gotten a good crewneck sweater with wide horizontal bands of varying shades of grey and olive green. But he was a dedicated dater and skater and now needed another one. He no longer allowed Mom to press his pants, she might carelessly iron a double crease into them, so he ironed all his own clothes meticulously and was no stranger to Dad's Brylcreem or his sports jacket. Those whom I sought to impress could care less about the crease in my pants. Still, I pressed them as carefully as Wayne did his, and I wanted a red V-neck sweater just like I saw in the new Coke ads. Andy wanted one too and by New Year's we looked like our own advertisement.

✦

I received another visitation from Jimmy Beehan, the Dark Angel from grade three. He caught up to me just past Marty's Restaurant on my way home. As we crossed the intersection to Pennywell Road, he leaned into me, his head bent conspiratorially.

"I've got a good one for you."

"A good what?"

"A joke, boy, a joke. Did you ever hear this one before?"

He paused before delivering his prize.

"Ruptured Balls by One Hung Low."

I paused, uncertain.

"Get it? Ruptured Balls by One Hung Low. You know what ruptured balls are right?"

"No."

"Well, geez boy, you know if you get hit in the balls playing soccer or something, you can rupture your balls and ruin yourself, then one of them hangs down lower than the other one, see? Ruptured Balls by One Hung Low."

My stomach turned over and I felt immediately sick.

"Oh yeah, good one," I offered weakly.

"Yeah, well, see you," and he vanished into his house, his work done.

I raced home to my bedroom, whipped my pants down and had a look. Yes, yes, one of my balls did hang lower than the other one. God no! I was ruined. How had it happened? Not on the soccer pitch or the basketball court. How? Perhaps I had been too aggressive with the nylons. It was all Sextus' fault. That was the end of the nylons, I thought, but what could I do to fix it? Was I ruined for life? I couldn't proceed on Jimmy Beehan's say-so, I had to have a professional opinion. But this must be done in the strictest secrecy. Mom and Dad must never know, and after all, doctors were sworn to secrecy, weren't they? Didn't they take an oath?

I went through the telephone book and settled on an unfamiliar name with an office in Rawlins Cross, just down from St. Bon's, and made an appointment. It took several weeks to collect the fifteen dollars for the fee, and I was early for the appointment.

"Can I have your name, please?" asked the receptionist pleasantly.

"Yes, of course, it's Walker, David Walker," I said, announcing my new pseudonym.

"And your parents'?"

"Oh, that doesn't matter."

"What?"

"Well, they're out of town right now."

"Okay. And what do you want to see the doctor about today?"

I stared back at her.

"I'll tell the doctor."

"All right then, he'll see you now," she smiled unevenly.

"I think I may have ruptured myself accidentally," I confessed, once alone with the doctor.

"Oh, what happened? Did you get a kick there or something?"

"Yes, playing soccer."

"Well, that happens. Let's have a look. Um hum, um hum, no there's nothing wrong there," he concluded.

"But one of my testicles is lower than the other one."

"Yes, that's perfectly normal. Just about everyone is like that. No, they're not ruptured at all."

I felt my body relax and life return after weeks of bloodless anxiety.

"That's great," I almost sang out. "That's really good. I was just worried."

"Well, no need to worry."

"Good, good. Thank you. Will I pay the receptionist?"

"Oh, you can just fill out this form," he said, walking out with me, "and your parents will . . ."

"No!"

"What?"

"No, that's all right, I'll just pay the fifteen dollars."

"But really you don't need to. Your parents . . ."

"No, that's all right, I'll pay it."

And I flung the damp, well-handled bills onto the reception-ist's desk.

"But we don't even have your address."

They both gaped at me as I backed away from them.

"I'll call it in," I shouted back as I ran out of the office.

It was such a relief to know I had not ruined myself for life. At least something was normal. I even forgave Jimmy Beehan his wretchedly inaccurate joke, but really, I thought, I absolutely must avoid any more run-ins with the Dark Angel.

$\mathcal{K}$eeping $\mathcal{U}p$ . . .

Our cousin Joan had already fled to the Canadian Army by the time Auntie Vera moved off Mount Royal Avenue. At first she and Uncle Ron rented an apartment on Sudbury Street, and then a house on Topsail Road, where I visited on weekends and played with her neglected budgie, Sweetie Pie. Finally she decided to leave Newfoundland, Bowring's, Ron and Sweetie Pie altogether and join Buddy in Montana. Losing Vera was unimaginable for Mom and for all of us although we could see her hopeless situation well enough.

Before she left for the States, lamenting her own situation and the fate of her children, Auntie Vera said to us in her sincerest tones: "You guys are so lucky to have your dad for a father because believe me not everyone has a father that cares about his children like your dad cares about you boys. My kids didn't have that, and that's the truth, and that's not nice. So you don't know how lucky you are, right? You know that don't you, Greg? Yes, you're good boys. What a great family you've got. And you too, of course, Ada, God, I almost forgot you."

"That's all right, Vera, don't mind me," said Mom, tears welling in her eyes.

"But you know what I mean, Ada."

"Yes, yes, I do."

"I am really going to miss coming here and all of you guys a lot. Come here and give me a big hug before I go. Don't cry now, Greg, we'll see each other again, I promise."

Once in Montana, Vera had no difficulty getting a job in a department store, but did not stay long with Buddy and Irene. She bought a car and struck out alone across the Nevada desert for the land of her dreams. She was carried along by her own grit and determination and the kindness of strangers, who fixed her over-heated car in the middle of the desert. In Los Angeles she soon secured herself a good job at the United California Bank in Beverly Hills, and an apartment in Van Nuys. She sent us many pictures of herself in her Hollywood fashions, posing alongside her new white convertible in her new platinum-blond bouffant and capris, looking like Doris Day. She was our American aunt now and we stared in awe at this new Vera in her exotic surroundings.

In our mother's life, we slowly came to understand, there was something unfulfilled and unsatisfied. Dad was devoted to her and called her Lovey. But despite Dad's dahlias and dedication, and all the breakfasts and dinners he cooked, and all the parties and all the laughs, and treating her like a queen until he snapped, still there was something missing. Vera might think she had the perfect family, but there it was: she was still a house-wife in the West End with four boys, who, however agreeable, must all still be fed, and turned out clean and well dressed. She had wanted to go to university and had the marks for it too, but Pop would not support the idea. She loved to read and draw, and she painted pretty watercolour portraits of us all when we were small. She loved the movies and took us off with her to her favourites. And she was beautiful, she still had her figure and she longed for the wider world.

The colour pictures of Vera, the "movie star" in sunny Hollywood, did nothing to calm this restless spirit, and her gaze, lingering over the little snaps, showed the faintest trace of dissatisfaction and longing in the wake of her exclamations of approval.

Well, if Vera was going to Hollywood, then Mom was at least getting off Mount Royal Avenue. She had seen a mouse, and then another one. Dad set traps and I announced that I wanted to skin them and collect the pelts, my supply from Ewing Fur Factory having dried up. Mom screamed at the thought and became more obsessed with relocating than ever. The time had finally come to "move up" and Dad had to kick in and start looking for a house on his rounds, in the East End, of course. He was completely on side with Mom's desire to move and, like the constant renovations and improvements, hoped the new address would satisfy her restless need for change.

There was another catalyst for this move besides Vera's adventures. Mom was pregnant again. This was a shock to us, and she confided in me and Wayne that it was a surprise to them as well, after all, Mom was now forty years old.

"Pregnant at my age! Imagine. I'll probably have to wear flats the rest of my life," she moaned.

Wayne and I were sympathetic though it took a while for us to catch onto the physics of pregnancy. Another boy was naturally anticipated without undue enthusiasm. Although Uncle Bob now had the son he and Aunt Mil had been trying for, with four boys behind them, Mom and Dad did not tantalize themselves again with visions of a baby girl.

We were not the only ones moving off Mount Royal Avenue. The Braces were building a new bungalow on University Avenue, close to Dr. Brace's new job. He went in the evenings to clean up after the carpenters, and sometimes he took Wayne and me with him. We were very impressed by the curved corner to the dining room they had created by soaking and bending a sheet of Gyproc. The Braces were more relaxed now and even Mrs. Brace managed a friendly word to me on the site of the new bungalow.

All of us were on the lookout for a house in the East End. Several possibilities had faded—too expensive, no garden. Dad knew all the real estate people and consequently every house on the market as soon as it came out. Nothing escaped him, but still, what it was that Lovey was looking for had so far failed to materialize.

★

The end of the school year was coming, as was the annual Christian Brothers' Grammar School Track and Field Meet, which St. Bon's must win. But Brother Murphy needed more boys for the team. He spoke to his friends Brother Pigott and Brother Rogers. My cast was long gone, leaving me almost ambidextrous, but I was not at all convinced I needed to risk joining the track team, and I hoped Dad would not get wind of Brother Murphy's need for new members. But Brother Rogers took the task on himself.

"You're too proud, my son, that's your problem," he said, psychoanalyzing me one afternoon as we walked around the campus.

"No, I'm not," I shot back.

"Yes, you're just afraid you're going to look bad with John Byrne and Jim Power."

"Maybe."

"Well, that is just stupid pride. You've got to forget everyone else, my son. They don't care about what you're doing. They're just worried about themselves. And you're fast. You can almost get away from me," he said, nudging me on the shoulder.

"Oh, I can get away from you."

"Let's see then," he demanded, grabbing up his soutane in his right hand. "Come on, I'll get to the other end before you."

We tore down the campus. I got ahead of him right away. I could see him out of the corner of my eye. He yanked his soutane higher and passed me, his white sports socks flashing under his black pants. He was ahead of me. Impossible. I gave whatever I had left and kept going until I caught up with him as we crossed the path at the other end of the field.

"Oh," gasped Brother Rogers, "you almost beat me."

"I did," I choked. "I got you."

"No, no. Almost. Almost. Oh, you're fast though. I bet with a bit of practice and a bit of coaching, you could even beat Pat Royal."

"Pat Royal?"

Brother Pigott also insisted that both Andy and I try out for the team and signed us both up with Brother Murphy. Andy was powerful and was put on the shot put and javelin, and I made the running team, and there I was with Pat Royal, Denis Barry, Jim Power, Dennis Neville and Eric Healey. No one could have been more surprised, or pleased, or nervous than me. Practice was brutal and my chest felt like it was stuffed full of hot peppermint nobs. Most of the time I could hardly breathe, let alone run. But I managed to keep up and was put into the fifty- and hundred-yard dash and the high jump. I was good on the short hops. Not so good on the long hauls, yet. But there were still two places on the relay team to be filled and I found myself in a run-off with Pat Royal and Dennis Neville and Jim Power. It was a tough race and two laps of the campus longer than I was used to.

Pat took the lead, followed by Jim Power with Dennis Neville and me together at the back. We were all running full out. I overtook Jim near the end of the first lap and moved up on Pat. In the last turn, he looked over his shoulder, a flash of concern in his eyes as I came up and edged alongside of him. He whipped his head back, stuck it out and seemed to lengthen his long, steady stride, pulling ahead of me. Despite my best effort, he crossed the finish line a good two heads in front of me. I was disappointed but I could not mind too much. He was such an excellent runner. We all collapsed on the ground, and I was on the relay team. At the big meet, at St. Pat's Ballpark on Carpasian Road, with the stands full, I won the fifty- and hundred-yard dash, Andy won the shot put, and the team won the relay and the meet. Brother Rogers and Brother Pigott could not have been more pleased. All these glories were later recalled at the Sports Day awards ceremony where trophies were handed out all round, and Dad said, "I told you so. All you have to do is try."

This was a technical gain. I knew he would approve of my victory as much as I felt he disapproved of me, and so we were once again on more or less neutral ground. Dad was further convinced I had now turned the page on sports and might even try out for soccer or hockey. He began reporting the scores of last night's game with renewed enthusiasm, and I was even moved by his genuine delight to respond, although Wayne's more spontaneous reaction generally carried the moment.

It was also not possible to avoid every Hockey Night in Canada on Saturday nights. Brought to us by none other than Imperial Oil, the Founder of the Feast, it had every claim on our family loyalty, so some weekends it was just easier to sit through a period or two. I appreciated Mahovlich's skill and got to like Big M with the small, shy voice, but the Rocket was too much like Dad to stir any affection in me. I made the effort, but all in all I would rather go play Mass or read The Hardy Boys, but I could not get away without comment.

"Don't go now. You're gonna miss the power play with Richard and Belliveau," Dad sang out, hands clapping in antic- ipation, "ding diddle-ing diddle-ing diddle-ing. My son, I can't see how you could not like hockey. Hockey is the ultimate sport. What do you think, Wayne?"

"Oh yeah," Wayne agreed wholeheartedly.

Even Kerry agreed, and little Beni, sitting in the brown chair of the new sofa set, rocking back and forth, or rockin' and rollin' as he called it, had his eyes trained on the puck through his thick glasses. Beni had already worn a bald spot in the top of the new chair from banging the back of his head against it, and he got quite carried away during the game. Mom had used every reprimand and psychological trick that she and *Chatelaine* magazine could think of to break him of the habit before the chair was ruined and no longer fit to move to our new house, wherever that might be.

*

Dad came home with a possibility.

"Lovey, there's a house that's just come on the market on Pine Bud Avenue."

Now of all the streets in the East End that Mom longed to live on, Pine Bud Avenue, with its smart homes and elegant trees and lush gardens was perhaps the choicest, and her favourite.

"We'll take it, Bill," she said instantly.

"Wait now, Lovey, you haven't even heard the price yet."

"How much are they asking for it?"

"Twenty-seven thousand dollars, and that's two thousand more than our top dollar."

"We'll take it."

"You haven't seen it yet."

"I know, Bill. But I don't need to see it. I want it. Who's selling it?"

"Alex Hickman owns it."

"Let's call him up, Bill."

"I think we should at least look at the house first. We've looked at everything else, inside and out."

"No, no, this is Pine Bud Avenue, Bill. There's nothing wrong with that house. Someone else will snap it up, and that's a good price for Pine Bud Avenue."

"I suppose it is but . . ."

"Definitely, definitely, Bill," insisted Mom. "Call him up right now. Look, do you know him?"

"I know him."

Mom was activated and in full battle mode, no obstacle would stand in her way, and Dad, overwhelmed by the clarity of her vision, quickly became her foot soldier and put in the call to Alex Hickman. Yes, it was still on the market, just on the market, in fact. How did Bill know? Yes, the asking price was $27,000, and, yes, Bill and Ada could have it for that price. With Dad being no stranger to the art and language of a contract it was all agreed to there and then, in less than ten minutes, after months of careful looking and inspecting and rejecting. And it was very well done indeed, because less than one hour later, a Mr. Moores from Carbonear, who was looking for a place for his children to stay while going to the university, called and offered Mr. Hickman $30,000 for the house, sight unseen. But Mr. Hickman stood by his agreement with Dad. Mom had been entirely correct and they had bought their dream house with less than an hour to spare.

It was official. We would be moving to Pine Bud Avenue. Well, almost official. Mom and Dad would need financing from their backer, Mr. Foster, who had financed Mount Royal Avenue for them. Mr. Foster had a beautiful house and garden with crabapple trees on St. Clare Avenue, and Wayne and I were now glad we had not been caught by him on our last crabapple raid. Mom felt sure that Mr. Foster would see the value of Pine Bud Avenue and be willing to make the investment, and here again she was proved correct. They still had to sell Mount Royal Avenue, and had to get $18,000 for it to swing the deal. All these concerns came out as we piled into the Pontiac and went to look at the house they had just agreed to buy.

To begin with, it was not a large house, smaller than Mount Royal, in fact. It was a pale green two-storey and Mom was pleased enough with its generous corner windows and broad

front bay window. It sat on a splendid corner lot at Sycamore
Place and Pine Bud, surrounded by the stately Caledonian
pines, from which the avenue got its name, as well as sycamores
of course, and dogberry trees. It had a front yard, a side garden
and a backyard on Sycamore Place, where Camp Alexander
housed American forces during the War.

The houses on Sycamore, Beech, Elm, Chestnut and the other
"Tree" streets were similar to ours and had been constructed
after the War by the Newfoundland Housing Corporation. Bungalows or two-storeys, large or small, they were all built of fine
BC lumber, and were very substantial, with hardwood floors
and lots of windows. On Pine Bud Avenue there were older and
grander structures, like the old McNicholas house, with its elegant mansard roof and large grounds. The avenue had been an
old country road and the pines had been planted by Redemp-
torist missionaries cloistered on what was now Chestnut Place.

Our corner lot measured up nicely, but the kitchen and dining room were only a kitchenette and dinette, really. The living
room was large and there was a full basement. The bedrooms
were smaller than at Mount Royal. Wayne and I would still have
to share a room but we didn't care. We loved Pine Bud Avenue.
It was exactly where we all wanted to be. Not a three-minute
walk past the end of Sycamore Place and along the beautiful
Rennie's River was Andy's house. Richard Simms and Michael
Harrington were also just around the corner, and, for Wayne,
the fantastic Toni McGrath was a mere stone's throw away.

We had arrived. This was where Mom's economies had been
heading. For this, Kelsey's milk and Mrs. Nash's eggs had gone
by the wayside, as Dad picked up the contracts from the bungalows that were now occupying their farmlands. Together they
had navigated us to 4 Pine Bud Avenue.

But we were not there yet. And so back to familiar old Mount
Royal Avenue we went. It looked well-worn to us now with its
crowded houses, and a little sad. Old friends had their own lives

and we saw less of each other. Brace was gone to University Avenue. The street was full of other, smaller children playing hopscotch and hide-and-seek in Basteaus' driveway, but the Basteaus were gone.

Sometimes we still gathered, Bruce Tizzard and Lioney and Jimmy Wadden and I, under the pole light by Jimmy's house, where Jimmy showed us how to make someone pass out.

"You just breathe in and out real deep and fast ten times and then hold your breath and get someone to stand behind you and squeeze you around the chest in a bear hug as hard as they can for a couple of seconds and you'll pass out."

"What? Go unconscious?"

"Just for a couple of seconds."

We all huffed and puffed, and I squeezed Jimmy, and Bruce squeezed me and lifted me off the ground until I got dizzy and fell to the pavement when he finally let me go.

Out of the Frying Pan

It was the end of Mount Royal Avenue. It was the end of grade eight. It was the end of St. Bonaventure's College. The last Sports Day had arrived. It was the end of everything and we gathered under a high, blue, June sky to mark the passing of more than one hundred years of College history, and wonder at the future. St. Bon's would, from that day, be a grammar school only, no longer a college. Two new high schools for boys had been built to take the swelling numbers of students: Brother Rice High School, further down Bonaventure Avenue, and Gonzaga High School, in our new neighbourhood.

Our new address put me in Gonzaga with Andy and my other friends, but we lost almost all the rest of the class to Brother Rice. Perhaps our greatest loss was our new friend John Whalen. John was a good athlete and one of the boys, but he was very witty and liked to hang around with me and Andy for a good laugh. Thoughtful and fair, and very loyal, John was a prince. He came with us on our long walks to Logy Bay, and on the way home I doused him with ketchup and dragged him

347

along the side of the road in an effort to stop passing cars. But despite a convincing performance from both of us, we failed to persuade any motorists of our distress. We also failed to persuade John to switch schools and come with us to Gonzaga. We tried, but he was reluctant to seek any special dispensation, and he was loyal to his other friends, Pat and Denis and John Byrne, all headed for Brother Rice.

The building that eventually became Brother Rice High School was originally intended to be Gonzaga High School for the Jesuits who were coming from Canada to run it. The new building was fitted with an elevator and other extra features for the Jesuits. But this building was also next to the Christian Brothers' existing schools and in their traditional territory, and it was obviously built to a better standard than the other new boys' high school, still unfinished just off Elizabeth Avenue on Smithville Crescent, which was meant for them. The Brothers were inflamed and held their ground against the Archdiocese. They would get the better school in their territory, or they would leave. And in this, the first battle between the Irish Christian Brothers and the Society of Jesus, the Brothers won. And so it happened that the Jesuits, and Gonzaga, went to Smithville, and we went with them.

The last Sports Day was glorious and sunny. For the last time, the senior boys marched in formation onto the campus and led the student body, with batons spinning and clubs swinging, in synchronized calisthenics, to the rhythm of the Mount Cashel Boys Band, installed onstage at the northwest corner of the field. Further down on the west side an enclosure, covered in canvas, faced the field and the school beyond. Here, seated on ornately carved chairs sat Archbishop Skinner and his retinue alongside Lieutenant-Governor Outerbridge and his wife. Victors of the day's many competitions were escorted, smudged and sweating, to kneel and kiss the Episcopal ring, and shake the viceregal hand of Sir Leonard Outerbridge, among the

general smiles, knowing nods and chuckling comments of the
Arch-Episcopal enclosure.

All around, crowds of students and their families thronged.
We bought hot dogs and soda at the stands, and there was cotton candy and wheels of chance. We had done well that year
with Brother Pigott and today in the races. The day was everything we had wanted. Andy and I strolled around the teeming
campus with Eddie Taylor and Richard Simms, Mike Harrington and Billy Cooper, all of whom would be going to Gonzaga
as well. John Whalen was still with us. We tried to squeeze in as
much play with him as possible before the end and Andy took
pictures of me and John around the campus, posing in fake
fights to everyone's amusement. There were turkey teas, cold
plates with hot tea, provided by the Ladies Auxiliary in the
afternoon and served in the boarders' and the Brothers' cafete-
ria, but we chose to treat ourselves to the best chips and burgers
and shakes at Marty's Restaurant on Freshwater Road, and we
felt very sophisticated and mature indeed.

When the year was finally done and the building empty of students, I went down the hall alongside the dining room and rang
for one of the maids.

"I want to see Brother Rogers."

"I'll ring for him. Wait up there."

I went up the short steps into the front hall and foyer and sat
in the waiting room, the middle of which was occupied by a
large, heavily carved, square oak table, surrounded by matching
high-backed chairs with red leather seats. The same tall, bright
window as was in our old classroom interrupted the gloom. In
the far off hall I heard five bells for Brother Rogers, one-two,
one-two-three, and soon the skip of his feet over the stairs and
the swish of his soutane turning into the room.

"Hi, Br."

"I knew it was you. I have something for you."

He gave me a holy picture, laminated, and a St. Christopher medal.

"Here's something to remember me by. You've done very well and I expect you to do even better with the Jesuits."

"I'll try."

"You better. Come back and visit me now."

"Oh, I will."

"No, you won't come back here. You're gone now. Just like all the rest."

"No, I will come back."

"No, you won't."

"Yes, I will. Really."

"You promise?"

"I promise."

"All right then. I'll hold you to that. Better say goodbye now."

"Thanks, Br, for everything."

"That's enough of that," he flushed. "You don't have to thank me for anything."

He smiled, flushing more.

"Thanks anyway. Goodbye, Br."

I did come back to that room, which was so alien to both of us and to any spontaneous exchange. I went for many visits. He was never anxious for me to leave, though there was little left to say. Brother Rogers eventually left the Brothers and we lost touch until many years later when he and his wife came to one of my shows.

✤

On a fine day at the end of July we finally left Mount Royal Avenue for the last time and arrived at 4 Pine Bud Avenue for good, all except Mom and the new baby who were at St. Clare's

Hospital. With the timely and generous help of his new friend Barron MacDonald at NECCO Construction, Dad had an extension built on the back of the new house. The kitchenette was now a proper kitchen that we could all fit into, and the dinette was now a proper dining room. It smelled of fresh paint and sunshine and our spirits soared. The very next day Mom came home from the hospital with the newest addition to the family.

When the nurses told her she had a girl, Mom thought they were joking and didn't believe them. It was only when they laid the baby girl in her arms that she absorbed the truth. Dad, more than ready to absorb it, was beaming. He had a nice new home and a beautiful new daughter. Surely these were auspicious signs for a new era. Now he and Bob really were like one of Dad's stories. "There were two friends, and one had four girls and one boy, the other had four boys and one girl." This rare and precious girl child they called Susan Marie, and she was the only one of us to be called by her first name—well, Susan Hayward was a wonderful actress, after all. We were as excited about the new baby as Mom and Dad and we all attended the Christening and took turns holding her. It seemed only fitting that we should have a sister to round out the family and appropriate to our new genteel address.

It was a lovely walk along the river to Andy's house and I made the trip frequently. The summer was passing quickly with only the minor irritation of Scout camp and a fresh resolve to quit it next year.

Gonzaga High School was not finished construction when we arrived for the first day of class in grade nine. There were only six grade nine classes and four grade ten classes that first year. All the grade eleven students stayed with the Brothers at Rice for graduation, and so Wayne and I were finally in separate schools.

We crowded expectantly into the new hallway lined with shining, coloured lockers. A buzz of excitement filled the air as students looked around, checking for friends and surveying the new arrivals from Torbay and Pouch Cove. Suddenly from the far end of the hallway came the sound of a loud bang and shouts. The lively buzz turned to a murmur as the sounds grew louder. There was another loud bang, the sound of a boy being slammed into the shiny new lockers. And then we heard it. It was unmistakable, the old familiar sound of the strap. Our hearts sank.

We had had a very good year with Brother Pigott, and before that with Brother Rogers and Brother McGoohan, and now we expected something else, perhaps something more mature, more sophisticated from these highly educated and famous Jesuits.

But he came upon us with his arm raised and his strap swinging wildly, his flat face distorted and red with anger. Shrieking and screaming he descended on us, the very hound from Hell. This ghastly apparition was the Reverend Father Holland, SJ, and the very first member we had ever seen of the Society of Jesus, that Prince of Peace so endlessly betrayed. The appearance of this dark, hysterical figure troubled our hearts greatly, and though we had hoped for more and were ready for better, I am sad to report that it was rather a case of out of the frying pan and into the fire.

Epilogue

OUR LITTLE CLASS from St. Bon's was a remarkable one and Brother Clancy, now an old man in upstate New York, still remembers the names of all the boys in it, according to Jimmy Duggan, who is in regular contact with him, and the picture of our grade four play comes from him.

I asked Andy Squires if he objected to my portrayal of his childhood sufferings.

"No, Greg," he said, still defiant. "It all happened. Tell it like it was, boy. I tell my children and grandchildren all about it."

Sean Power died young. Danny Williams became premier of Newfoundland and Labrador and I think we were all very proud of that.

My old friend Wayne Brace became a psychiatrist in an all-out effort to maintain sanity. Jimmy "Hot Dog" Wadden bought our old house at 18 Mount Royal Avenue, and my vital statistics are within his hearth now. Bonnie Tizzard found me on Facebook a few weeks ago and asked me if I remembered all the good times we used to have on the street. She and Lorna

353

Brace are now anxiously awaiting the publication of this book, and I hope they will not be disappointed. I had not seen Barbara Lynn since that grey day with Carl and the snowmen, but through Bonnie I tracked her down to tell her about the book.

"Barbara Lynn," I said, "I was going to ask if you wanted to play house tomorrow?"

"Well, I'd probably say yes," she answered.

Her voice still had the lively ring of youth, and we picked up where we had left off.

"Do you remember when you borrowed my big tricycle in grade two to enter the tricycle race at the St. Bon's Sports Day?"

"Oh no, I had forgotten that."

"Yes, you decorated it with blue and yellow crepe paper streamers, and rode off down Pennywell Road to school like you had the world by the tail," and she laughed.

Brother Rogers and I are still in touch. He is "Ed" for good now, and I asked him to read "Teacher's Pet." At first he and his wife were doubtful about tales told out of school, but, after reading it, he gave me his approval, as did Denis Barry and Pat Royal, which pleased me no end.

Andy Jones and I continued to be best friends and acted together in many wonderful dramatic productions at Gonzaga, which proved to have more blessings than was first indicated. We were parted for university, but I reunited with him and his sister Cathy, and, along with Mary Walsh, Diane Olsen, Whitey, and our dear friend Tommy Sexton, we formed the CODCO comedy troupe, which became a successful television series on CBC in the late '80s and early '90s. And our friendship survived even that. Bill Cooper and I became great friends again in high school. During university we hitchhiked around Europe together and sold our blood for food on the Costa Brava. He is now a dedicated teacher in Labrador.

At Memorial University of Newfoundland in St. John's I fell in with an exciting crowd of actors and musicians and met

Whitey, a.k.a. Mary Magdalene Perpetua White, from Carbonear. She was a most unusual person and the first girl to wear
jeans at MUN. I was intrigued by her. We became fast friends,
and spent many long evenings together discussing Dostoevsky,
Oscar Wilde, Jean Genet and my own homosexuality until one
night we found ourselves in bed together. Her boyfriend was the
handsome and talented guitarist Sandy Morris, who was also a
fan of Jean Genet, which astonished me, and I was forced to fall
in love with him as well. We eventually became a family. We
stayed together for many years and had two children together,
our beautiful sons, Django and Dashi. The three of us were also
a professional team and together we created the *Wonderful
Grand Band* television series for CBC. Sandy did the music for
the *CODCO* series as well, while Whitey was the manager and
much more for both companies.

My parents' romance continued to be tempestuous. Dad was
busier than ever with another promotion at work, running the
Scouts and then calling the big bingo game for the Archdiocese
at the BIS, the Benevolent Irish Society, on weekday evenings.
Mom countered with more frequent trips to visit Auntie Vera in
California, often taking Susan with her. Their friends and parties increased in number and frequency until they cut out drinking on weekdays, but that didn't stop the get-togethers. The
little house on Pine Bud Avenue was a full one, with Dad and
Mom and their friends carrying on upstairs, and me and my
brothers and our friends downstairs in the rec room, our club-
house, and there were plenty of good times to be had.

However, our parents, who were largely mystified by us as
children, became more challenged by us as we grew to adult
size. We happily confronted them on all philosophical, religious
and social grounds, and when they could rise to that challenge

we came close to being that modern family they so aspired to be. But the past cannot easily be disowned and the hairline cracks of alienation from Mount Royal widened to open fractures and even fights on lovely Pine Bud. These fault lines had deeper roots than we realized.

Dad was always very afraid that we might turn out like Uncles Jim or Eugene or Bren, not amount to anything and bring shame on him. As we grew to Jim and Eugene's height before his eyes, this fear became almost a phobia, and he fought first with Wayne, and then with Kerry, with the same bitterness and intensity he had fought with his own brothers in their store years ago, until I believed he thought Wayne and Kerry were them.

"What the hell do you mean getting in this hour of the morning?"

"I was out," Wayne answered the minimum possible.

"You whoremaster. You're out all night, drinking, beating the path, with I don't know what kind of girls."

"It's not what you think."

"It's what I know. You're just like your Uncle Jim and Eugene and you're doing the same thing as them, and you'll end up the same way."

Dad tried the same fight with me but the dynamic was all wrong.

"And what are you doing out all night with your friends?"

"We were up all night talking."

"Talking?"

"Yes, talking."

He didn't understand it, but he knew I was telling the truth.

We were not Jim or Eugene, or even Bren or Tom, but our parents did not know exactly who we were, and they lacked both the freedom and the time to find out. In the end, it was not a happy home and we stayed away as much as we could.

I, of course, had the Joneses, while Wayne found a second home at Carole King's house on Cornwall Crescent. The Kings were Protestant and he was very popular with Carole's father and mother. Wayne had found his Protestant Princess.

All the girls were wild about Kerry, who inherited all of Dad's good looks, infectious charm and mercurial nature. His life is a colourful one and could fill another book. Beni complained loudly about having to follow in the footsteps of Wayne, me and the ever-popular Kerry. But he set his own course and, true to his original promise, became a professional clown. He married Whitey's younger sister Marian . . . "two brothers married two sisters."

Susan, our new sister, was a great joy to Dad, and he at last had a child with whom he could express his affectionate nature. But Mom was strangely challenged by this beautiful, athletic, strong-willed and much-longed-for daughter, and their relationship was a difficult one.

Most of us left home early but returned for regular visits, and we laughed and joked about the past at Christmas reunions as though we were that perfect family in the photo albums.

Uncle Bob died of cancer in his early fifties. Dad visited him every day for the last year for his life, and when he died, Mom wailed. "Bob is gone! It will never be the same again."

And in this she was proved correct again.

Mrs. Jones did not live into old age either. She died suddenly and before we could fully appreciate the great impact of her generous heart and loving soul on our young lives.

Several years ago it was my sad chore to move Dad and Mom into St. Patrick's Mercy Home, where Daddy Lone had died years before. Dad, with advanced Parkinson's but still with his wits about him, planned it all with me, his final act of care for Lovey. Mom was greatly troubled by depression and alcohol, and had lost her short-term memory entirely. She was still tall and glamorous, however, and covered for her memory loss with great skill.

"What did you have for lunch today, Mom?"

"Oh, your father and I don't eat much these days, Greg. Just some little thing will do us."

In the nursing home, everyone thought at first that Mom was a visitor, there to look after Dad, but they soon realized the opposite was true.

On the last day in their almost-empty apartment, Dad found an old box of cassette tapes of his favourite songs—"Danny Boy," "North to Alaska," "Big John" and other songs I had found so corny as a teenager. We were there alone and I put "North to Alaska" by Johnny Horton in the cassette player for him. Dad stood, stooped and shaking slightly, in the centre of the empty room. He began to sway and snap his wrist in time to the music, smiling as always. His eyes half-closed, he looked far back to those sunny times when he and Bob and the old gang had laughed and sung together over Old Sam. As I saw that smile and watched him rock back and forth, tears came to my eyes and ran freely down my face, and when the song was over, Dad turned to me with some surprise.

"My God, Greg, I never thought I'd see you cry for those songs."

Yes, Daddy, yes. But it's not the songs I'm crying for. To his crowd, Dad was "Danny Boy," and when he died, the remnants of that happy gang stood round his grave and sang the song to him one last time. On his gravestone my brothers and sister and I had carved the inscription "Gone to the Gullies" and he truly was.

Mom is by herself now and she finds it hard to be alone . . . Mommy Lone. I pick her up at the nursing home and take her for drives in the car, which she loves. We take long walks together around Bowring Park, skipping over the ice in the winter, laughing at the wind, and feeding the ducks and laughing at the little children in the summer. She is like a young girl herself now and her mind ranges playfully over the past, which is still open to her.

"Pop used to come here after he retired, you know. He'd sit by the statue of Peter Pan and play his mandolin guitar or his accordion, and all the little kids would gather around and listen to him. Then he'd walk on to another spot and play some more and all the kids would follow him. They called him the Pied Piper of Bowring Park . . . my, that was a long time ago now, Greg."

"Yes, Mommy . . . another lifetime."

*

Our memories are the bread crumbs that lead us home.
Without them we stand bereft and alone.

Acknowledgments

I WOULD LIKE TO THANK Marian Frances White for introducing me to Joan Clark, and Joan Clark for her kind advice and introduction to my editor, Diane Martin. Helen Peters and Judy (Lynch) Cameron read an early version of the manuscript and I thank them for their suggestions. I also especially want to thank Andy Jones for his warm and wholehearted encouragement at a crucial time, Denis Barry for his friendship and support and Jimmy Duggan, who gave me the photo of our grade four class play. And special thanks to my brothers, Wayne, Kerry and Beni, and my sister, Susan, for all the laughs and all the talks. I greatly appreciate the work of the editorial staff at Knopf Canada, especially Diane Martin for seeing this book through with me to the end, all the way to the remote community of Cow Head in fact, where we finally met.

Illustrations

Except where noted, these photographs are from the author's collection.

p. xii   The Author (in grade four).

p. 1   Imperial Oil Picnic. Dad on left, me in harness, Wayne with head covered, 1951.

p. 3   The Walkers. From left to right: Len, Auntie Vera (holding Buddy), Ray, Arthur B. (Pop), Mary (Nanny) and Ada (Mom) (standing).

p. 11   The Basketball Champion. William S. Malone (Dad), around nineteen years old.

p. 23   Scouting with the Fourth St. Edward's Troop at It'll Do in Mount Pearl. Dad is kneeling in front, seated in the centre is E. B. Foran and to his left is Gandhi Royal, c. 1937.

p. 29   The Young Couple. Bill and Ada (Dad and Mom). *Photo by Ladd Bursey.*

GREG MALONE is an actor who was a co-founder of the New-foundland satirical comedy troupe, CODCO. When one of his CODCO partners, Tommy Sexton, died of HIV/AIDS in the early '90s, Greg campaigned for AIDS awareness. He is also an environmental activist and performs regularly in theatre and film. He lives in St. John's.